Japan's Economic Challenge

Garland Reference Library
of Social Science
(vol. 425)

JAPAN'S ECONOMIC CHALLENGE

A Bibliographic Sourcebook

Michael Keresztesi
Gary R. Cocozzoli

GARLAND PUBLISHING, INC. • NEW YORK & LONDON
1988

Library of Congress Cataloging-in-Publication Data

Keresztesi, Michael.
  Japan's economic challenge: a bibliographic sourcebook / Michael
Keresztesi, Gary R. Cocozzoli.
     p. cm. — (Garland reference library of social science ;
  vol. 425)
  Includes indexes.
  ISBN 0-8240-6608-1
  1. Japan—Economic conditions—1945-   —Bibliography.
  2. Japan—Economic policy—1945-   —Bibliography. I. Cocozzoli,
Gary R. II. Title. III. Series: Garland reference library of social science ;
v. 425
Z7165.J3K45   1988
[HC462.9]
016.330952'04—dc19   88-322
                                                                            CIP

Printed on acid-free, 250-year-life paper
Manufactured in the United States of America

to Jeanne

CONTENTS

VII

Contents

Contents

Contents

Contents

PREFACE

Japan's rapid emergence as an industrial giant
after the devastation of World War II is often seen as
one of the most enigmatic events in recent history.
What has propelled this island nation to rise from
defeat, overtaking older industrial countries of the
West, to assume global leadership in many key sectors
of the economy of the world in such a short period of
time?

Along with the rapid expansion of its productive
capacity, Japanese export trade has undergone an
explosive growth. By the early 1980's, Japanese goods
had penetrated practically every corner of the planet
and forced their competitors out of their previous
positions. Japan's financial strength has increased
correspondingly, and the Japanese financial
establishment has begun to demand increasingly greater
shares of the international financial markets.

Japan's evolving economic prowess attracted the
attention of social scientists of various specialities
long before the country attained its present status.
Researchers have sought insights primarily into the
underlying historical, social, and cultural processes.
The results of their quests have found articulation in
a large quantity of scholarly monographs and writings
in learned periodical publications.

The spectacular successes of the Japanese economy
in past years has engendered wide discussion and debate
in America as well as in Europe, focusing on the
question of why Western industry has been overtaken by
the Japanese. Among the many aspects, the emphasis on
new technology, sophisticated production management

1

Preface

methods in large Japanese plants, unique manpower
management approaches and practices, and most of all, a
centrally formulated national industrial policy, have
been pointed to by students and observers as being the
chief contributory factors.

Government officials and industrial leaders in the
United States and other Western nations, feeling the
damaging effects of Japanese competition on their own
economies both at home and abroad, have began to wonder
whether Japanese methods could be transferred and
adapted to their own production processes.

While the debate over emulating Japanese methods is
still going on, it has become increasingly obvious that
Japan's ascent to industrial and financial might cannot
be attributed to a few isolated factors. The intrinsic
nature of the Japanese economic challenge, in all its
dimensions, is tied up with the country's history,
social and political structure and cultural values. It
is the result of complex forces which have been at work
for long historical periods, the study and
understanding of which require a broad conceptual
approach and a sophisticated intellectual framework.

In past decades, a multitude of academic,
professional, and journalistic writings in English and
foreign literature has addressed the issues and
problems that surround Japan's economic challenge.
Collectively, these writings chronicle the historical,
social, and cultural background of Japan's spectacular
industrial take-off. They describe, analyze, and
interpret the diverse manifestations of Japan's
economic challenge. While the volume of this
literature has been growing, the bibliographic
organization of this material has not kept pace.

At the inception of the present project, no
bibliography could be found on this topic. It was thus
the purpose of this undertaking to assemble a pool of
references in English to help interested professionals
and students in their quest for facts, background

2

information, evidence, analyses, interpretations, and opinions on a variety of subjects pertinent to the generic concept of "Japan's economic challenge." Over 3000 citations have been culled from a wide section of scholarly, professional, trade, technical, and journalistic literature and press in the English language.

To provide some conceptual unity for this widely divergent material, a broad subject-framework was designed encompassing germane writings ranging from the historical, social, and cultural setting on the one end of the topical spectrum, to current responses to the Japanese economic challenge, on the other. Chronologically, few citations go farther back than 1940, with the bulk originating from the late 1970s to the mid-1980s. The cut-off date is June 1987.

An effort was made to cite an item only once in the listing, although often the breadth of an item's coverage might have warranted its citation in several subject categories. For this reason, the subject arrangement serves mainly as a broad organizational device. In order to aid the user in conducting narrowly defined subject searches and to mine the contents of this sourcebook productively, a "topical locator" has been included. Intended to be more detailed and analytical than an ordinary subject index, the "topical locator" appears in the front of the book to provide ready guidance to the user.

The front matter also includes a listing of the sources of periodical articles, giving the reader some idea of the scope of this compilation and the provenance of the citations. Issues, which have come to the forefront in America only in the late 1970s and early 1980s, as for example, productivity, Quality Circles, robotics, etc., tend to cluster in the periodical literature of those years. This explains the unevenness in the distribution of the material among the various topical areas.

Preface

Despite some unavoidable omissions and flaws in an undertaking of this kind, it is hoped that the present work will be a useful guide of first instance to the many who seek answers to the far-reaching problems generated by the challenge of Japan.

GLOSSARY AND ABBREVIATIONS

Amae - Expectation of a mutual dependence; a relationship in which the subordinate member may presume the good will of a superior.

Amakudari - Describes a pervasive pattern whereby government officials retire at age 55 and often take top level positions in business.

ASEAN - Association of Southeast Asian Nations.

BOJ - Bank of Japan.

Chu - Notion of loyalty.

Daimyo - Generic term applied to the largest landholding military lords in pre-modern Japan.

Danchi - Modern housing project; apartment complex.

Denshinho - Law on Extraordinary Measures for the Promotion of Electronic Industries.

Dozoku - Extended family; descriptive of social attitudes in the context of a business enterprise.

Edo - Old name for the city of Tokyo.

Edo Period - 1600-1868, the early modern period in the history of Japan; also referred to as the Tokugawa Period.

Fukko Kinyu Kinko - Reconstruction Finance Corporation.

Glossary

IBJ - Industrial Bank of Japan.

Ie or Iye - A concept designating the household,
    extended family, and family kinship.

Japan Inc. - Refers to the fusion of government and
    business in the promotion of industry and trade
    for the achievement of overall national
    objectives.

JDB - Japan Development Bank.

JEIDA - Japan Electronic Industry Development
    Association.

JETRO - Japan External Trade Organization.

JIS - Japan Industrial Standards.

JIT - see Just-In-Time.

Jomukai - A conclave of key members of a company's
    top management who hold decision-making
    authority.

JRDC - Japan Research Development Corporation.

Junjo - (Literally: "the proper order of things") A
    reference to a system of social advancement in
    pre-war Japan in which only people with proper
    family background and connections could become
    members of the Japanese elite.

Just-In-Time - "Kanban" in Japanese; a manufacturing
    system based on the precise coordination and
    timing of parts, materials, and processes in
    the assembly room. Large inventories of parts
    are not required, as they are ordered from the
    parts suppliers as needed.

Kanban - see Just-In-Time.

Kazoku - Paternalistic approaches to management.

6

Keiei - Corresponds to Western corporate management.

Keiretsu - Linked groups of private business enterprises; often, loose groupings of former subsidiaries of the pre-war industrial and financial combines called **Zaibatsu** (q.v.), which emerged after the dissolution of the Zaibatsu during the American military occupation.

Kidenho - Law of Extraordinary Measures for the Promotion of Electronics and Machinery Industry.

Kigyo Kumai - Enterprise unionism.

Kijoho - Law on Extraordinary Measures for the Promotion of Specific Machinery and Information Industry.

Kokuryoku - "National Strength."

Kokusai Denshin Denwa - Japan's international telecommunications monopoly.

LTCB - Long Term Credit Bank of Japan.

Meiji Era - 1868-1912, the beginning of the modern period of Japan during which the country was transformed from feudalism to a modern industrial power.

MITI - Ministry of Trade and Industry.

Mitsui - A large industrial group.

NCB - Nippon Credit Bank.

Nenko - A wage and promotion system based on seniority and long service.

Glossary

Oyabun-Kobun - A pattern of dependency relationship,
e.g., parent--child, master--apprentice,
superior--subordinate, which implies strong
personal ties in work and employment situations
leading to mutual benefit and social support.

QC - see Quality Circle.

Quality Circle - Small group of volunteers from the
same work area of an industrial enterprise who
meet regularly to address product quality,
productivity, and related problems, and to
solve them through such techniques as
brainstorming, chart and diagram analysis,
etc.

Ringi - The system of decision-making by consensus; a
process of decision-making from the bottom up;
collective decision-making.

Ringisho - Corporate planning document in a Japanese
enterprise circulated among the respective
workers for information and comment.
Subsequently the document is submitted to top
executives for authorization.

Samurai - Elite warrior class in feudal Japan; many
early business enterpreneurs were Samurai who
preserved and transferred feudal values into the
world of business, adapting them to modern
organization and technology.

Senpai-Kohai - Senior-junior relationship.

Shogun - Feudal military dictator of an area or
region.

Shogunate - Designates "military government" which
was pervasive in Japan from 1192 to 1867.

Shudan - Group oriented approaches to management
based on a specifically developed code of

8

ethics that bind group members together.

Shukko - A system of transfer of employees from a parent firm to a branch for a variety of reasons; e.g., demotion, or saving the employee from dismissal during slowdowns.

Shushin-Koyo - Permanent, life-long employment.

Sogo Shosha - Large general trading companies.

Tetsuri - A tenet of managerial thinking based on a combination of principle and truth; a Buddhist teaching.

Theory Z - Expounded by W. G. Ouchi, it describes a management philosophy recommended to American enterprises for solving some of their managerial problems. A Z-type company is characterized by relatively low task specialization, low turnover of labor, and cooperative relations among employees and work units. Theory Z emphasizes long term employment, individual responsibility, informal control, and wholistic concerns of management, including concern for the welfare not only of the employed individual, but of his family as well.

Tokugawa Period - 1600-1868, the feudalist period in Japanese history during which time the foundations were formed that made the rapid industrialization of the country possible in the following historical period, the Meiji Era from 1868 through 1912.

Tsukiai - A personal relationship cultivated as a result of social necessity or a feeling of obligation.

Wa - Concord, harmony; a managerial approach emphasizing cooperation in the workplace rather

Glossary

than submission to authority.

Yokkakari - Cycle of dependence.

Zaibatsu - Large family-owned and controlled industrial, commercial, and financial combines formally dissolved after World War II.

Z Theory - see Theory Z.

SOURCES OF PERIODICAL ARTICLES

Academy of Management Journal
Mississippi State, USA

Across the Board
New York, NY USA

Administrative Science Quarterly
Ithaca, NY USA

Advanced Management Journal
Cincinnati, OH USA

Advertising Age
Chicago, IL USA

Africa. An International Business, Economic
and Political Monthly
London, UK

Agricultural History
Berkeley, CA USA

Akron Business and Economic Review
Akron, OH USA

American Anthropologist
Washington, DC USA

American Chamber of Commerce in Japan Journal
Tokyo, Japan

American Chamber of Commerce Journal
Washington, DC USA

Sources of Articles

American Economic Review
New York, NY USA

American Federationist
Washington, DC USA

American Import/Export Management--Global
  Trade Executive
Philadelphia, PA USA

American Journal of Economics and Sociology
New York, NY USA

American Journal of Sociology
Chicago, IL USA

American Metal Market
New York, NY USA

American Political Science Review
Washington, DC USA

American Scholar
Washington, DC USA

American Shipper
Jacksonville, FL USA

American Sociological Review
New York, NY USA

Ampo
Tokyo, Japan

Annals of the American Academy of Political and
  Social Science
Philadelphia, PA USA

Annals of the Hitotsubashi Academy
Tokyo, Japan

Arizona Business
Tempe, AZ USA

Asia Pacific Community
Tokyo

Asia Pacific Journal of Management
Singapore, Singapore

Asia Scene/Business Japan
Tokyo, Japan

Asian Affairs
Dacca, Bangladesh

Asian Affairs
London, UK

Asian Affairs
New York, NY USA

Asian Business
Hong Kong, Hong Kong

Asian Development Review
Manila, Philippines

Asian Finance
Hong Kong, Hong Kong

Asian Forum
Washington, DC USA

Asian Monetary Monitor
Hong Kong, Hong Kong

Asian Profile
Hong Kong, Hong Kong

Asian Studies
Queson City, Philippines

Sources of Articles

Asian Survey
Berkeley, CA USA

Atlanta Economic Review
Atlanta, GA USA

Australian Geographical Studies
Armidale, NSW Australia

Automotive Industries
Radnor, PA USA

Banker
London, UK

Banker's Magazine
London, UK

Barron's
New York, NY USA

Beijing Review
Beijing, China

British Journal of Industrial Relations
London, UK

Brookings Papers on Economic Activity
Washington, DC USA

Brooklyn Journal of International Law
Brooklyn, NY USA

Bulletin for International Fiscal Documentation
Amsterdam, Netherlands

Bulletin of Concerned Asian Scholars
San Francisco, CA USA

Business America
Washington, DC USA

Business and Economic Review
Columbia, SC USA

Business (Atlanta)
Atlanta, GA USA

Business and Society Review
Boston, MA USA

Business Economics
Washington, DC USA

Business Forum
Los Angeles, CA USA

Business History
London, UK

Business History Review
Boston, MA USA

Business Horizons
Bloomington, IN USA

Business Japan
Tokyo, Japan

Business Quarterly
London, Ont Canada

Business Week
New York, NY USA

California Management Review
Los Angeles, CA USA

Cambridge Journal of Economics
London, UK

Canadian Banker and ICB Review
Toronto, Ont Canada

Sources of Articles

Canadian Business
Toronto, Ont Canada

Canadian Business Review
Ottawa, Ont Canada

CA Magazine
Toronto, Ont Canada

Capital and Class
London, UK

Car and Driver
New York, NY USA

Case Western Reserve Journal of International Law
Cleveland, OH USA

Cato Journal
San Francisco, CA USA

Center Magazine
Santa Barbara, CA USA

Chain Store Age
New York, NY USA

Challenge
New York, NY USA

Chemical Business
New York, NY USA

Chemical Marketing Reporter
New York, NY USA

Chemical Week
New York, NY USA

Coal Age
New York, NY USA

Columbia Journal of Transnational Law
New York, NY USA

Columbia Journal of World Business
New York, NY USA

Commentary
New York, NY USA

Comparative Political Studies
Beverly Hills, CA USA

Comparative Studies in Society and History
Ann Arbor, MI USA

Communications News
Cleveland, OH USA

Computers and People
Newtonville, MA USA

Conference Board Record
New York, NY USA

Congressional Quarterly
Washington, DC USA

Credit and Financial Management
New York, NY USA

Current
Plainfield, NY USA

Current History
Philadelphia, PA USA

Data Management
Park Ridge, IL USA

Datamation
New York, NY USA

Sources of Articles

Decision Sciences
Atlanta, GA USA

Dentsu Japan Marketing/Advertising
Tokyo, Japan

Department of State Bulletin
Washington, DC USA

Developing Economies
Tokyo, Japan

Director
Calcutta, India

Director
London, UK

Distribution
Mainz, West Germany

Dollars and Sense
Somerville, MA USA

Dun's Business Month
Chicago, IL USA

Econometrica
Chicago, IL USA

Economia & Lavoro
Padova/Venice, Italy

Economic Activity
Nedland, Australia

Economic and Industrial Democracy
London, UK

Economic Bulletin
Tokyo, Japan

Economic Development and Cultural Change
Chicago, IL USA

Economic Eye
Tokyo, Japan

Economic History Review
Norwich, UK

Economic Journal
London, UK

Economic Record
Melbourne, Australia

Economic Review -- Bank of Israel
Jerusalem, Israel

Economic Review -- Kansallis Osake Pankki
Helsinki, Finland

Economica
London, UK

Economie Appliquee
Paris, France

Economist
London, UK

EDP Analyser
Bethesda, MD USA

Electronic Business
Newton, MA USA

Electronic News
New York, NY USA

Electronics World
New York, NY USA

Sources of Articles

Empirical Economics
Heidelberg, West Germany

Engineering News-Record
New York, NY USA

Esquire
New York, NY USA

Ethnology
Pittsburgh, PA USA

Euromoney
London, UK

European Economic Review
Amsterdam, Netherlands

EXIM Review
Japan, Tokyo

Explorations in Entrepreneurial History/
Explorations in Economic History
San Diego, CA USA

Far Eastern Economic Review
Hong Kong, Hong Kong

Far Eastern Quarterly/Journal of Asian Studies
Ann Arbor, MI USA

Federal Reserve Board of San Francisco Economic Review
San Francisco, CA USA

Finances et Developpement -- IMF
Washington, DC USA

Fleet Owner
New York, NY USA

Food Research Institute Studies
StanFord, CA USA

Forbes
New York, NY USA

Foreign Affairs
New York, NY USA

Foreign Policy
New York, NY USA

Fortune
Chicago, IL USA

Fuji Bank Bulletin
Tokyo, Japan

Futures
Guildford, UK

Futurist
Washington, DC USA

Geographical Review
New York, NY USA

Gestion 2000
Louvain-la-Neuve, Belgium

Global Trade Executive
Philadelphia, PA USA

Handling and Shipping Management
Cleveland, OH USA

Harper's
New York, NY USA

Harvard Business Review
Boston, MA USA

Harvard International Law Review
Cambridge, MA USA

Sources of Articles

Harvard Journal of Asiatic Studies
Cambridge, MA USA

Harvard Law Review
Cambridge, MA USA

Hastings International and Comparative Law Review
San Francisco, CA USA

Health Care Management Review
Rockville, MD USA

Higher Education
Amsterdam, Netherlands

History of Political Economy
Durham, NC USA

Hitotsubashi Journal of Economics
Tokyo, Japan

Human Organization
New York, NY USA

Human Relations
London, UK

Human Resource Management
Chettenham, Vic Australia

Human Resource Management
New York, NY USA

Inc.
Boston, MA/Boulder, CO USA

Indian Economic Journal
Bombay, India

Indian Journal of Economics
Allahabad, India

Industrial and Labor Relations Review
New York, NY USA

Industrial Development
Atlanta, GA USA

Industrial Development
Karachi, Pakistan

Industrial Engineering
Norcross, GA USA

Industrial Management
Norcross, GA USA

Industrial Management
Oakville, Ont Canada

Industrial Management and Data Systems
Bradford, W Yorkshire UK

Industrial Quality Control
Milwaukee, WI USA

Industrial Relations
Quebec, Canada

Industry Week
Cleveland, OH USA

Institutional Investor
New York, NY USA

Inter-Economics
Hamburg, West Germany

Interfaces
Providence, RI USA

Internal Auditor
Altamonte Springs, FL USA

Sources of Articles

International Affairs
London, UK

International Economic Review
Philadelphia, PA USA

International Journal of Comparative Sociology
Dharwar, India

International Journal of Contemporary Sociology
New Delhi, India

International Journal of Intercultural Relations
Elmsford, NY USA

International Journal of Operations and
  Production Management
Bradford, W Yorkshire UK

International Journal of Production Research
Basingstoke, Hants UK

International Journal of the Sociology of Law
London, UK

International Labour Review
Geneva, Switzerland/New York, NY USA

International Labor Relations Review
Ithaca, NY USA

International Management
New York, NY USA

International Monetary Fund Staff Papers
Washington, DC USA

International Organization
Boston, MA USA

International Review
Osaka, Japan

International Review of Applied Psychology
London, UK

International Social Science Journal
UNESCO Paris, France

International Studies of Management and Organization
Armonk, NY USA

Industrial Marketing Management
New York, NY USA

Iron Age
Radnor, PA USA

Japan Economic Journal-Nihon Keizai Shimbun
Tokyo, Japan

Japan Economic Journal
Washington, DC USA

Japan Quarterly
Tokyo, Japan

Japanese Economic Studies
Armonk, NY USA

Japanese Finance and Industry Quarterly Survey
Tokyo, Japan

Japanese Psychological Research
Tokyo, Japan

Journal of Accounting, Auditing, and Finance
Boston, MA USA

Journal of Applied Psychology
Washington, DC USA

Sources of Articles

Journal of Asian and African Studies
Toronto, Canada

Journal of Asian Studies
Ann Arbor, MI USA

Journal of Banking and Finance
Amsterdam, Netherlands

Journal of Business
Chicago, IL USA

Journal of Business, Finance and Accounting
Oxford, UK

Journal of Business Strategy
Boston, MA USA

Journal of Commerce and Commercial
New York, NY USA

Journal of Commonwealth and Comparative Politics
Leicester, UK

Journal of Comparative Economics
New York, NY USA

Journal of Consumer Affairs
Columbia, MO USA

Journal of Consumer Research
Los Angeles, CA USA

Journal of Contemporary Business
Seattle, WA USA

Journal of Cross-Cultural Psychology
Newbury Park, CA USA

Journal of Development Economics
Amsterdam, Netherlands

Journal of East Asian Affairs
Seoul, S Korea

Journal of Economic Behavior and Organisation
Amsterdam, Netherlands

Journal of Economic History
New York, NY USA

Journal of Economic Issues
Lincoln, NE USA

Journal of Economic Studies
Bradford, W Yorkshire, UK

Journal of Energy and Development
Boulder, CO USA

Journal of Family History
Greenwich, CT USA

Journal of Farm Economics/American Journal
 of Agricultural Economics
Ames, IA USA

Journal of General Management
London, UK

Journal of Human Resources
Madison, WI USA

Journal of Industrial Economics
Oxford, England

Journal of Industrial Relations
Sydney, Australia

Journal of Information Science
Amsterdam, Netherlands

Journal of International Affairs
New York, NY USA

Sources of Articles

Journal of International Business Studies
Newark, NJ USA

Journal of International Economics
Amsterdam, Netherlands

Journal of Japanese Studies
Seattle, WA USA

Journal of Japanese Trade and Industry
Tokyo, Japan

Journal of Management Studies
Oxford, UK

Journal of Marketing
Chicago, IL USA

Journal of Marriage and the Family
Minneapolis, MN USA

Journal of Money, Credit and Banking
Columbus, OH USA

Journal of Northeast Asian Studies
Washington, DC USA

Journal of Occupational Psychology
Leicester, UK

Journal of Political Economy
Chicago, IL USA

Journal of Politics
Gainsville, FL USA

Journal of Portfolio Management
New York, NY USA

Journal of Post Keynesian Economics
New York, NY USA

Journal of Psychology
Washington, DC USA

Journal of Purchasing and Materials Management
Oradell, NJ USA

Journal of Small Business Management
Morgantown, WV USA

Journal of Social Issues
Ann Arbor, MI USA

Journal of Social Psychology
Provincetown, MA USA

Journal of Systems Management
Cleveland, OH USA

Journal of the American Statistical Association
Washington, DC USA

Journal of the Operational Research Society
Elmsford, NY USA

Journal of World Trade Law
London, UK

Keio Business Review
Tokyo, Japan

Keio Economic Studies
Tokyo, Japan

Keio Journal of Politics
Tokyo, Japan

Keizai Kagaku
Tokyo, Japan

Keizai Kenkyu
Tokyo, Japan

Sources of Articles

Kobe Economic and Business Review
Kobe, Japan

Kobe University Annals of the School of
  Business Administration
Kobe, Japan

Kobe University Economic Review
Kobe, Japan

Kredit und Kapital
Berlin,West Germany

KSU Economic and Business Review
Kyoto, Japan

Kyklos
Berne, Switzerland

Kyoto University Economic Review
Kyoto, Japan

Labor Law Journal
Chicago, IL USA

Labour and Society
Geneva, Switzerland

Law and Policy in International Business
Washington, DC USA

Leviathan
Paris, France

Long Range Planning
Oxford, UK

Maclean's
Toronto, Canada

Management Accounting
London, UK

Management Decisions
Bradford, W Yorkshire   UK

Management Focus
New York, NY USA

Management Solutions
New York, NY USA

Management Today
London, UK

Management Review
Melbourne, Australia

Management World/Management Success
Willow Grove, PA USA

Managerial Planning/Managerial Review
Oxford, UK

Marriage and Family Living
Meinrad, IN USA

Marketing News
Chicago, IL USA

McKinsey Quarterly
New York, NY USA

Mergers and Acquisitions
Philadelphia, PA USA

Michigan Law Review
Ann Arbor, MI

Millennium
London, UK

Sources of Articles

Mini-Micro Systems
Newton, MA USA

Monthly Labor Review
Washington, DC USA

Monthly Review
New York, NY USA

Monumenta Nipponica
Tokyo, Japan

MSU Business Topics
Lansing, MI

Multinational Business
London, UK

National Food Review
Washington, DC USA

National Productivity Review
New York, NY USA

National Real Estate Investor
Atlanta, GA USA

National Review
New York, NY USA

National Westminster Bank Quarterly Report
London, UK

Nation's Business
Washington, DC USA

New England Business
Dublin, NH USA

New Leader
New York, NY USA

New Republic
New York, NY USA

New Scientist
London, UK

New Times
Moscow, USSR

New York Review of Books
New York, NY USA

New York Times
New York, NY USA

New York Times Magazine
New York, NY USA

New York University Journal of Law and Politics
New York, NY USA

Northern California Review of Business and Economics
Chico, CA USA

OECD Observer
Paris, France/Washington, DC USA

Omni
New York, NY USA

Orbis
Philadelphia, PA USA

Ordo
Bonn/Stuttgart, West Germany

Organisation Studies
Berlin, West Germany

Organizational Behavior and Human Performance/
Organizational Behavior and Human Decision Processes
San Diego, CA USA

Sources of Articles

Organizational Dynamics
New York, NY USA

Oriental Economist
Tokyo, Japan

Osaka Economic Papers
Osaka, Japan

Oxford Economic Papers
Oxford, UK

Pacific Affairs
Oxford, UK

Pacific Basin Quarterly
Los Angeles, CA USA

Pacific Community
Newton, MA USA

Pakistan Horizon
Karachi, Pakistan

Past and Present
Oxford, UK

People Weekly
New York, NY USA

Personnel
Paris, France

Personnel Administrator
Alexandria, VA USA

Personnel Journal
Swarthmore, PA USA

Personnel Management
London, UK

Personnel Psychology
Baltimore, MD USA

Personnel Review
Bradford, W Yorkshire   UK

Phi Delta Kappan
Bloomington, IN USA

Philippine Economic Journal
Manila, Philippines

Physics Today
New York, NY USA

Policy Studies
Beverly Hills, CA USA

Political Science Quarterly
New York, NY USA

Political Studies
Oxford, UK

Politico
Pavia, Italy

Population Research and Policy Review
Amsterdam, Netherlands

Populi
New York, NY USA

Production and Inventory Management Review
   and APICS News
Hollywood, FL USA

Psychology Today
New York, NY USA

Sources of Articles

Public Finance
The Hague, Netherlands

Public Interest
New York, NY USA

Public Opinion Quarterly
Princeton, NJ USA

Public Personnel Management
Alexandria, VA USA

Public Policy
Cambridge, UK

Public Relations Quarterly
Rhinebeck, NY USA

Purchasing
Newton, MA USA

Quality Progress
Milwaukee, WI USA

Quarterly Journal of Economics
Cambridge MA USA

Quarterly Review of Economics and Business
Champaign, IL USA

Real Estate Review
Boston, MA USA

Reason
Santa Monica, CA USA

Research in Population Economics
Greenwich, CT USA

Research Management
Lancaster, PA USA

Research Policy
Amsterdam, Netherlands

Restaurant Business
New York, NY USA

Review of Economic Studies
Edinburgh, U.K.

Review of Economics and Statistics
Cambridge, MA USA

Revue Economique
Paris, France

Rice University Studies
Houston, TX USA

Risk Management
New York NY USA

Rivista Internazionale di Scienze
   Economiche e Commerciali
Milan/Padova, Italy

SAIS Review
Washington DC USA

Sales and Marketing Management
New York, NY USA

Sales and Marketing Management
Luton, UK

SAM Advanced Management Journal/Advanced
   Management Journal
Cincinnati, OH USA

Scholastic Update
New York, NY USA

Sources of Articles

Science
Washington, DC USA

Science and Public Policy
London, UK

Science News
Washington, DC USA

Scientific American
New York, NY USA

Senior Scholastic
New York, NY USA

Site Selection Handbook
Norcross, GA USA

Sloan Management Review
Cambridge, MA USA

Small Group Behavior
Newbury Park, CA USA

Social Research
New York, NY USA

Social Science Information
Paris, France

Social Security Bulletin
Washington, DC USA

Social Service Review
Chicago, IL USA

Society
New Brunswick, NJ USA

Sociological Quarterly
Carbondale, IL USA

Sociologus
Berlin, West Germany

Sociology and Social Research
Los Angeles, CA USA

Sociology of Work and Occupations
Newbury Park, CA USA

South
London, UK

Southeast Asian Affairs
Singapore, Singapore

Southern Economic Journal
Chapel Hill, NC USA

Southwestern Journal of Anthropology/Journal of
  Anthropological Research
Albuquerque, NM USA

Staff Papers, International Monetary Fund
Washington, DC USA

Stanford GSB
Stanford, CA USA

Strategic Management Journal
Chichester, Sussex UK

Studia Diplomatica
Brussels, Belgium

Studies of Broadcasting
Tokyo, Japan

Sumitomo Bank Review
Tokyo, Japan

Sumitomo Quarterly
Tokyo, Japan

Sources of Articles

Supervision
Burlington, IA USA

Supervisory Management
New York, NY USA

Technological Forecasting and Social Change
New York, NY USA

Technology Review
Cambridge, MA USA

Telephony
Chicago, IL USA

Textile Industries
Atlanta, GA USA

Three Banks Review
Edinburgh, UK

Time
New York, NY USA

Training
Minneapolis, MN USA

Training and Development Journal
Alexandria, VA USA

Trialogue
New York, NY USA

UCLA Pacific Basin Law Journal
Los Angeles, CA USA

United States Banker
Cos Cob, CT USA

Urban Land
Washington, DC USA

Urbanisme
Paris, France

US News and World Report
Washington, DC USA

Venture
New York, NY USA

Vision
Paris, France

Vital Speeches of the Day
Mt. Pleasant, SC USA

Wall Street Journal
New York, NY USA

Ward's Auto World
Detroit, MI USA

Waseda Economic Papers
Tokyo, Japan

Western Economic Journal
Huntington Beach, CA USA

Wilson Quarterly
Washington, DC USA

Working Woman
New York, NY USA

World Development
Elmsford, NY USA

World Economy
London, UK

World Politics
London, UK

Sources of Articles

World Press Review
Farmingdale, NY USA

World Today
London, UK

Worldwide Projects and Installation Planning
Westport, CT USA

Yale Review
New Haven, CT USA

TOPICAL LOCATOR

----Suppliers   EA-26
----Technology   GD-15

BALANCE OF PAYMENTS   A-3, CF 77, DG-4, DG-24, DG-25,
     EC-37

Balance of Trade   see   TRADE, BALANCE OF

Bank of Japan   see CENTRAL BANK

BANKING   DB-6, DB-25, DB-39, DH-1, DH-13, DH-15, DH-16,
     DH-18, DH-26, DH-41
----History   DH 45

BANKRUPTCY   GA-32
----Prediction   GA-25

BANKS, COMMERCIAL   DH-32

BASEBALL BATS   EC-22

BAUXITE   EC-124

BEEF   GD-11

BEHAVIORAL PATTERNS   BD-18, BD-21

BENEFITS   (see also BONUS)   FH-4

BERGSTEN, C. FRED   EC-55

BIBLIOGRAPHIES   A-29, A-34, A-37, BA-14

BIOGRAPHY   A-5
----Directory   A-41

BIRTHRATE   BC-66

BLUE COLLAR WORKERS   (see also LABOR AND LABORING
     CLASSES)   FF-3, FF-13
----and Tradition   FF-3

CAPITALISM, RURAL   CB-51

CAREERS AND CAREER DEVELOPMENT   (see also RECRUITMENT;
   and TRAINING AND DEVELOPMENT)
----Corporate   FC-7
----Corporate, in U.S.   FC-7
----in Management   FG-5, FG-8, HA-2

CENTRAL BANK (Japan)   DB-33, DH-11, DH-12

CHEMICALS AND CHEMICAL INDUSTRY   GD-36

CHILD DEVELOPMENT   BC-1

CHILDREN   BC-49, BD-34

CHINA (Communist)   BF-6, BF-12, CA-16

CHOSHU   BA-9, BC-39

CHRYSLER CORP.   GD-64, JC-38, JC-65, JC-68

CITIES   BC-6, BC-34

City Life   see CITIES

CLASS STRUGGLE   BB-43

COLLECTIVE INTERDEPENDENCE   DC-40

Commercial Agreements   see TREATIES

COMMERCIAL POLICY   EA-13, EA-14, EA-15, EA-17, EA-19,
   EA-22, EA-68, EA-69

COMMODITIES   CF-7

COMMUNALISM   BC-44

COMMUNICATION IN BUSINESS   (see also
   ORGANIZATIONS)   HB-44, HD-68
----Rules for   HB-21

Community-Based Industries see INDUSTRIES,
    COMMUNITY-BASED

COMPANIES (see also BUSINESS; also
    CORPORATIONS) GB-2, GB-3, GB-4, GB-6, GB-19,
    GB-20, GB-21, GB-27
----Directories A-6, A-7, A-12, A-13, H-8
----Economic Analysis GB-1
----Outsiders in GB-30
----in U.S (see CORPORATIONS, JAPANESE IN THE U.S.)

COMPANY TRAINING PROGRAMS (see also TRAINING AND
    DEVELOPMENT) FG-11

COMPETITION (see also BUSINESS COMPETITION) CD-7

COMPETITION, INTERNATIONAL (see also TRADE RIVALRY;
    also U.S. AND JAPAN) CF-15, CF-21

Competition, Trade see TRADE RIVALRY

Computer Aided Design see CAD-CAM

Computer Aided Manufacturing see CAD-CAM

COMPUTER INDUSTRY (see also ELECTRONICS
    INDUSTRY) DD-8, DD10

CONFLICT RESOLUTION DA-63, HB-45, HD-88

CONFLICTS, SOCIAL BC-71

CONGLOMERATES (see also ZAIBATSU) DB-23

CONSENSUS (see also RINGI SYSTEM;
    DECISION-MAKING) GB-13

CONSERVATISM
----of Business Organization EA-10

CONSTRUCTION PROJECTS
----U.S. Excluded from   EC-153

CONSUMPTION   CA-55, DG-29, FE-13

CONTRACT   CD-9, CD-10

CONVERGENCE HYPOTHESIS   DA-41, FC-9, HB-13

Cooperation, Industrial   see INDUSTRIAL COOPERATION

COPPER   EC-124

CORN OIL   EC-45

CORPORATE CHARITY   GB-15

CORPORATE CONTROL   CD-9

CORPORATE CULTURE   EG-6

CORPORATE FINANCE   DH-25, GA-13, GA-14, GB-23, GB-24
----U.S. Compared   GB-24

CORPORATE PLANNING   CD-7, GB-18, GC-3, GC-6, GC-11,
    GC-12

CORPORATE REFORMS   GC-5

CORPORATE STRATEGIES   DA-78, EA-62, GB-6, GB-37, GB-40,
    GC-1, GC-4, GC-7, GC-9, GC-10
----Canon Co.   GC-10

CORPORATE STRUCTURE   GB-37, GB-40, HD-3

CORPORATIONS, FOREIGN (IN JAPAN) (see also JOINT
    VENTURES)   DJ-2, DJ-5, DJ-7, DJ-14, DJ-19, DJ-20,
    DJ-21
----Laws   DJ-3
----Management   DJ-1, FA-3
----Operations   DJ-1
----Policies   DJ-3

DANFORTH, JOHN C.   EC-55

DAIMYO   CB-39

DANCHI   BD-16

Darwinism, Economic   see ECONOMIC DARWINISM

DEBENTURES, CORPORATE   EG-29

DECISION-MAKING   (see also RINGI SYSTEM)   GB-7, GB-17,
    GD-69, HB-28, HB-56, HB-68, HB-69, HB-80

----Cultural Aspects   HA-21

----Traditional   HA-41

----U.S. Compared   HB-22

DEFENSE POLICY
----Post WWII   BB-39

DEMING, W. EDWARDS   HA-8, HB-19, IC-53, IC-56, IC-59

DEMOCRACY   BC-11, BC-24, BD-56

 ----Industrial   FH-10

DEPENDENCE   BD-9, BD-50, CA-77, GB-29

DEPRESSION (Business)   CE-3

DEREGULATION
----Finance   DG-8, DG-10

DEVELOPING COUNTRIES   (see also ECONOMIC RELATIONS WITH
    DEVELOPING COUNTRIES)   BF-23, CH-35, CH-37

DEVELOPMENT PROCESS   CF-15

DICTIONARIES
----Geography   A-23
----History   A-23
----Biography   A-5

DIRECTORIES   A-6, EA-7
----Automobile Industry   A-20
----Business   A-7
----Companies (Japan)   A-12, A-13
----Electronics   A-18
----Japanese Firms in U.S. and Canada   A-12, A-13
----Japanese Imports   A-9, A-38
----Japanese Start-up Ventures   A-10
----Industrial Groupings in Japan   A-10
----Information Service   A-27
----Overseas Investment   A-25
----Pharmaceutical Industries   A-26
----Professional Associations   A-14
----Publishers (Japan)   A-21
----Trade   A-23, A-36

DIGNITY   HC-7

Diplomacy, Economic   see ECONOMIC DIPLOMACY

DIPLOMATS, JAPANESE   BB-45

Dispute Resolution   see CONFLICT RESOLUTION

DISTRIBUTION SYSTEM   DB-4, DB-28, DK-12, GD-7

DIVERSIFICATION, CORPORATE   GC-8

DOING BUSINESS WITH THE JAPANESE   CD-1, CD-3, CD-4,
    CD-5, CD-10, CE-1, CE-2, CD-9, CE-10, CE-14, CE-15,
    CE-16, CE-17, CE-18, CE-19, CE-21, CE-23, CE-25,
    CE-26, CE-28, CE-31, CE-32, CE-33, CE-35, DC-5

DUESENBERY MODEL   FE-8

DUMPING   EA-1, EB-6, EB-10, EB-11, EB-12, EB-13, EB-20,
    EB-32, EC-110, EB-163, EE-11, GD-54, JB-12

Earning   see WAGES AND EARNING

East Asia   see ASIA, EAST

ECONOMETRIC MODEL   CB-43, CF-53, DA-48

Economic Assistance   see   FOREIGN AID

ECONOMIC BUREAUCRACY   (see also MITI; also JETRO)   DC-4

ECONOMIC COMPETITION   DA-17

ECONOMIC CONDITIONS   CF-37, CF-48, CF-67, CF-71, CF-72,
    CF-78, CF-84, CF-90, EC-143

ECONOMIC CONTROL   CA-53, CA-73

ECONOMIC CYCLES   CA-41, CF-86

ECONOMIC DARWINISM   GB-11

ECONOMIC DEMOCRACY   DA-15

ECONOMIC DEPENDENCE   CA-20, CA-22

ECONOMIC DEVELOPMENT   BA-11, BB-15, BD-43, CA-16,
    CA-24, CA-36, CA-43, CA-49, CA-50, CA-52, CA-66,
    CA-68, CB-13, CB-45, CB-46, CC-16, CC-17, CC-21,
    CC-22, CC-23, CE-5, CF-52, CF-59, DA-9, DA-11,
    DA-39, DA-71, EA-57, HA-10
----Financing   DA-60

ECONOMIC DUALISM   DA-80, DB-1 DG-18

Topical Locator

ECONOMIC GROWTH   CA-73, CA-74, CA-79, CB-2, CB-8, CB-9,
     CB-10, CB-30, CB-47, CE-13, CF-22, CF-23, CF-35,
     CF-57, CF-86, CF-98, DA-17, DA-26, DA-42, DC-6,
     DG-7, DG-11, DH-49, EA-46, EA-57
----Pre-WWII CB-17, CB-19, CB-35
----Statistical Analysis CA-69
----Theory DA-26
----U.S. Compared CG-14, CG-18

ECONOMIC GROWTH PATTERNS   CA-62, CB-20, CF-80

ECONOMIC HEGEMONY   CA-72, CF-97, CG-5, DA-18, DA-35,
     DB-17, DH-44, JA-21, JA-23, K-36

ECONOMIC HISTORY   BA-26, BA-27, BB-32, BB-40, CA-6,
     CA-21, CA-26, CA-27, CA-32, CA-40, CA-42, CA-45,
     CA-49, CA-50, CA-52, CB-34, CB-43, CB-49, CB-50,
     CC-9, DB-45, DH-43

ECONOMIC OPTIONS   CF-17, CF-27, CF-28, CF-29, CF-31,
     CF-40, DA-53, DE-7

ECONOMIC PLANNING   BB-42, BD-49, DA-9, DA-17, DA-36,
     DA-49, DA-54, DA-61, DC-41
----West Germany Compared DA-72

ECONOMIC POLICY   CF-93, DA-11, DA-14, DA-15, DA-45,
     DA-51, DA-53, DA-59, DC-25, EA-29, EA-74, EC-158,
     IA-29

ECONOMIC PROSPECTS   CF-8, CF-19, CF-24, CF-27, CF-32,
     CF-41, CF-45, CF-70, CF-72, CF-74, CF-81, CF-89,
     DA-33, DA-85, DC-16

ECONOMIC RECOVERY   CF-26, DA-2, DG-31, EA-55

ECONOMIC RELATIONS
----with Africa CH-14
----with ASEAN CH-3, CH-4, CH-28
----with Asia CH-9
----with Australia CH-8
----with Canada CH-12, ED-5

EMPLOYMENT CHARACTERISTICS
----U.S.-Japan Compared FC-9

Employment, Permanent see RINGI SYSTEM

EMPLOYMENT POLICY FC-1

EMPLOYMENT PRACTICES BC-58, CF-39, DA-32, DB-40, FA-2,
    FA-3, FC-3, FC-9, FC-10, FC-13, FC-15, FC-21,
    FC-42, FH-11

EMPLOYMENT STRUCTURE FC-32, FC-35

ENCYCLOPEDIAS A-28

ENERGY POLICY CF-14, DE-1, DE-4, DE-5, DE-10, DE-12,
    DE-13

ENERGY PROBLEMS DE-2, DE-7, DE-11

ENERGY RESOURCES CF-14, DE-3, DE-14
----Demand by Japan DE-13
----and Economic Growth DE-8

ENTERPRISE SIZE CE-4

ENGINEERS FG-7

ENLIGHTENMENT BA-6

ENTRANCE EXAMINATIONS BC-72

ENTREPRENEUR AND ENTREPRENEURSHIP BC-46, BC-50, CA-67,
    CA-71, CB-6, CB-31

ENTERPRISE UNIONS (see also LABOR UNIONS) FC-15,
    FD-17

ENVIRONMENT CA-34

ENVIRONMENTAL LAW DF-1

ENVIRONMENTALISM   DF-2, EA-10

EQUALITY   BD-7

EQUILIBRIUM ANALYSIS   EC-168
----European Communities   EC-168
----Japan   EC-168
----U.S. Trade   EC-168

ESTABLISHMENT SIZE
----Labor Coefficient   FA-13

ETHICS   BD-13

Ethos   see JAPANESE ETHOS

ETIQUETTE   (see also DOING BUSINESS IN JAPAN; also
     NEGOTIATING STYLE)   CD-3, CD-4, CD-5, CE-16

EXCHANGE RATE   DG-1, DG-24, DH-27, DH-46, EA-26, EA-27,
     EA-28, EA-35, EA-36, EA-79, EB-8, EC-29
----Productivity Approach   EA-36

EXECUTIVES, SELECTION OF   HA-23

EXPORT-PUSH   EC-13

EXPORT QUOTAS
----Automobiles   EC-26

EXPORTS   (see also IMPORTS; also TRADE)   EB-8, EB-9,
     EB-16, EB-17, EB-21, EB-23, EB-24
----Performance   EA-59
----Post-WWII expansion   EB-22
----to Europe   EB-4
----to U.S.   EX-13, EC-72, EC-81, EC-82, EC-89, EC-93

EXPORT CARTELS   EB-15

FACTOR ENDOWMENT   IE-6

FACTOR PROPORTIONS   EA-71

FACTORIES, JAPANESE (see also INDUSTRIAL
     ENTERPRISE) FA-3, GB-22
----Automobile GD-9
------Social Structure GA-22, GD-15
----Modernization IB-6
----Organizational Structure GB-26
----Social Organization FA-1, FA-19
----Technical Operations GB-25

FACTORY LEGISLATION DC-14

FAMILY BC-55, BC-73, BC-75, GB-14

FAMILY LIFE BA-13

FAMILY PLANNING BC-4

FAMILY FARMING CC-5

FARMING EMPLOYMENT CC-5

FERTILITY CA-63

FIBERS GD-30

FINANCE CA-47, DB-2, DH-14, DH-15, GC-15
----Local DH-22
----Private DH-17

FINANCE, INTERNATIONAL EG-13

FINANCIAL DEVELOPMENT CE-8, DC-20

Financial Market see MONEY MARKET (see also CAPITAL
     MARKET)

FINANCIAL OPERATIONS DH-11, DH-13, DH-15, DH-18
----Theory of DH-18

FINANCIAL POLICY   CA-64, CE-8, DA-84, DG-20, DG-28,
    DG-34, DH-12, DH-27, DH-28, DH-34, DH-39, DH-40,
    DH-42, DH-43, DH-46, DH-52, DH-56, EA-45, EG-24

FINANCIAL REFORM   DH-51

FINANCIAL REPORTING   CD-2, DH-8, DK-1

FINANCIAL STRUCTURE
----and Bankruptcy   GA-32

FINANCIAL SYSTEM   DB-24, DB-25, DB-35, DB-42, DH-5,
    DH-10, DH-16, DH-21, DH-41
----History   DB-45, DH-45

FISCAL POLICY   CG-20, DG-3, DG-13, DG-15, DG-17, DG-22,
    DG-30, DG-31, DG-34, DH-33

FOOD   BC-60
----Control of   DC-11

FOREIGN AID, JAPANESE   CH-40, EG-1, EG-4
----Policy   EG-4

FOREIGN EXCHANGE   DH-4, EA-68
----Theory   DH-4

FOREIGN EXCHANGE MARKET   DH-36

FOREIGN EXCHANGE RESERVES   DG-20

Foreign Investments in Japan   see INVESTMENTS, FOREIGN
    IN JAPAN

FOREIGN POLICY (JAPAN)   BB-27, BF-19, BF-22

FOREMAN SYSTEM   FA-19

FREE ENTERPRISE   DC-42

FUCHI, K.   GD-57

FUJI BANK
----Quality Circles   IC-69

GATT (General Agreement on Tarrifs and Trade)   DG-21,
     EC-2

GENERAL MOTORS   EC-115, EF-80
----Just-in-Time   JC-8, JC-29, JC-33

GEOGRAPHY   A-2, BA-12, CA-23, CA-28

GOVERNMENT AND BUSINESS   (see also GOVERNMENT GUIDANCE;
     also MITI) DA-58, DA-62, DA-63, DC-1, DC-4, DC-5,
     DC-6, DC-7, DC-27, DC-28, DC-37, DC-28

GOVERNMENT AND GOVERNMENT CONTROL   BC-36, CF-38, CF-87,
     DC-4, DC-10, DC-11, DC-21, DC-22, DC-23, DC-24,
     DC-26, DC-34, DC-39, DC-42, DH-43, DL-1, EA-68

GOVERNMENT ENTERPRISES   BD-33a, CB-41, DB-12

GOVERNMENT GUIDANCE   (see also GOVERNMENT AND BUSINESS;
     and MITI) DA-32, DA-37, DA-58, DA-83, DA-83, DC-4,
     DC-6, DC-36, DC-42, DC-43

GREAT BRITAIN   BB-3, BF-5, BF-11
----Economy Compared with Japan   CH-32
----Industry   DA-13
----Treaties and Agreements   CH-24, CH-30

GROUP   BC-12, BC-76, BD-55, BD-65, GD-24
----Loyalty   FC-27

GROUPISM   BC-76, CA-59, DA-27, GB-7

HAKUTO   EC-44

HARMONY   BC-23, CF-33, IA-39
----in the Workplace   FH-46
----in Competition   HA-22

Topical Locator

HIGH TECHNOLOGY   A-10, BD-46, DD-1, ID-3, ID-6, ID-11,
    ID-15, ID-16, ID-17, ID-18, ID-19, ID-20, ID-21,
    ID-23, ID-24, ID-28, ID-29, ID-30
----Directory   A-10
----Effect on Employment in Japan   FC-23
----Industrial Policy   DC-29
----Laws and regulations   EC-56
----Trade Friction   Ec-128
----U.S. Strategy   DD-1, JA-17, JA-19

HIGH TECHNOLOGY INDUSTRIES   DD-5, DD-9, ID-25
----Competition   ID-34

History, Economic   see ECONOMIC HISTORY

HISTORY (GENERAL) BA-14, BA-20, BA-24, BA-25, BC-7,
    BA-28
----Bibliography   A-34
----Biographical Dictionaries   A-5
----Dictionaries   A-33

HISTORY (MEIJI PERIOD 1808-1912)   BA-8, BA-9, BA-23,
    BA-30, BB-17, BB-40, BD-31, CB-6, CB-24, CB-31,
    CB-37, CB-41, CB-42, CB-52, CC-25, HC-8

HISTORY (MODERN PERIOD 1868--) BA-1, BB-4, BB-25,
    BB-29

HISTORY (POST-WWII PERIOD 1945--) BF-14, BF-15

HISTORY (TOKUGAWA PERIOD 1603-1868)   BA-15, BA-29, BD-10,
    CA-9, CB-27, CB-31, CB-50

HITACHI   GC-31

HOARDING   EA-10

HONDA   GD-32

HOUSING
----Finance   DG-11

IMPORTS   EA-17, EA-18, EB-3, EB-7, EB-14, EB-18, EB-20,
    EC-19, EC-134
----Automobiles ED-44
----Beef EB-19
----Non-fuel Minerals   ED-4
----Oil ED-4
----Oranges EB-19
----Telephones EC-141

INAMORI, K.   CF-50

INCOME
----Distribution of   DA-12

INCOME SECURITY   FD-15

INCOME TAX   DG-12

INCOMES POLICY   DG-9

INDIA   CE-8, CF-25

INDIVIDUALISM   BC-59

INDUSTRIAL COOPERATION   CF-33, CF-38, DC-42

Industrial Democracy   see DEMOCRACY, INDUSTRIAL

INDUSTRIAL DEVELOPMENT   BD-33a, CA-23, CA-28, CF-56,
    DA-3, DA-10, DA-34, DA-47, DA-63, DA-64, DA-80,
    DA-82, HA-53
----Social Aspects   BC-13, BC-14

INDUSTRIAL EQUIPMENT   DA-67

INDUSTRIAL GROUPINGS   (see also KEIRETSU)   A-11, DB-3,
    DB-5, DB-39, DC-33
----Directories   A-11

INDUSTRIAL KNOWLEDGE   DA-13

INDUSTRIAL MANAGEMENT   DB-16

ITAMI, HIROYUKI   JA-33

IYE   CA-59

JAPAN (COMPARATIVE VIEW)   BA-10, BB-6, BB-21, BC-65,
    CF-92, GA-2

JAPAN (GENERAL TREATMENT)   BA-10, BA-12, BA-16, BA-17,
    BA-19, BB-1, BB-5, BB-7, BB-8, BB-13, BB-16, BB-19,
    BB-20, BB-23, BB-24, BB-28, BB-29, BB-30, BB-31,
    BB-35, BB-36, BB-44, BC-12, BE-7, BF-4, CA-39,
    CB-28, CH-36, GA-1, HA-54

JAPAN (INTERNATIONAL RELATIONS)   BE-7, BF-1, BF-8,
    BF-9, BF-16, CB-48, CH-17

JAPAN (LEGAL SYSTEM)   CA-18

JAPAN (WORLD ROLE)   BE-7, BF-2, BF-3, BF-7, BF-10,
    BF-18, BF-21, CA-15, CE-11, CE-12, CF-6, CF-9,
    CF-10, CF-64, CF-65, CH-1, CH-13, CH-14, EC-148

Japan-U.S. Relations   see U.S.-JAPAN RELATIONS

"JAPAN, INC."   (see also MITI)   DC-40

Japanese Corporations in the United States   see
    CORPORATIONS, JAPANESE

JAPANESE ETHOS   BD-24

JAPANESE MANAGERS IN THE U.S.   (see also CORPORATIONS,
    JAPANESE) HB-14, HB-15, HB-16, HB-52, HD-16, HD-21,
    HD-38, HD-45, HD-46, HD-75, HD-93

JAPANESE MIND   BD-4, BD-22, BD-23, BD-54

JETRO   DB-23, EC-53

JOB PAY   HA-45

Topical Locator

----United States HD-1, HD-3, HD-8, HD-19, HD-23,
    HD-24, HD-25, HD-30, HD-31, HD-32, HD-36, HD-38,
    HD-40, HD-42, HD-46, HD-47, HD-49, HD-51, HD-57,
    HD-58, HD-59, HD-60, HD-63, HD-64, HD-67, HD-68,
    HD-69, HD-71, HD-72, HD-73, HD-74, HD-78, HD-79,
    HD-80, HD-85, HD-87, HD-91, HD-92, HD-94, HD-95,
    HD-98, IA-13
----the West HD-6, HD-39, HD-52, HD-90

MANAGEMENT (CRITICAL VIEW) HA-25, HA-30, HA-36, HA-42,
    HA-43, HA-66, HB-11, HB-39, HB-42, HB-50, HB-51,
    HB-63, HB-66, HB-77, HB-82, HB-83, HD-84

MANAGEMENT DEVELOPMENT HB-6, HD-61

MANAGEMENT INFORMATION SYSTEM ID-5

MANAGEMENT (LEGAL ASPECTS) HA-60

MANAGEMENT, PARTICIPATIVE (see also WORKER
    PARTICIPATION; also RINGI SYSTEM) HA-6, HB-18,
    HB-25, HB-37, HB-53

MANAGEMENT PHILOSOPHY DB-37, HA-14, HA-19, HA-29,
    HD-76
----British Response HD-76

MANAGEMENT PRACTICES CD-1, CD-6, DA-3, DA-69, DC-8,
    FA-18, FH-19, FH-20, HB-9, HB-17, HB-23, HB-26,
    HB-27, HB-83, HB-84, HB-85, HB-86, HD-11, HD-98
----Compared GB-2
----U.S. Compared HA-15

MANAGEMENT OF PUBLIC ENTERPRISES CA-51

MANAGEMENT (SOCIO-CULTURAL ASPECTS) HA-62, HA-63,
    HA-67

MANAGEMENT STYLE DB-3, HB-1, HB-27, HB-36, HB-38,
    HB-47, HB-48, HB-68, HB-74, HD-19, HD-48, HD-49,
    HD-98

MANAGEMENT SYSTEM, JAPANESE   CA-47, HA-42, HB-32, HD-51
----History   HC-8

MANAGEMENT, SCIENTIFIC   HA-40

MANAGEMENT THEORIES   HA-36, HA-37, HA-47, HA-48, HA-49,
    HA-50, HA-52

Management Training   see TRAINING AND DEVELOPMENT; also
    MANAGERS

Managerial Attitudes   see ATTITUDES, MANAGERIAL

MANAGERIAL CAREER DEVELOPMENT   (see also TRAINING AND
    DEVELOPMENT)   HB-81, HC-1

MANAGERS
----American (of Japanese Ancestry)   HA-28
----Generalists   HD-10
----Motivation of   HB-24
----Specialists   HD-10

MANCHURIA   BB-41, CB-26

MANPOWER POLICY   FA-16, FC-2

MANPOWER UTILIZATION   DA-3

MANSFIELD, MIKE   JA-62

MANUFACTURING ESTABLISHMENTS   CE-4

MARKET STRUCTURE, JAPANESE   CA-60, DA-32, DB-3, DB-4

MARKET, JAPANESE   DD-21, DJ-10, DK-2, DK-3, DK-8, DK-9,
    DK-10, DK-12, DK-14, DK-15, DK-17, DK-18, EA-63,
    EA-81
----East Asian Products   DK-15
----Grievances   EA-63
----Openness   EA-63

PERSONNEL MANAGEMENT   FA-2, FG-6, FG-12, FH-41, HC-5,
    HC-12, HC-13, HC-14, HD-69
----Japanese, in Britain   HC-3
----Japanese, in U.S.   HC-2
----Lessons for the West   JD-2
----Problems   HC-10, HD-70
----Productivity   HC-15
----Public Sector   HC-6
----U.S. Compared   HC-12

PERSONNEL ROTATION   GA-17, GA-18

PHARMACEUTICAL INDUSTRY
----Directories   A-26

PHILLIPS CURVE   FE-15

PHILOSOPHY   BD-23

POLITICAL PARTICIPATION   BC-74

POLITICAL THOUGHT   BA-15

POLITICS   BB-26, BB-33, BB-34, BB-37, BB-38, BC-3,
    BC-7, BC-11, BC-24, BC-32, BC-45, BD-33a

POPULATION   BB-15, BB-47, BC-21, BC-49, BC-66, CA-76,
    FA-8
----Aging   FC-26

PRESSURE GROUPS   BC-51

PRICE FIXING   EA-10

PRICE MOVEMENTS   FE-9

PRICES AND PRICING   DA-16, FE-4, FE-5, FE-7, FE-11,
    FE-12, FE-13, FE-14, FE-16, FE-17
----Agricultural   FE-15
----Changes   FA-20
----Construction   FE-18
----U.S. Compared   FE-2, FE-3

RECONSTRUCTION (Post WWII) BB-10, DA-43

REBELS BC-9

RECRUITMENT
----and Higher Education FG-2

Re-employment see AMUKADARI

REGULATIONS
----Foreign Investments DL-1

RELIGION BC-10, CA-9

RELIGIOUS MOVEMENTS BC-10

RESEARCH AND DEVELOPMENT IE-4, IE-12, IE-13, IE-15,
    IE-17, IE-19
----Imports of Technology IE-4

RESEARCH HANDBOOK A-40

Research, Economic see ECONOMIC RESEARCH

RESEARCH AND DEVELOPMENT DC-43

RETAILING GA-16, GD-7, GD-37

RETIREMENT (see also AMUKUDARI)
----Early FC-29
----Government Officials HC-9
----Re-employment HC-9

REVOLUTION
----Aristocratic BB-46
----Bourgeois BA-30

RINGI SYSTEM BC-70, CA-61, CD-1, CF-33, CF-39, DA-63,
    DC-8, EI-2, HA-23

RINGISHO CD-1

Topical Locator

TAXATION, UNITARY   DJ-15

TECHNICAL ASSISTANCE   CH-40

TECHNICAL INFORMATION
----Role in Competitiveness with Japan   ID-7

TECHNICAL SKILLS   GD-38

TECHNOCRACY   GB-5

TECHNOECONOMICS   ID-8

TECHNOLOGICAL CHANGE   DA-41

TECHNOLOGICAL CO-OPERATION   ID-13

TECHNOLOGICAL DEVELOPMENT   DA-32

TECHNOLOGICAL IMPLICATION, THEORY OF   ID-26

TECHNOLOGY ACQUISITION   DC-26

TECHNOLOGY TRANSFER   DB-3, ED-9, GA-29, HB-60, IA-29

TECHNOLOGY   IE-3, JA-31
----Automobile Assembly   GD-15
----Exports   ID-40
----Global View   JB-3
----International Co-operation   JB-3
----Steel   GD-14

TECHNOLOGY AND SCIENCE   (see also HIGH
     TECHNOLOGY)   BD-24, CA-57, ID-9, ID-10, ID-11,
     ID-12, ID-33, ID-35, ID-36
----Information and Documentation   ID-14

TECHNOLOGY, IMPACT OF   CF-87, CF-95
----Automobile Factory   GA-22

TECHNOPOLIS   ID-6

TECHNORIVALRY   JA-60

TELEVISION SETS   GD-46

TETSURO, WATSUJI   BD-38

TEXTILE INDUSTRY   DD-19, GC-34, GD-45, JA-5

THEORY Z (see also TYPE-Z ORGANIZATIONS) DB-37, HA-7,
    HA-39, HA-47, HA-48, HA-49, HA-52, HA-55, HA-58,
    HA-64, HA-65, HD-56, HD-65, HD-66, JC-14, K-9
----Critical View   JC-15

Tokugawa Period see HISTORY (TOKUGAWA PERIOD)

TOKUGAWA SHOGUNATE   CB-44

TOKYO   CC-11, CC-26

TOKYO ROUND   EA-38

TOGETHERNESS (Organizational)   (see also
    GROUPISM)   HB-72

TOSHIMICHI, OKUBO   BB-18

TOYOTA   GD-16, GD-18
----Robotics   TD-2
----Toyota Production System GD-16, IB-7, IB-32,
    IB-33, IB-34, IB-35, IB-40, IB-49

TRADE   BF-17, BF-23, CB-7, CB-29, DA-10, DA-16, EA-16,
    EA-21, EA-37, EA-38, EA-64, ED-24
----Directories   A-23, A-36
----Instability   DG-1
----Pre-WWII   CB-4, CB-33
----Statistics   A-19, A-22
----Western Media   EA-23

TRADE, BALANCE OF DG-14, DG-23, DG-32, EC-17, EC-18,
    EC-24, EC-57, EC-58, EC-75, EC-78, EC-142, EC-154,
    EC-160, JA-39

TRADE BARRIERS (see also TRADE, FOREIGN) EA-49,
    EE-20, EE-24, EE-26
----Japan (to others) EA-65, EC-11, EC-36, EC-62,
    EC-65, EC-76, EC-80, EC-120, EC-129, EC-131,
    EC-167, ED-141, EE-4, EE-5, EE-19, EE-21, EE-32,
    EE-32, GD-41
----U.S. EC-80, EC-120, EE-11

TRADE CONFLICT EC-95, EC-99, EC-100, EC-101, EC-102,
    EC-114, EC-126, EC-133, EC-137, EC-140, EC-141,
    EC-144, EC-146, EC-152, EC-161, EC-165, EE-6,
    EE-10, EE-22, EE-23
----Electronics EC-39
----with Europe DC-21
----with U.S. DC-21, EC-20, EC-21, EC-22, EC-23,
    EC-27, EC-35, EC-41, EC-42, EC-51, EC-54, EC-58,
    EC-60, EC-61, EC-63, EC-69, EC-70, EC-84, EC-85,
    EC-92

TRADE CONTROL DJ-6
----Law EA-68

TRADE DEFICIT (see also TRADE, BALANCE OF) EC-18,
    EC-24, EC-25, EC-31, EC-37, EC-66, EC-74, EC-90,
    EC-103, EC-131, EC-151

TRADE EXPANSION EA-2, EA-8

TRADE, FOREIGN CF-76, EA-9, EA-11, EA-46, EA-54, EA-56
----with Europe EB-4
----Third World EB-1

TRADE, INTERNATIONAL CF-15, CF-18, EA-41, EA-42,
    EB-17, EC-6, EC-8, EC-119
----Steel EC-6
----White Paper ED-2, ED-3

TRADE-INVESTMENT CYCLE ED-6

TRADE LIBERALIZATION EA-4, EA-22, EA-34, EA-39, EA-63,
    EB-18, EB-19, EC-46

TRADE NEGOTIATIONS   EA-64, EC-2, ED-22

TRADE POLICY (see also COMMERCIAL POLICY)   CB-42,
    CF-20, CF-51, CF-76, EA-2, EA-3, EA-6, EA-22,
    EA-24, EA-25, EA-30, EA-31, EA-32, EA-33, EA-38,
    EA-40, EA-43, EA-44, EA-46, EA-47, EA-48, EA-50,
    EA-57, EA-65, EA-73, EA-78, EA-80, EA-81, EA-82,
    EB-2, EC-67, EC-68, EC-90, EC-91, EC-112, ED-8,
    ED-26
----Agricultural   CH-18

TRADE PRACTICES   EA-2, EA-5, EA-60, EA-75, EA-84,
    EA-84, EC-50, ED-31
----in Middle East   EA-5

TRADE PRACTICES, UNFAIR   EA-50, DC-3

TRADE RECIPROCITY   EC-107, EC-123, ED-35

TRADE RELATIONS WITH
----Africa   ED-20
----ASEAN   ED-1, ED-37
----Brazil   ED-22
----Canada   ED-23
----Developing Countries   ED-46
----Europe   ED-36
----Europe, Eastern   ED-28, ED-45
----Europe, Western   CE-29, ED-39, JB-6
----Far East   ED-33
----India   ED-38
----Indonesia   ED-42
----International   CH-38, EA-72, ED-21, ED-32, ED-34,
    ED-40, EG-19, JA-15, JA-16, JA-18
----Middle East   DE-13

TRADE RELATIONS, U.S.-JAPAN   CE-30, CF-20, CG-1, CG-2,
    CG-3, CG-4, CG-5, DC-21, DE-13, EA-67, EA-85, EC-1,
    EC-4, EC-9, EC-12, EC-14, EC-15, EC-16, EC-34,
    EC-43, EC-52, EC-53, EC-59, EC-71, EC-73, EC-74,
    EC-86, EC-97, EC-111, EC-136, EC-169, ED-10, ED-11,
    ED-12, ED-13, ED-14, ED-15

Topical Locator

U.S.--JAPAN RELATIONS (GENERAL) BE-1, BE-5, BE-6,
    BE-8, BE-9, BE-10, BE-12, BE-14, BE-15, BE-16,
    BE-17, BE-18, BE-22, BE-25, CG-6, CG-7, CG-9,
    CG-10, CG-11, CG-12, EA-51, EC-64, EC-88, EC-109
----Defense EC-106
----Prospects EC-104, EC-108

URBANIZATION BB-47, CA-58, CC-24, CC-26, CC-27

VALUES, JAPANESE BD-39, BD-52, CA-9

VALUES, SOCIAL (see also MANAGERIAL VALUES) BD-39,
    CB-55, CF-59
----Employee Attitudes, U.S.-Japan Compared FA-21
----in Management Innovation HA-34
----Workers HB-70, HB-71

VEHICLE SAFETY GD-49

VENDOR RELATIONS HB-78

VENTURE CAPITAL DH-35

VILLAGE BB-2

VOLUNTARY EXPORT RESTRAINT (see also AUTOMOTIVE
    INDUSTRY--Quotas) EC-159, EE-8
----Agreement EC-94

Wa see HARMONY

WAGE DETERMINATION FD-18

WAGE STRUCTURE DB-48, FD-10, FD-17, FD-19

WAGES AND EARNING FA-20, FC-25, FD-2, FD-8, FD-11,
    FD-12, FD-14, FE-9, FE-12, FE-17
----U.S. Compared FD-9

Warehouse Productivity see INVENTORY CONTROL

WEALTH, DISTRIBUTION OF DG-16

XEROX CORP.
----Productivity IA-44
----Quality Control IC-50

YAMAHA GD-20   YEARBOOKS, STATISTICAL A-22

YEN CA-40, DG-15, DG-19, DH-3, DH-24, DH-44, DH-46,
    DH-52, EA-26, EA-27, EA-28, EA-35, EA-45, EA-79,
    EB-7, EC-29, EC-87, EC-164, ED-17, EG-15, EG-23,
----Valuation DH-52

YANASE GD-23

YOKKAHARI GB-29

YOKICHI, FOKUZAWA BA-6

ZAIBATSU CB-1, CB-53, DB-3, DB-39, DC-38, GD-69,
    HA-40, HB-30

ZEN CD-12

CHAPTER 1

A. REFERENCE MATERIALS

A 1.   Anderson, Alun M. SCIENCE AND TECHNOLOGY IN JAPAN. Harlow, England: Longman; distributed by Gale Research, 1984. 421pp.

A 2.   Association of Japanese Geographers. GEOGRAPHY OF JAPAN. Tokyo: Teikoku-Shoin, 1980. 440pp.

A 3.   Bank of Japan. BALANCE OF PAYMENTS. Tokyo, monthly.

A 4.   Bank of Japan. ECONOMIC STATISTICS OF JAPAN. Tokyo, annual.

A 5.   BIOGRAPHICAL DICTIONARY OF JAPANESE HISTORY. Tokyo: Kodansha International, 1978. 655pp.

A 6.   COMPLETE DIRECTORY OF JAPAN: 1986-87. New York: International Culture Institute, 1986. 1074pp.

A 7.   DIAMOND'S JAPAN BUSINESS DIRECTORY 1987. Tokyo: Diamond Lead Co., 1987. 1500pp.

A 8.   DIRECTORY: AFFILIATES AND OFFICES OF JAPANESE FIRMS IN U.S.A. AND CANADA. Tokyo: Japan External Trade Association; distributed by Gale Research Co., 1986. 559pp.

Reference Materials

A 9. DIRECTORY OF JAPANESE IMPORTERS BY PRODUCT. New York: UNIPUB, 1985. 919pp.

A 10. HIGH-TECH START-UP VENTURES IN JAPAN: AN INDEX TO 500 SELECT COMPANIES. Tokyo: Japan Economic Journal; New York: distributed by UNIPUB, 1984. 256pp.

A 11. INDUSTRIAL GROUPINGS IN JAPAN 1986-87. 7th ed. Tokyo: Dodwell Marketing Consultants, 1986. 531pp.

A 12. JAPAN COMPANY HANDBOOK: NEWEST DATA ON 1104 BIG LISTED COMPANIES. Tokyo: Oriental Economist, 1985; New York: distributed by UNIPUB, 1985. 1174pp.

A 13. JAPAN DIRECTORY 1987. Tokyo: Japan Press, 1987. 2 vols., 1800pp.

A 14. JAPAN DIRECTORY OF PROFESSIONAL ASSOCIATIONS 1984-1987. Tokyo: Intercontinental Marketing, 1984. 349pp.

A 15. JAPAN ECONOMIC ALMANAC. Tokyo: Japan Economic Journal; New York: distributed by UNIPUB. annual.

A 16. JAPAN ELECTRONICS ALMANAC 1987. Philadelphia: distributed by IPS, 1987. 411pp.

A 17. JAPAN ENGLISH PUBLICATIONS IN PRINT 1985-86. Tokyo: Intercontinental Marketing; New York: distributed by UNIPUB, 1985. 366pp.

A 18. JAPAN ELECTRONICS BUYERS' GUIDE 1987. 25th ed. Philadelphia: distributed by IPS, 1987. 4 vols.

A 19. Japan. Ministry of Finance. THE SUMMARY REPORT; TRADE OF JAPAN. Tokyo, annual.

A 20. Japan Motor Industry Federation. GUIDE TO THE MOTOR INDUSTRY OF JAPAN 1987. Philadelphia: distributed by IPS, 1987. 290pp.

A 21.   JAPAN PUBLISHERS DIRECTORY.   Philadelphia:
distributed by IFS, 1986. 200pp.

A 22.   JAPAN STATISTICAL YEARBOOK.   Tokyo: Bureau of
Statistics, annual.   v.1-- 1941--.

A 23.   JAPAN TRADE DIRECTORY, 1986-87.   Tokyo: Japan
External Trade Organization; distributed by Gale
Research, 1986.

A 24.   Japanese Economic Research Center. LIST OF
JAPANESE ECONOMIC AND BUSINESS PERIODICALS IN ENGLISH.
3rd rev. ed.   Tokyo: The Center, 1973. 56pp.

A 25.   JAPANESE OVERSEAS INVESTMENT; A COMPLETE
LISTING BY FIRMS AND COUNTRIES, 1984-85.   Tokyo: The
Oriental Economist, 1984.

A 26.   JAPANESE PHARMACEUTICAL AND RELATED FIRMS
1984-86. 2nd ed.   Tokyo: Intercontinental Marketing,
1985. 300pp.

A 27.   JAPANESE TECHNICAL INFORMATION SERVICE: 1)
Current Japanese Research; 2) Japanese Technical
Abstracts; 3) Japanese Technical Abstracts, Quarterly
Index.   Ann Arbor, Mich.: University Microfilms, 1986.

A 28.   KODANSHA ENCYCLOPEDIA OF JAPAN. Toyo; New
York: Kodansha International, 1983. 9 volumes.

A 29.   Komiya, Ryutaro, comp.   A BIBLIOGRAPHY OF
STUDIES IN ENGLISH ON THE JAPANESE ECONOMY. Tokyo:
University of Tokyo Press, 1966. 52pp.

A 30.   Liesner, Thelma. ECONOMIC STATISTICS
1900-1983: UNITED KINGDOM, UNITED STATES OF AMERICA,
FRANCE, GERMANY, ITALY, JAPAN. New York: Facts On File,
1985. 142pp.

A 31. NIPPON: A CHARTERED SURVEY OF JAPAN, 1985/86. Tokyo: Kokusei-sha Corp., 1985. (annual) 357pp.

A 32. Nunn, Godfrey Raymond. JAPANESE PERIODICALS AND NEWSPAPERS IN WESTERN LANGUAGES: AN INTERNATIONAL UNION LIST. Kondon: Mansell, 1979. 235pp.

A 33. Papinot, Edmond. HISTORICAL AND GEOGRAPHICAL DICTIONARY OF JAPAN. 2 vols. New York: Frederick Ungar Pub. Co., 1964.

A 34. Rosovsky, Henry, comp. QUANTITATIVE JAPANESE ECONOMIC HISTORY; AN ANNOTATED BIBLIOGRAPHY AND A SURVEY OF U.S. HOLDINGS. Berkeley, Calif.: Center for Japanese Studies of the Institute for International Relations of the Institute of Business and Economic Research, University of California, 1961. 173pp.

A 35. Smith, Betty, and King, Shirley V. JAPANESE JOURNALS IN ENGLISH: A LIST OF JAPANESE SCIENTIFIC, TECHNICAL AND COMMERCIAL JOURNALS. London: British Library; Wolfeboro, N.H.: Longwood Publishing Group, 1985. 138pp.

A 36. STANDARD TRADE INDEX OF JAPAN 1987-88. 31st ed. Tokyo: Japan Chamber of Commerce and Industry, 1987. 1445pp.

A 37. Tada, H. A SELECTED BIBLIOGRAPHY ON SOCIO-ECONOMIC DEVELOPMENT OF JAPAN. Part 1: ca.1600-1940. New York: UNIPUB, 1980. 156pp.

A 38. 2000 IMPORTERS OF JAPAN. Tokyo: Japan External Trade Organization; New York: distributed by UNIPUB, 1984.

A 39. U. S. Library of Congress, comp. JAPANESE NATIONAL PUBLICATIONS IN THE LIBRARY OF CONGRESS. Washington, D.C.: U.S. Government Printing Office, 1981.

A 40.   Washington Researchers, Ltd. HOW TO FIND
INFORMATION ABOUT JAPANESE COMPANIES AND INDUSTRIES.
Washington, D.C.: Washington Researchers, Ltd., 1985.
340pp.

A 41.   WHO'S WHO IN JAPAN, 1984-85. Hong Kong:
International Culture Institute; distributed by Gale
Research, 1986. Biennial. 1083pp.

v.

CHAPTER 2

B. GENERAL WORKS; HISTORY,
SOCIETY, CULTURE, FOREIGN RELATIONS

BA. Historical Background

Monographic Works

BA 1.   Beasley, William G. THE MODERN HISTORY OF
JAPAN. 3rd ed.   New York: St. Martin's Press, 1981.
358pp.

BA 2.   Beckmann, George M. THE MODERNIZATION OF
CHINA AND JAPAN. New York: Harper and row, 1963. 724pp.

BA 3.   Befu, Harumi. JAPAN: AN ANTHROPOLOGICAL
INTRODUCTION. San Francisco: Chandler, 1971. 210pp.

BA 4.   Bisson, Thomas A. ASPECTS OF WARTIME
ECONOMIC CONTROL IN JAPAN. New York: Institute of
Pacific Relations, 1945. 108pp.

BA 5.   Bisson, Thomas A. JAPAN'S WAR ECONOMY. New
York: Institute of Pacific Relations, 1945. 267pp.

BA. Historical Background

BA 6.   Blacker, Carmen. THE JAPANESE ENLIGHTENMENT:
A STUDY OF THE WRITINGS OF FUKUZAWA YUKICHI. Cambridge:
Cambridge University Press, 1964. 185pp.

BA 7.   Braddon. Russell. JAPAN AGAINST THE WORLD,
1941-2041: THE HUNDRED YEAR WAR FOR SUPREMACY. New
York: Stein and Day, 1983. 256pp. Also known as THE
OTHER HUNDRED YEARS WAR: JAPAN'S BID FOR SUPREMACY,
1941-2041. London: Collins, 1983. 246pp.

BA 8.   Burks, Ardath W. THE MODERNIZERS: OVERSEAS
STUDENTS, FOREIGN EMPLOYEES, AND MEIJI JAPAN. Boulder,
Colo.: Westview Press, 1985. 450pp.

BA 9.   Craig, Albert M. CHOSHU IN THE MEIJI
RESTORATION. Cambridge, Mass.: Harvard University
Press, 1961. 385pp.

BA 10.   Craig, Albert M., ed.   JAPAN: A COMPARATIVE
VIEW. Princeton, N.J.: Princeton University Press,
1979. 437pp.

BA 11.   Datta, Amlan. A CENTURY OF ECONOMIC
DEVELOPMENT OF RUSSIA AND JAPAN. Calcutta: The World
Press, 1963. 187pp.

BA 12.   Dempster, Prue. JAPAN ADVANCES. A
GEOGRAPHICAL STUDY. 2nd ed.   London: Methuen, 1969.
332pp.

BA 13.   De Vos, George, and Wagatsuma, Hiroshi. THE
HERITAGE OF ENDURANCE. Berkeley: University of
California Press, 1984. 500pp.

BA 14.   Dower, John W. JAPANESE HISTORY AND CULTURE
FROM ANCIENT TO MODERN TIMES: SEVEN BASIC
BIBLIOGRAPHIES. Manchester, Eng.: Manchester
University Press, 1984. 232pp.

BA 15.   Earl, David Magarey. EMPEROR AND NATION IN
JAPAN: POLITICAL THINKERS OF THE TOKUGAWA PERIOD.
Seattle: University of Washington Press, 1964. 270pp.

BA 16.   Gibney, Frank. JAPAN: THE FRAGILE
SUPERPOWER. Rev. ed. New York: Norton, 1979. 378pp.

BA 17.   Hall, John W. JAPAN: FROM PREHISTORY TO
MODERN TIMES. New York: Dell, 1986. 397pp.

BA 18.   Hall, John W., and Beardsley, Richard K.
TWELVE DOORS TO JAPAN. New York: McGraw-Hill, 1965.
649pp.

BA 19.   Kobayashi, Maurie K. JAPAN: THE MOST
MISUNDERSTOOD COUNTRY. Tokyo: Japan Times, 1984. 165pp.

BA 20.   Morton, W. Scott. JAPAN: ITS HISTORY AND
CULTURE. New York: McGraw-Hill, 1984. 304pp.

BA 21.   Nakamura, Hajime. WAYS OF THINKING OF
EASTERN PEOPLES; INDIA, CHINA, TIBET, JAPAN. Honolulu:
East-West Center Press, 1964. 712pp.

BA 22.   Norbeck, Edward. CHANGING JAPAN. 2nd ed.
New York: Holt Rinehart and Winston, 1976. 108pp.

BA 23.   Norman, E. Herbert. JAPAN'S EMERGENCE AS A
MODERN STATE: POLITICAL AND ECONOMIC PROBLEMS OF THE
MEIJI PERIOD. New York: Institute of Pacific Relations,
1940. 254pp.

BA 24.   Reischauer, Edwin O. THE JAPANESE.
Cambridge, Mass.: Belnap Press, 1977. 443pp.

BA 25.   Sansom, George Bailey. JAPAN: A SHORT
CULTURAL HISTORY. New York: D. Appleton-Century, 1943.
654pp.

BA 26.   Sumiya, Mikio, and Taira, Koji, eds. AN
OUTLINE OF JAPANESE ECONOMIC HISTORY 1603-1940: MAJOR
WORKS AND RESEARCH FINDINGS. Tokyo: University of Tokyo
Press, 1979. 372pp.

BA. Historical Background

BA 27. Thomas, Andrew Frank, and Koyama, Soji. COMMERCIAL HISTORY OF JAPAN. Tokyo: Yuhodo, 1936. 168pp.

Articles

BA 28. Aichi, Kiichi. "Japan's Legacy and Destiny of Change." FOREIGN AFFAIRS v.48 Oct. 1969 pp.21-38.

BA 29. Chor, Kee Il. "Tokugawa Feudalism and the Emergence of the New Leaders of Early Modern Japan." EXPLORATIONS IN ENTREPRENEURIAL HISTORY v.9 Dec. 1956 pp.72-90.

BA 30. Eidus, Kh. "Meiji Ishin as an Incomplete Bourgeois Revolution in Japan." INTERNATIONAL CONGRESS OF ORIENTALISTS v.5 1963 pp.409-414.

BB. Modern Period

Monographic Works

BB 1. Austin, Lewis, ed. JAPAN: THE PARADOX OF PROGRESS. New Haven: Yale University Press, 1976.

BB 2. Beardsley, Richard K.; Hall, John K.; and Ward, Robert E. VILLAGE JAPAN. Chicago: University of Chicago Press, 1959. 498pp.

BB 3. Beasley, William G. GREAT BRITAIN AND THE OPENING OF JAPAN: 1834--1858. London: Luzac & Co., 1951. 223pp.

BB 4.   Beasley, William G., ed.   MODERN JAPAN:
ASPECTS OF HISTORY, LITERATURE AND SOCIETY. London:
Allen & Unwin, 1975. 296pp.

BB 5.   Brzezinski, Zbigniew K. THE FRAGILE BLOSSOM;
CRISIS AND CHANGE IN JAPAN. New York: Harper & Row,
1972. 153pp.

BB 6.   Buck, Trevor. COMPARATIVE INDUSTRIAL
SYSTEMS: INDUSTRY UNDER CAPITALISM, CENTRAL PLANNING
AND SELF-MANAGEMENT. New York: St. Martin's Press,
1982. 177pp.

BB 7.   Buckley, Roger. JAPAN TODAY. New York:
Cambridge University Press, 1985. 139pp.

BB 8.   Burks, Ardath W. JAPAN: A POSTINDUSTRIAL
POWER. 2nd, updated ed.   Boulder, Colo.: Westview
Press, 1984 263pp.

BB 9.   Burks, Ardath W. JAPAN: PROFILE OF A
POSTINDUSTRIAL POWER. Boulder, Colo.: Westview Press,
1981. 260pp.

BB 10.   Cohen, Jerome B. JAPAN'S ECONOMY IN WAR AND
RECONSTRUCTION. Minneapolis: University of Minnesota
Press, 1949. 545pp.

BB 11.   Courdy, Jean-Claude. THE JAPANESE: EVERYDAY
LIFE IN THE EMPIRE OF THE RISING SUN. New York: Harper
& Row, 1984. 269pp.

BB 12.   Fukutake, Tadashi. JAPANESE SOCIETY TODAY.
2nd ed.   Tokyo: University of Tokyo Press, 1981. 165pp.

BB 13.   Grossberg, Kenneth A., ed.   JAPAN TODAY.
Philadelphia: Institute for the Study of Human Issues,
1981. 118p.

BB 14.   Halliday, Jon, and McCormack, Gavan.
JAPANESE IMPERIALISM TODAY, "CO-PROSPERITY IN GREATER

BB. Modern Period

EAST ASIA". New York: Monthly Review Press, 1973. 279pp.

BB 15. Hama, Hidehiko. POPULATION PROBLEMS AND NATIONAL DEVELOPMENT PLANS IN JAPAN--POST-WAR TRENDS. New York: United Nations, 1981. 25pp.

BB 16. Ike, Nobutaka. JAPAN: THE NEW SUPERSTATE. San Francisco: W. H. Freeman, 1974. 121pp.

BB 17. Ishii, Ryosuke. JAPANESE LEGISLATION IN THE MEIJI PERIOD. Tokyo: Pan-Pacific Press, 1958. 741pp.

BB 18. Iwata, Masakazu. OKUBO TOSHIMICHI: THE BISMARCK OF JAPAN. Berkeley and Los Angeles: University of California Press, 1964. 376pp.

BB 19. Kahn, Herman. THE EMERGING JAPANESE SUPERSTATE: CHALLENGE AND RESPONSE. Englewood Cliffs, N.J.: Prentice-Hall, 1979. 274pp.

BB 20. Lederer, Emil, and Lederer-Seidler, Emy. JAPAN IN TRANSITION. New Haven: Yale University Press, 1938. 260pp.

BB 21. Matsuoka, Toshio, ed. JAPAN 1980: AN INTERNATIONAL COMPARISON. Tokyo: Japan Institute for Social and Economic Affairs, 1980. 62pp.

BB 22. Morris, Ivan, ed. JAPAN 1931-1945: MILITARISM, FASCISM, JAPANISM? Boston: D.C. Heath, 1965. 77pp.

BB 23. Nippon Steel Corp. NIPPON: THE LAND AND ITS PEOPLE. Tokyo: Gakuseisha, 1982 350pp.

BB 24. No, Toshio, and Gordon, Douglas H., eds. MODERN JAPAN: LAND AND MAN. 2nd ed. Tokyo: Teikoiu-Shoin, 1978. 146pp.

BB 25.   Nozomu, Kawamura, THE MODERNIZATION OF JAPANESE SOCIETY, 1869--1945. Tokyo: Japan Foundation, 1982. 41pp.

BB 26.   Pempel, T. J. POLICY AND POLITICS IN JAPAN: CREATIVE CONSERVATISM. Philadelphia: Temple University Press, 1982. 330pp.

BB 27.   Scalapino, Robert A. THE FOREIGN POLICY OF MODERN JAPAN. Berkeley: University of California Press, 1977. 426pp.

BB 28.   Seward, Jack. THE JAPANESE. Tokyo: Simpson-Doyle, 1971. 232pp.

BB 29.   Shiba, Kinpei. OH, JAPAN! YESTERDAY, TODAY AND PROBABLY TOMORROW. Tenerden: Paul Norbury, 1979. 236pp.

BB 30.   Shiratori, Rei, ed.   JAPAN IN THE 1980s. Tokyo: Kodansha, 1982. 290pp.

BB 31.   Shiratori, Rei. JAPAN TODAY. Manchester: Manchester University Press, 1987.

BB 32.   Takizawa, Matsuyo. THE PENETRATION OF MONEY ECONOMY IN JAPAN AND ITS EFFECTS UPON SOCIAL AND POLITICAL INSTITUTIONS. New York: Columbia University Press, 1927. 159pp.

BB 33.   Thayer, Nathaniel B. HOW THE CONSERVATIVES RULE JAPAN. Princeton, N.J.: Princeton University Press, 1969. 349pp.

BB 34.   Tsuneishi, Warren M. JAPANESE POLITICAL STYLE: AN INTRODUCTION TO THE GOVERNMENT AND POLITICS OF MODERN JAPAN. New York: Harper & Row, 1966. 226pp.

BB 35.   United States. Department of State. Bureau of Public Affairs. Office of Public Communication. JAPAN. Publication 7770, Background Notes. May, 1983. 8pp.

BB. Modern Period

BB 36. Velen, Elizabeth, and Velen, Victor A.,
eds. THE NEW JAPAN. New York: H. W. Wilson, 1958.
203pp.

BB 37. Ward, Robert E. JAPAN'S POLITICAL SYSTEM.
2nd ed. Englewood Cliffs, N.J.: Prentice-Hall, 1978.
253pp.

BB 38. Ward, Robert E., and Rustow, Dankwart A.
POLITICAL MODERNIZATION IN JAPAN AND TURKEY. Princeton,
N.J.: Princeton University Press, 1964.

BB 39. Weinstein, Martin E. JAPAN'S POSTWAR
DEFENSE POLICY, 1947--1968. New York: Columbia
University Press, 1971. 160pp.

BB 40. Westney, D. Eleanor. IMITATION AND
INNOVATION: THE TRANSFER OF WESTERN ORGANIZATIONAL
PATTERNS TO MEIJI JAPAN. Cambridge, Mass.: Harvard
University Press, 1987. 256pp.

BB 41. Yoshihashi, Takehiko. CONSPIRACY AT MUKDEN:
THE RISE OF THE JAPANESE MILITARY. New Haven: Yale
University Press, 1963. 274pp.

Articles

BB 42. Fukui, Harahiro. "Economic Planning in
Postwar Japan." ASIAN SURVEY v.12 1972 pp.327-348.

BB 43. Ichimuro, Muto. "Class Struggle in Postwar
Japan; Its Past, Present, and Future." AMPO (Tokyo)
v.14 no.3 1982 pp.19-27.

BB 44. "Japan: A Nation in Search of Itself." TIME
v.122 Aug 1, 1983 pp.16-78. (Special Issue.)

BB 45. Mushakoji, Kinhide. "Thought and Behavior of Japanese Diplomats." JOURNAL OF SOCIAL AND POLITICAL IDEAS IN JAPAN v.4 Apr. 1966 pp.19-25.

BB 46. Smith, Thomas Carlyle. "Japan's Aristocratic Revolution." YALE REVIEW v.50 1964 pp.370-383.

BB 47. Taeuber, Irene Barnes. "Urbanization and Population Change in the Development of Modern Japan." ECONOMIC DEVELOPMENT AND CULTURAL CHANGE v.9 Oct. 1960 pp.1-28.

BC. The Social and Political Context

Monographic Works

BC 1. Azuma, Hiroshi, et al. CHILD DEVELOPMENT AND EDUCATION IN JAPAN. San Francisco: W. H. Freeman, 1986. 400pp.

BC 2. Beauchamp, Edward R. LEARNING TO BE JAPANESE: SELECTED READINGS ON JAPANESE SOCIETY AND EDUCATION. Hamden, Conn.: Linnet Books, 1978. 408pp.

BC 3. Benjamin, Roger, and Ori, Kan. TRADITION AND CHANGE IN POSTINDUSTRIAL JAPAN: THE ROLES OF THE POLITICAL PARTIES. New York: Praeger, 1981. 192pp.

BC 4. Coleman, Samuel. FAMILY PLANNING IN JAPANESE SOCIETY. Princeton, N.J.: Princeton University Press, 1983 269pp.

BC 5. Dore, Ronald Phillips, ed. ASPECTS OF SOCIAL CHANGE IN MODERN JAPAN. Princeton, N.J.: Princeton University Press, 1967. 474pp.

BC 6.   Dore, Ronald Phillips. CITY LIFE IN JAPAN: A STUDY OF A TOKYO WARD. Berkeley: University of California Press, 1958. 472pp.

BC 7.   Dower, John W., ed.   ORIGINS OF THE MODERN JAPANESE STATE: SELECTED WRITINGS OF E. H. NORMAN. New York: Pantheon Books, 1975. 497pp

BC 8.   Fukutake, Tadashi. THE JAPANANESE SOCIAL STRUCTURE: ITS EVOLUTION IN THE MODERN CENTURY. Translated by Dore, Ronald P. Tokyo: University of Tokyo Press; New York: Columbia University Press, 1983. 232pp.

BC 9.   Hane, Mikiso. PEASANTS, REBELS, AND OUTCASTS: THE UNDERSIDE OF MODERN JAPAN. New York: Pantheon, 1982. 297pp.

BC 10.   McFarland, H. Neill. THE RUSH HOUR OF THE GODS: A STUDY OF NEW RELIGIOUS MOVEMENTS IN JAPAN. New York: Macmillan, 1967.

BC 11.   Maki, John M. GOVERNMENT AND POLITICS IN JAPAN: THE ROAD TO DEMOCRACY. New York: Frederick A. Praeger, 1961. 275pp.

BC 12.   Matsumoto, Yoshiharu Scott. CONTEMPORARY JAPAN; THE INDIVIDUAL AND THE GROUP. Philadelphia: American Philosophical Society, 1960. 75pp.

BC 13.   Maurette, Fernand. SOCIAL ASPECTS OF INDUSTRIAL DEVELOPMENT IN JAPAN. Geneve: ILO, 1934. 69pp.

BC 14.   Monroe, Wilbur F., and Sakakibara, Eisuke. THE JAPANESE INDUSTRIAL SOCIETY, ITS ORGANIZATIONAL, CULTURAL, AND ECONOMIC UNDERPINNINGS. Austin, Texas: Bureau of Business Research, University of Texas at Austin, 1977. 74pp.

BC 15.   Mouer, Ross E. JAPANESE SOCIETY: INDUSTRIALIZATION, INTERNATIONALIZATION AND SOCIAL

CHANGE. Tokyo: Japan Foundation, 1982. 41pp.

BC 16.   Nakane, Chie. HUMAN RELATIONS IN JAPAN.
Tokyo: Ministry of Foreign Affairs, 1972. 86pp.

BC 17.   Nakane, Chie. JAPANESE SOCIETY. Berkeley:
University of California Press. 1970. 157pp.

BC 18.   Palmore, Erdman Ballagh. THE HONORABLE
ELDERS: A CROSS-CULTURAL ANALYSIS OF AGING IN JAPAN.
Durham, N.C.: Duke University Press, 1975. 148pp.

BC 19.   Palmore, Erdman Ballagh, and Maeda,
Daisaku. THE HONORABLE ELDERS REVISITED: A REVISED
CROSS-CULTURAL ANALYSIS OF AGING IN JAPAN. Durham,
N.C.: Duke University Press, 1985 135pp.

BC 20.   Passin, Herbert. SOCIETY AND EDUCATION IN
JAPAN. Tokyo: Kodansha, 1983. 347pp.

BC 21.   Penrose, Ernest F. POPULATION THEORIES AND
THEIR APPLICATION, WITH SPECIAL REFERENCE TO JAPAN.
Stanford, Calif.: Stanford University Press, 1934.
347pp.

BC 22.   Plath, David W., ed.   WORK AND LIFECOURSE
IN JAPAN. Albany, N.Y.: State University of New York
Press, 1983. 267pp.

BC 23.   Rohlen, Thomas P. FOR HARMONY AND STRENGTH:
JAPANESE WHITE-COLLAR ORGANIZATION IN ANTHROPOLOGICAL
PERSPECTIVE. Berkeley: University of California Press,
1974. 285pp.

BC 24.   Scalapino, Robert A. DEMOCRACY AND THE
PARTY MOVEMENT IN PREWAR JAPAN: THE FAILURE OF THE
FIRST ATTEMPT. Berkeley: University of California
Press, 1962. 471pp.

BC 25.   Singleton, John. NICHU: A JAPANESE SCHOOL.
New York: Holt, Reinhart & Winston, 1967. 125pp.

BC. Social & Political Context

BC 26. Smethurst, Richard J. A SOCIAL BASIS FOR PREWAR JAPANESE MILITARISM: THE ARMY AND THE RURAL COMMUNITY. Berkeley, Calif.: University of California Press, 1974. 202pp.

BC 27. Smith, Robert J. JAPANESE SOCIETY: TRADITION, SELF, AND THE SOCIAL ORDER. Cambridge; New York: Cambridge University Press, 1983. 176pp.

BC 28. Steiner, Kurt. LOCAL GOVERNMENT IN JAPAN. Palo Alto, Calif.: Stanford University Press, 1965. 564pp.

BC 29. Sugimoto, Yoshio, and Mouer, Ross. JAPANESE SOCIETY: STEREOTYPES AND REALITIES. Melbourne: Japanese Studies Center, 1982. 41pp.

BC 30. Sumiya, Mikio. SOCIAL IMPACT OF INDUSTRIALIZATION IN JAPAN. Tokyo: Japanese Commission for UNESCO, 1963. 278pp.

BC 31. Taylor, Jared. SHADOWS OF THE RISING SUN: A CRITICAL VIEW OF THE "JAPANESE MIRACLE." New York: Morrow, 1983. 336pp.

BC 32. Totten, George O. THE SOCIAL DEMOCRATIC MOVEMENT IN PREWAR JAPAN. New Haven, Conn.: Yale University Press, 1966. 455pp.

BC 33. Tsurumi, Kazuko. SOCIAL CHANGE AND THE INDIVIDUAL: JAPAN BEFORE AND AFTER DEFEAT IN WORLD WAR II. Princeton, N.J.: Princeton University Press, 1970. 441pp.

BC 34. Vogel, Ezra F. JAPAN'S NEW MIDDLE CLASS: THE SALARY MAN AND HIS FAMILY IN A TOKYO SUBURB. Berkeley and Los Angeles: University of California Press, 1963. 299pp.

BC 35. Von Mehren, Arthur Taylor., ed. LAW IN JAPAN: THE LEGAL ORDER IN A CHANGING SOCIETY. Cambridge, Mass.: Harvard University Press, 1963.

BC 36. Woronoff, Jon. INSIDE JAPAN, INC. Tokyo: Lotus Press, 1982. 273pp.

BC 37. Woronoff, Jon. THE JAPAN SYNDROME: SYMPTOMS, AILMENTS, AND REMEDIES. New Brunswick, N.J.: Transaction Books, 1986. 230pp.

BC 38. Woronoff, Jon. JAPAN, THE COMING SOCIAL CRISES. Tokyo: Lotus Press, 1980. 369pp.

BC 39. Yazaki, Takeo. THE JAPANESE CITY: A SOCIOLOGICAL ANALYSIS. Rutland, Vt.: Japan Publications Trading Co., 1963. 105pp.

Articles

BC 40. Abegglen, James C., and Mannari, Hiroshi. "Leaders of Modern Japan: Social Origins and Mobility." ECONOMIC DEVELOPMENT AND CULTURAL CHANGE v.9 no.1, part 2 Oct. 1960 pp.109-134.

BC 41. Ahl, David H. "Japanese Cramming Schools Leave Little Time for Play." CREATIVE COMPUTING v.10 Aug. 1984 p.78.

BC 42. Atsumi, R. "Tsukiai--Obligatory Personal Relationships of Japanese White-Collar Company Employees." HUMAN ORGANIZATION v.38 no.1 1979 pp.63-70.

BC 43. Befu, Harumi. "Ritual Kinship in Japan: Its Variability and Resiliency." SOCIOLOGUS v.14 1964 pp.150-169.

BC 44. Bennett, John, and Ishino, Iwao. "Tradition, Moderninity and Communalism in Japan's Modernization." JOURNAL OF SOCIAL ISSUES v.24 no.4 1968 pp.25-45.

BC 45. Campbell, John C. "The 'Old People Boom' and Japanese Policy Making." JOURNAL OF JAPANESE STUDIES v.5 pp.321-357.

BC 46. Checkland, S. G. "The Entrepreneur and the Social Order: The Japan Business History Society Conference, 6-9 January 1975." BUSINESS HISTORY v.17 no.2 1975 pp.176-188.

BC 47. Dore, Ronald Phillips. "Talent and the Social Order in Japan." PAST AND PRESENT no.21 Apr. 1962 pp.60-72.

BC 48. Harari, Ehud, and Ziera, Yoram. "Attitudes of Japanese and Non-Japanese Employees--A Cross National Comparison in Uni-National And Multinational Corporations." INTERNATIONAL JOURNAL OF COMPARATIVE SOCIOLOGY v.18 no.3-4 1977 pp.228-241.

BC 49. Hashimoto, Masanori. "Demand for Children in Japan During Modernization." in Simon, Julian L., and Da Vanzo, Julie, eds. RESEARCH IN POPULATION ECONOMICS A Research Annual, vol.2. Greenwich, Conn.: JAI Press, 1979. pp.295-320.

BC 50. Hirschmeier, J. "Entrepreneurs and the Social Order: America, Germany and Japan, 1870-1900." in International Conference on Business History (2nd: 1976: Fuji Education Center) SOCIAL ORDER AND ENTREPRENEURSHIP: PROCEEDINGS OF THE SECOND FUJI CONFERENCE. Tokyo: University of Tokyo Press, 1977. pp.3-41.

BC 51. Ishida, Takeshi. "Pressure Groups in Japan." JOURNAL OF SOCIAL AND POLITICAL IDEAS IN JAPAN v.2 Dec. 1964 pp.108-111.

BC 52.   Ishida, Takeshi. "The Development of
Interest Groups and the Pattern of Modernization in
Japan." PAPERS ON MODERN JAPAN 1965 Canberra: Research
School of Pacific Studies, Australian National
University. pp. 1-17.

BC 53.   "Japanese Society Through the Eyes of Three
Generations." JAPAN QUARTERLY v. 26 Jan. /Mar. 1979
pp. 53-84.

BC 54.   Kawai, Takao. "Studies on Social Mobility
in Postwar Japan; Their Development and Problems." KEIO
JOURNAL OF POLITICS v. 5 1984 pp. 27-51.

BC 55.   Kiefer, Christie W. "The Psychological
Interdependence of Family, School, and Bureaucracy in
Japan." AMERICAN ANTHROPOLOGIST v. 72 no. 1 1970 pp. 66+.

BC 56.   Koh, B. C. , and Kim, Jae-On. "Paths to
Advancement in Japanese Bureaucracy." COMPARATIVE
POLITICAL STUDIES v. 15 no. 3 Oct. 1982 pp. 289-313.

BC 57.   Kubota, Akira. "Japan: Social Structure and
Work Ethic." ASIA PACIFIC COMMUNITY no. 20 1983
pp. 35-65.

BC 58.   Kubota, Akira. "Japanese Employment System
and Japanese Social Structure." ASIA PACIFIC COMMUNITY
v. 15 Winter 1982 pp. 96-120.

BC 59.   Levy, Marion J. , Jr. "Some Aspects of
'Individualism' and the Problem of Modernization in
China and Japan." ECONOMIC DEVELOPMENT AND CULTURAL
CHANGE v. 10 Apr. 1962 pp. 225-240.

BC 60.   Lindstrom, David E. "Japan Needs U. S.
Surplus Food." JOURNAL OF FARM ECONOMICS v. 37 Feb. 1955
pp. 125-127.

BC. Social & Political Context

BC 61. Marsh, Robert M., and Mannari, Hiroshi. "Lifetime Commitment in Japan: Roles, Norms and Values." AMERICAN JOURNAL OF SOCIOLOGY v.76 Mar. 1971 pp.795-812.

BC 62. Naoi, Atsushi, and Schooler, Carmi. "Occupational Conditions and Psychological Functioning in Japan." AMERICAN JOURNAL OF SOCIOLOGY v.90 Jan. 1985 pp.729-752.

BC 63. Norbeck, Edward, and Befu, Harami. "Japanese Uses of Terms of Relationship." SOUTHWESTERN JOURNAL OF ANTHROPOLOGY v.14 no.1 pp.66-86 1958.

BC 64. Ohmae, Kenichi. "Japan: from Stereotypes to Specifics." McKINSEY QUARTERLY Spring 1982 pp.2-33.

BC 65. Oishi, Y. "Recognizing Differences for Mutual Understanding." JAPAN QUARTERLY v.30 Apr./Jun. 1983 pp.145-147.

BC 66. Okazaki, Yoichi. "Coping with the Declining Birthrate." ECONOMIC EYE v.2 Dec. 1981 pp.20-23.

BC 67. Ravitch, D. "Japan's Smart Schools." NEW REPUBLIC v.194 Jan. 6-13 1986 pp.13-15.

BC 68. Smith, Thomas Carlyle. "Landlords' Sons in the Business Elite." ECONOMIC DEVELOPMENT AND CULTURAL CHANGE v.9 Oct. 1960 pp.93-108.

BC 69. Steven, Rob. "The Japanese Bourgeoisie." BULLETIN OF CONCERNED ASIAN SCHOLARS v.10 Apr./June 1979 pp.2-24.

BC 70. Takagi, K. "A Social Psychological Approach to the Ringi-System." INTERNATIONAL REVIEW OF APPLIED PSYCHOLOGY v.18 no.1 1968/1969 pp.53-58.

BC 71.   Totten, George O. "Labor and Agrarian
Disputes in Japan Following World War I." ECONOMIC
DEVELOPMENT AND CULTURAL CHANGE v.9 Oct. 1960
pp.187-212.

BC 72.   Vogel, Ezra F. "Entrance Examinations and
Emotional Disturbances in Japan's Middle Class." in
Smith, R. J. and Beardsley, Richard K., eds. JAPANESE
CULTURE: ITS DEVELOPMENT AND CHARACTERISTICS. Chicago:
Aldine, 1962.

BC 73.   Vogel, Ezra F., and Vogel, Suzanne H.
"Family Security, Personal Immaturity, and Emotional
Health in a Japanese Family." MARRIAGE AND FAMILY
LIVING v.23 1961 pp.161-166.

BC 74.   White, James W. "Civic Attitudes, Political
Participation, and System Stability in Japan."
COMPARATIVE POLITICAL STUDIES v.14 Oct. 1981
pp.371-400.

BC 75.   Yamane, Tsureo, and Nonoyama, Hisaya.
"Isolation and the Nuclear Family and Kinship
Organization in Japan: A Hypothetical Approach to the
Relationships between the Family and Society." JOURNAL
OF MARRIAGE AND THE FAMILY v.29 1967 pp.789-796.

BC 76.   Zander, A. "The Value of Belonging to a
Group in Japan." SMALL GROUP BEHAVIOR v.14 no.1 1983
pp.3-14.

BD. The Cultural Setting

Monographic Works

BD 1.   Benedict, Ruth. THE CHRYSANTHEMUM AND THE
SWORD: PATTERNS OF JAPANESE CULTURE. Boston: Houghton
Mifflin Co., 1946. 324pp.

BD. Cultural Setting

BD 2.   Blaker, Michael. JAPANESE INTERNATIONAL
NEGOTIATING STYLE. Studies of the East Asian Institute.
New York: Columbia University Press, 1977. 253pp.

BD 3.   Brown, Delmer M. NATIONALISM IN JAPAN: AN
INTRODUCTORY HISTORICAL ANALYSIS. Berkeley: University
of California Press, 1955. 336pp.

BD 4.   Christopher, Robert. THE JAPANESE MIND; THE
GOLIATH EXPLAINED. New York: Simon & Shuster, 1983.
352pp.

BD 5.   Condon, John, and Kurata, Keisuke. IN SEARCH
OF WHAT'S JAPANESE ABOUT JAPAN. Tokyo: C.E. Tuttle,
1974. 148pp.

BD 6.   Connaghan, Charles J. THE JAPANESE WAY:
CONTEMPORARY INDUSTRIAL RELATIONS.. Ottawa, Ont.:
Labour Canada, 1982.

BD 7.   Cummings, William K. EDUCATION AND EQUALITY
IN JAPAN. Princeton, N.J.: Princeton University Press,
1980. 305pp.

BD 8.   De Vos, George A. SOCIALIZATION FOR
ACHIEVEMENT: ESSAYS ON THE CULTURAL PSYCHOLOGY OF THE
JAPANESE. Berkeley, Calif.: University of California
Press, 1973. 613pp.

BD 9.   Doi, Takeo. THE ANATOMY OF DEPENDENCE.
Bester, John, trans.   Tokyo: Kodansha International,
1973. 170pp.

BD 10.   Dore, Ronald Phillips. EDUCATION IN
TOKUGAWA JAPAN. London: Routledge & Kegan Paul, Ltd.,
1965. 346pp.

BD 11.   Fields, George. FROM BONSAI TO LEVIS--WHEN
WEST MEETS EAST: AN INSIDER'S ENTERTAINING, SURPRISING
ACCOUNT OF HOW THE JAPANESE LIVE. ed.   by Forman, Gail.
New York: Macmillan, 1984. 256pp.

BD 12.   Gibney, Frank. FIVE GENTLEMEN OF JAPAN: THE PORTRAIT OF A NATION'S CHARACTER. New York: Farrar, Straus, and Young, 1953. 373pp.

BD 13.   Hall, Robert. SHUSHIN: THE ETHICS OF A DEFEATED NATION. New York: Bureau of Publications, Teachers College, Columbia University, 1949. 244pp.

BD 14.   Hasegawa, Nyozekan. THE JAPANESE CHARACTER: A CULTURAL PROFILE. Bester, John, trans.   Tokyo: Kodansha International, 1982, c1965.   157pp.

BD 15.   Jansen, Marius B., ed.   CHANGING JAPANESE ATTITUDES TOWARDS MODERNIZATION. Princeton, N.J.: Princeton University Press, 1965.

BD 16.   Kiefer, Christie W. "Personality and Social Change in a Japanese Danchi." PhD Dissertation, University of California Berkeley, 1970.

BD 17.   Lebra, Takie Sugiyama, and Lebra, William P., eds.   JAPANESE CULTURE AND BEHAVIOUR: SELECTED READINGS. Rev. ed.   Honolulu: University of Hawaii Press, 1986. 292pp.

BD 18.   Lebra, Takie Sugiyama. JAPANESE PATTERNS OF BEHAVIOR. Honolulu: East--West Center Press, 1976. 312pp.

BD 19.   Leestma, Robert, et al.   JAPANESE EDUCATION TODAY: A REPORT FROM THE U.S. STUDY OF EDUCATION IN JAPAN. Washington, D.C.: U.S. Department of Education; U.S. Government Printing Office, 1987. 95pp.

BD 20.   Mannari, Hiroshi, and Befu, Harumi. THE CHALLENGE OF JAPAN'S INTERNATIONALIZATION: ORGANIZATION AND CULTURE. Tokyo: Kodansha International, 1985. 308pp.

BD. Cultural Setting

BD 21. Minami, Shinichiro. THE PSYCHOLOGY OF THE
JAPANESE PEOPLE. Trans. by Ikoma, Albert R. Honolulu:
East-West Center Press, 1970. 189pp.

BD 22. Moloney, James C. UNDERSTANDING THE
JAPANESE MIND. New York: Philosophical Library, 1954.
252pp.

BD 23. Moore, Charles A., ed. JAPANESE MIND:
ESSENTIALS OF JAPANESE PHILOSOPHY AND CULTURE.
Honolulu: East--West Center Press, 1967. 357pp. Papers
from the East--West Philosophers' Conferences of 1939,
1949, 1959, 1964.

BD 24. Morishima, Michio. WHY HAS JAPAN
"SUCCEEDED"?: WESTERN TECHNOLOGY AND THE JAPANESE
ETHOS. Cambridge, Mass.: Cambridge University Press,
1982. 218pp.

BD 25. Nagai, Michio. HIGHER EDUCATION IN JAPAN:
ITS TAKEOFF AND CRASH. Dusenbury, Jerry, translator.
Tokyo: University of Tokyo Press, 1971. 264pp.

BD 26. Okakura, Yoshisaburo. THE JAPANESE SPIRIT.
New York: J. Pott, 1905. 132pp.

BD 27. Ozaki, Robert S. THE JAPANESE: A CULTURAL
PORTRAIT. Rutland, Vt.: C.E. Tuttle, 1978. 328pp.

BD 28. Passin, Herbert. JAPANESE EDUCATION: A
BIBLIOGRAPHY OF MATERIALS IN THE ENGLISH LANGUAGE. New
York: Teachers College Press, 1970. 135pp.

BD 29. Pempel, T. J. PATTERNS OF JAPANESE
POLICYMAKING. Boulder, Colo.: Westview Press, 1978.
248pp.

BD 30. Plath, David W. THE AFTER HOURS: MODERN
JAPAN AND THE SEARCH FOR ENJOYMENT. Berkeley and Los
Angeles: University of California Press, 1964. 222pp.

BD 31.   Shibusawa, Keizo. JAPANESE LIFE AND CULTURE IN THE MEIJI ERA. Tokyo: Obunsha, 1958. 397pp.

BD 32.   Shively, Donald H., ed. TRADITION AND MODERNIZATION IN JAPANESE CULTURE. Princeton, N.J.: Princeton University Press, 1971. 689pp.

BD 33.   Smith, Robert J., and Beardsley, Richard K. JAPANESE CULTURE: ITS DEVELOPMENT AND CHARACTERISTICS. Chicago: Aldine Publishing Co., 1963, c1962.   193pp.

BD 33a.   Smith, Thomas C. POLITICAL CHANGE AND INDUSTRIAL DEVELOPMENT IN JAPAN: GOVERNMENT ENTERPRISE, 1868--1880. Stanford, Calif.: Stanford University Press, 1974, c.1955.   126pp.

BD 34.   White, Merry I. THE JAPANESE EDUCATIONAL CHALLENGE: A COMMITMENT TO CHILDREN. New York: Free Press, 1987. 210pp.

Articles

BD 35.   Azumi, K., and McMillan, C. J. "Culture and Organization Structure: a Comparison of Japanese and British Organizations." INTERNATIONAL STUDIES OF MANAGEMENT AND ORGANIZATION v.5 no.1 1975 pp.35-47.

BD 36.   Ballon, Robert J. "Non-Western Work Organizations." ASIA PACIFIC JOURNAL OF MANAGEMENT v.1 no.1 1983 pp.1-14.

BD 37.   Beasley, W. G. "Tradition and Modernity in Post-War Japan." ASIAN AFFAIRS (London) v.67 Feb. 1980 pp.5-17.

BD 38.   Bellah, Robert Neelly. "Japan's Cultural Identity: Some Reflections on the Work of Watsuji Tetsuro." JOURNAL OF ASIAN STUDIES v.24 Aug. 1965 pp.573-594.

BD. Cultural Setting

BD 39. Calista, Donald J. "Postmaterialism and Value Convergence; Value Priorities of Japanese Compared with Their Perceptions of American Values." COMPARATIVE POLITICAL STUDIES v. 16 no. 4 Jan. 1984 pp. 529-555.

BD 40. Chao, K-L, and Gorden, W. I. "Culture and Communication in the Modern Japanese Organization." In Jain, N., ed. INTERNATIONAL AND INTERCULTURAL COMMUNICATION ANNUAL. Falls Church, Va.: Speech Communication Association, 1979. v. 5 pp. 26-36.

BD 41. Cummings, W. K., and Kobayashi, V. N. "Education in Japan." CURRENT HISTORY v. 84 Dec. 1985 pp. 422-425+.

BD 42. DeVos, George, and Wagatsume, Hiroshi. "Status and Role Behavior in Changing Japan: Psychocultural Continuities." in Seward, Georgene, and Williamson, Robert, eds., SEX ROLES IN CHANGING SOCIETY New York: Random House, 1970.

BD 43. Dore, Ronald Phillips. "Education in Japan's Growth." PACIFIC AFFAIRS v. 37 Spring 1964 pp. 66-79.

BD 44. Dow, Tsung-I. "The Meaning of Confucian Work Ethic as the Source of Japan's Economic Power." ASIAN PROFILE v. 11 June 1983 pp. 219-230.

BD 45. El-Agraa, Ali M., and Inchii, Akira. "The Japanese Education System with Special Emphasis on Higher Education." HIGHER EDUCATION v. 14 Feb. 1985 pp. 1-16.

BD 46. Garr, D. "Pro-Tech Psychology." OMNI v. 7 June 1985 pp. 34+.

BD 47. Helm, L. "The High Price Japanese Pay for Success." BUSINESS WEEK Apr. 7, 1986 pp. 52-54.

BD 48.   Houser, M. "Are the Japanese Workaholics?"
PERSONNEL MANAGEMENT v. 13 Dec. 1981 pp. 38-42.

BD 49.   "How Japan Has 'Won' the Peace."
INTERNATIONAL MANAGEMENT v. 37 Apr. 1982 pp. 23-24.

BD 50.   Ishino, Iwao. "The Oyabun-Kobun: A Japanese
Ritual Kinship Institution." AMERICAN ANTHROPOLOGIST
v. 55 Dec. 1953 pp. 706+ .

BD 51.   "Japanese Schools: There Is Much We Can
Learn." U.S. NEWS AND WORLD REPORT v. 99 Sep. 2, 1985
p. 43.   (An interview with T. Bell)

BD 52.   Kazama, Daiji, and Akiyama, Tokoyo.
"Japanese Value Orientations; Persistence and Change."
STUDIES OF BROADCASTING v. 17 Mar. 1980 pp. 5-26.

BD 53.   Kazutoshi, Koshiro. "Perceptions of Work
and Living Attitudes of the Japanese." JAPAN QUARTERLY
v. 27 Jan. /Mar. 1980 pp. 46-55.

BD 54.   Kikuchi, M. "Creativity and Ways of
Thinking: the Japanese Style." PHYSICS TODAY v. 34 Sep.
1981 pp. 42-54+.   Discussion, v. 35 April 1982 pp. 91-94.

BD 55.   Klauss, R., and Bass, B. M. "Group
Influence on Individual Behavior Across Cultures."
JOURNAL OF CROSS-CULTURAL PSYCHOLOGY v. 5 no. 2 1974
pp. 236-246.

BD 56.   Odaka, K. "Traditionalism, Democracy in
Japanese Industry." INDUSTRIAL RELATIONS v. 3 no. 1 1963
pp. 95-103.

BD 57.   Rohlen, Thomas P. "Is Japanese Education
Becoming Less Egalitarian? Notes on High School
Stratification and Reform." JOURNAL OF JAPANESE STUDIES
v. 3 1977 pp. 37-70.

BD. Cultural Setting

BD 58.   Rohlen, Thomas P. "Japanese Education: If They Can Do It, Should We?" AMERICAN SCHOLAR v. 55 Winter 1985/1986 pp. 29-43.

BD 59.   Schinzinger, R. "Imitation and Originality in Japanese Culture." JAPAN QUARTERLY v. 30 July/Sep. 1983 pp. 281-288.

BD 60.   Schmidt, Helmut. "Japan's Next Challenges: Insularity, Insecurity, and the Need for a Cultural Rebirth." WORLD PRESS REVIEW v. 32 Jan. 1985 pp. 28-30.

BD 61.   Seligman, D. "Clever, Those Orientals." FORTUNE v. 105 May 3, 1982 p. 77.

BD 62.   Smith, L. "Creativity Starts to Blossom in Japan." FORTUNE v. 110 Oct. 29, 1984 pp. 144-153.

BD 63.   Stevenson, H. W., et al. "Mathematics Achievement of Chinese, Japanese and American Children." SCIENCE v. 231 Feb. 14, 1986 pp. 693-699.

BD 64.   White, M. I. "Japanese Education: How Do They Do It?" PUBLIC INTEREST no. 76 Summer 1984 pp. 87-101.

BD 65.   Whitehill, Arthur M. "Cultural Variations in Group Attraction." SOCIOLOGY AND SOCIAL RESEARCH v. 48 no. 4 1964 pp. 469-477.

BE. Japan and the United States; Comparative and General Perspective

Monographic Works

BE 1. Bendahmane, Diane B., and Moser, Leo, eds. TOWARD A BETTER UNDERSTANDING: UNITED STATES--JAPAN RELATIONS, September 28-29, 1983. Washington, D.C.: U.S. Government Printing Office, 1986. 150pp.

BE 2. Bereday, George Z. F., and Masui, Shigeo. AMERICAN EDUCATION THROUGH JAPANESE EYES. Honolulu: University Press of Hawaii, 1973. 279pp.

BE 3. Cleaver, Charles G. JAPANESE AND AMERICANS: CULTURAL PARALLELS AND PARADOXES. Minneapolis: University of Minnesota Press, 1976. 290pp.

BE 4. Condon, John C. WITH RESPECT TO THE JAPANESE: A GUIDE FOR AMERICANS. Yarmouth, Me.: Intercultural Press, 1984. 92pp.

BE 5. Goodman, Grant K., and Moos, Felix. THE UNITED STATES AND JAPAN IN THE WESTERN PACIFIC: MICRONESIA AND PAPUA NEW GUINEA. Boulder, Colo.: Westview Press, 1981. 289pp.

BE 6. Holland, Harrison, M. MANAGING DIPLOMACY: THE UNITED STATES AND JAPAN. Stanford, Calif.: Hoover Institution Press, 1984. 251pp.

BE 7. Japan Center for International Exchange. THE SILENT POWER: JAPAN'S IDENTITY AND WORLD ROLE. Tokyo: Simul Press, 1976. 251pp.

BE 8. Kitamura, Hiroshi, Murata, Ryohei; and Okazaki, Hisahiko. BETWEEN FRIENDS: JAPANESE DIPLOMATS LOOK AT JAPAN--U.S. RELATIONS. New York: Weatherhill, 1985. 220pp.

BE 9.   Kitamura, Hiroshi. PSYCHOLOGICAL DIMENSIONS OF U.S.-JAPANESE RELATIONS. Occasional Papers in International Affairs: No. 28. Cambridge, Mass.: Center for International Affairs, Harvard University, 1971. 46pp.

BE 10.   Lee, Chae-jin, and Sato, Hideo. U.S. POLICY TOWARD JAPAN AND KOREA. New York: Praeger, 1982. 208pp.

BE 11.   Lockwood, William W. TRADE AND TRADE RIVALRY BETWEEN THE UNITED STATES AND JAPAN. New York: Institute of Pacific Relations, 1936. 66pp.

BE 12.   Matsuyama, Yukio. A JAPANESE JOURNALIST LOOKS AT U.S.-JAPAN RELATIONS. Boulder, Colo.: Westview Press, 1984. 48pp.

BE 13.   Ogawa, Dennis M. FROM JAPS TO JAPANESE: THE EVOLUTION OF JAPANESE-AMERICAN STEREOTYPES. Berkeley: McCutchan, 1971. 167pp.

BE 14.   Osgood, Robert E.; Packard, George R., III; and Badgley, John H. JAPAN AND THE UNITED STATES IN ASIA. Baltimore: Johns Hopkins Press, 1968.

BE 15.   Reischauer, Edwin O. THE UNITED STATES AND JAPAN. 2nd ed. Cambridge, Mass.: Harvard University Press, 1965. 396pp.

BE 16.   Shiels, Frederick L. AMERICA, OKINAWA, AND JAPAN: CASE STUDIES FOR FOREIGN POLICY THEORY. Washington : University Press of America, 1980. 333pp.

BE 17.   U.S.--JAPAN RELATIONS: TOWARDS A NEW EQUILIBRIUM. Annual Review, 1982-1983, Program on U.S.--Japan Relations. Cambridge, Mass.: Center for International Affairs, Harvard University, 1983.

BE 18.   Valeo, Francis R., and Morrison, Charles E., eds. THE JAPANESE DIET AND THE U.S. CONGRESS. Boulder, Colo.: Westview Press, 1983. 212pp.

Articles

BE 19. Barnett, Robert W. "Occupied Japan: The Economic Aspect." in Harris, Seymour, ed. FOREIGN ECONOMIC POLICY FOR THE UNITED STATES. Cambridge, Mass.: Harvard University Press, 1948. pp.104-133.

BE 20. "Compliments and Cultures." PSYCHOLOGY TODAY v.19 Aug. 1985 p.27.

BE 21. Reisman, S. "Japan and the U.S.: the Conflict." CREATIVE COMPUTING v.10 Aug. 1984 pp.54-60.

BE 22. Sherman, William C. "The Evolution of the U.S.--Japan Alliance." SAIS (School of Advanced International Studies) REVIEW v.5 Winter/Spring 1985 pp.191-200.

BE 23. Shimahara, N. K. "Japanese Education and Its Implication for U.S. Education." PHI DELTA KAPPAN v.66 Feb. 1985 pp.418-421.

BE 24. "Survey Reveals American Attitudes toward Japan." BUSINESS JAPAN v.26 Feb. 1981 pp.26-31.

BE 25. Tsurumi, Yoshi. "Another Kind of Bond with America." JAPAN QUARTERLY v.29 Jan./Mar. 1982 pp.19-29.

BF. International Arena

BF. Japan in the International Arena

Monographic Works

BF 1.   Barnet, Richard J. THE ALLIANCE: AMERICA,
EUROPE, JAPAN; MAKERS OF THE POSTWAR WORLD. New York:
Simon & Schuster, 1983. 511pp.

BF 2.   Borton, Hugh, ed. JAPAN BETWEEN EAST AND
WEST. New York: Harper & Bros., 1957. 327pp.

BF 3.   Hall, Robert Burnett, Jr. JAPAN: INDUSTRIAL
POWER OF ASIA. 2nd ed. New York: D. Van Nostrand,
1976. 150pp.

BF 4.   Haring, Douglas G., ed. JAPAN'S PROSPECT.
Cambridge, Mass.: Harvard University Press, 1946.
474pp.

BF 5.   Hubbard, Gilbert E., comp. EASTERN
INDUSTRIALIZATION AND ITS EFFECT ON THE WEST, WITH
SPECIAL REFERENCE TO GREAT BRITAIN AND JAPAN. London:
Oxford University Press, 1935. 418pp.

BF 6.   Leng, Shao Chuang. JAPAN AND COMMUNIST
CHINA. New York: Institute of Pacific Relations, 1959.
166pp.

BF 7.   Mendl, Wolf. WESTERN EUROPE AND JAPAN
BETWEEN THE SUPERPOWERS. New York: St. Martin's Press,
1984. 181pp.

BF 8.   Ozaki, Robert S., and Arnold, Walter, eds.
JAPAN'S FOREIGN RELATIONS: A GLOBAL SEARCH FOR ECONOMIC
SECURITY. Boulder, Colo.: Westview Press, 1984. 225pp.

BF 9.   Passin, Herbert, and Curtis, Gerald. JAPAN
IN THE 1980s, II. Papers on International Issues: No.
6. Atlanta: Southern Center for International Studies,
1983. 72pp.

BF 10.   Sansom, George Bailey. THE WESTERN WORLD
AND JAPAN. New York: Alfred A. Knopf, 1951. 504pp.

BF 11.   Shimizu, Hiroshi. ANGLO--JAPANESE TRADE
RIVALRY IN THE MIDDLE-EAST IN THE INTER-WAR PERIOD.
London: Ithaca Press, 1986. 302pp.

BF 12.   Shirk, Susan L., ed.   THE CHALLENGE OF
CHINA AND JAPAN: POLITICS AND DEVELOPMENT IN EAST ASIA.
Woodside, N.Y.: Praeger, 1985. 533pp.

BF 13.   Wee, Mon-Cheng. THE CHRYSANTHEMUM AND THE
ORCHID: OBSERVATIONS OF A DIPLOMAT. Singapore: Maruzen
Asia, 1982. 167pp.

Articles

BF 14.   Borton, Hugh. "United States Occupation
Policies in Japan Since Surrender." POLITICAL SCIENCE
QUARTERLY v.62 June 1947 pp.250-257.

BF 15.   Borton, Hugh. "Preparation for the
Occupation of Japan." JOURNAL OF ASIAN STUDIES v.25
Feb. 1966 pp.203-212.

BF 16.   "The Japan Problem: It Will Not Go Away."
(six articles) WORLD PRESS REVIEW v.34 Aug. 1987
pp.12-19.

BF 17.   Kawata, F. "United Nations Conference on
Trade and Development and Japan." THE DEVELOPING
ECONOMIES v.2 1964 pp.290-301.

BF. International Arena

BF 18.   Lockwood, William W. "Japan's Response to the West: The Contrast with China." WORLD POLITICS v.9 Oct. 1956 pp.37-54.

BF 19.   Mochizuki, M. "Japan's Foreign Policy." CURRENT HISTORY v.84 Dec. 1985 pp.401-404+.

BF 20.   Nakane, Chie. "Social Background of Japanese in Southeast Asia." THE DEVELOPING ECONOMIES v.10 no.2 1972 pp.115-125.

BF 21.   Nakasone, Yasuhiro. "Japan's Choice: A Strategy for World Peace and Prosperity." ATLANTIC COMMUNITY REVIEW v.22 Fall 1984 pp.212-219.

BF 22.   Rothacher, Albrecht. "The Formulation of Japanese Foreign Policy." MILLENNIUM v.10 Spring 1981 pp.1-13.

BF 23.   Yoshihara, T. "Japan's Trade with Developing Countries." THE DEVELOPING ECONOMIES v.Preliminary Volume 1962 pp.106-120.

VI.

CHAPTER 3

C. BACKGROUND TO THE JAPANESE ECONOMY

CA. General Works

Monographic Works

CA 1.   Akao, Nobutoshi, ed.   JAPAN'S ECONOMIC
SECURITY. New York: St. Martin's Press, 1983. 279pp.

CA 2.   Allen, George C. JAPAN AS A MARKET AND
SOURCE OF SUPPLY. Oxford: Pergamon Press, 1967. 139pp.

CA 3.   Allen, George C. THE JAPANESE ECONOMY. New
York: St. Martin's Press, 1981. 226pp.

CA 4.   Allen, George C. JAPAN'S ECONOMIC EXPANSION.
London: Oxford University Press, 1965. 296pp.

CA 5.   Allen, George C. JAPAN'S ECONOMIC RECOVERY
POLICY. London: Macmillan, 1958. 215pp.

CA 6.   Allen, George C. A SHORT ECONOMIC HISTORY OF
MODERN JAPAN: WITH A SUPPLEMENTARY CHAPTER ON ECONOMIC
RECOVERY AND EXPANSION, 1945-1960. 2nd rev.   ed.
London: Allen & Unwin, 1962.   237pp.

CA. General Works

CA 7. Bank of Japan. OUTLINE OF JAPANESE ECONOMY AND FINANCE. Tokyo: The Bank of Japan, 1969. 69pp.

CA 8. Beardsley, R. K. STUDIES ON ECONOMIC LIFE IN JAPAN. Ann Arbor: University of Michigan Press, 1964. 124pp.

CA 9. Bellah, Robert N. TOKUGAWA RELIGION: THE VALUES OF PRE-INDUSTRIAL JAPAN. Glencoe, Ill.: The Free Press, 1957. 249pp.

CA 10. Bennett, John W., and Ishino, Iwao. PATERNALISM IN THE JAPANESE ECONOMY: ANTHROPOLOGICAL STUDIES OF OYABUN-KOBUN PATTERNS. Minneapolis: University of Minnesota Press, 1963. 307pp.

CA 11. Bieda, Ken. THE STRUCTURE AND OPERATION OF THE JAPANESE ECONOMY. New York: Wiley, 1971. 292pp.

CA 12. Blumenthal, Tuvia. SAVING IN POSTWAR JAPAN. Cambridge, Mass.: Harvard University Press, 1970. 117pp.

CA 13. Boltho, Andrea. JAPAN: AN ECONOMIC SURVEY, 1953-1973. New York: Oxford, 1975. 204pp.

CA 14. Cohen, Jerome B. JAPAN'S POSTWAR ECONOMY. Bloomington: Indiana University Press, 1958. 262pp.

CA 15. Committee for Economic Development. JAPAN IN THE FREE WORLD ECONOMY. Washington, D.C., 1963. 45pp.

CA 16. Cowan, Charles D. THE ECONOMIC DEVELOPMENT OF CHINA AND JAPAN. New York: Praeger, 1964. 255pp.

CA 17. Fodella, Gianni, ed. SOCIAL STRUCTURES AND ECONOMIC DYNAMICS IN JAPAN UP TO 1980. Milan: Luigi Bocconi University, Institute of Economic and Social Studies for East Asia, 1975. 322pp.

CA 18. Hahn, Elliott J. JAPANESE BUSINESS LAW AND THE LEGALSYSTEM. Westport, Conn.: Quorum Books, 1984. 208pp.

CA 19. Haitani, Kanji. THE JAPANESE ECONOMIC SYSTEM: AN INSTITUTIONAL OVERVIEW. Lexington, Mass.: Lexington Books, 1976. 190pp.

CA 20. Hollerman, Leon. JAPAN'S DEPENDENCE ON THE WORLD ECONOMY. Princeton, N.J.: Princeton University Press, 1967. 291pp.

CA 21. Honjo, Eijiro. THE SOCIAL AND ECONOMIC HISTORY OF JAPAN. New York: Russell & Russell, 1965, c1935. 410pp.

CA 22. Hoshii. Iwao. THE ECONOMIC CHALLENGE TO JAPAN. Tokyo; Philadelphia: Orient-West, 1964. 70pp.

CA 23. Kornhauser, David. JAPAN: GEOGRAPHICAL BACKGROUND TO URBAN-INDUSTRIAL DEVELOPMENT. 2nd ed. New York: Longman, 1982. 189pp.

CA 24. Minami, Ryoshin. THE TURNING POINT IN ECONOMIC DEVELOPMENT: JAPAN'S EXPERIENCE. Tokyo: Kinokuniya Bookstore Co.,1973. 330pp.

CA 25. Mitchell, Kate L. JAPAN'S INDUSTRIAL STRENGTH. New York: Institute of Pacific Relations, 1942. 94pp.

CA 26. Mizuno, Soji. EARLY FOUNDATIONS FOR JAPAN'S 20TH ECONOMIC EMERGENCE: A SHORT COMMERICAL HISTORY OF JAPAN. New York: Vantage, 1981. 102pp.

CA 27. Morley, James, ed. DILEMMAS OF GROWTH IN PREWAR JAPAN. Princeton, N.J.: Princeton University Press, 1971. 527pp.

CA 28. Murata, Kiyoji, and Ota, Isamu, eds. INDUSTRIAL GEOGRAPHY OF JAPAN. New York: St. Martin's Press. 1980. 205pp.

CA. General Works

CA 29. Nakamura, Takafusa. THE JAPANESE ECONOMY, GROWTH AND STRUCTURE. Tokyo: Tokyo University Press, 1978.

CA 30. Nakamura, Takafusa. THE POSTWAR JAPANESE ECONOMY: ITS DEVELOPMENT AND STRUCTURE. Tokyo: University of Tokyo Press; New York: Columbia University Press, 1981. 277pp.

CA 31. New York University. C.J. Devine Institute of Finance. THE JAPANESE ECONOMY. New York: New York University Graduate School of Business Administration, 1960. 43pp.

CA 32. Ohkawa, Kazushi, et al. GROWTH RATE OF THE JAPANESE ECONOMY SINCE 1878. Tokyo: Kinokuniya, 1957. 250pp.

CA 33. Okita, Saburo. JAPAN IN THE WORLD ECONOMY. Tokyo: Japan Foundation, 1975. 235pp.

CA 34. Olsen, Edward A. JAPAN: ECONOMIC GROWTH, RESOURCE SCARCITY, AND ENVIRONMENTAL CONSTRAINTS. Boulder, Colo.: Westview Press, 1978. 139pp.

CA 35. Organization for Economic Cooperation and Development. OECD ECONOMIC SURVEYS: JAPAN. Paris: The Organization, July 1984. 94pp.

CA 36. Otsuka, Katsuo. DUALISTIC ECONOMIC DEVELOPMENT IN JAPAN: A GUIDE TO THE STUDY OF THE JAPANESE ECONOMY. Nathan, Queensland: School of Modern Asian Studies, Griffith University, 1982. 37pp.

CA 37. Patrick, Hugh Talbot, and Rosovsky, Henry, eds. ASIA'S NEW GIANT: HOW THE JAPANESE ECONOMY WORKS. Washington: Brookings Institution, 1976. 943pp.

CA 38. Sato, Takeshi. BUSINESSMAN'S JAPAN: A SURVEY OF JAPAN'S "DIVINE WIND" ECONOMY IN THE 1960s. London: Michael Joseph, 1964. 175pp.

142

CA 39.   Sebald, William J., and Spinks, C. Nelson.
JAPAN: PROSPECTS, OPTIONS, AND OPPORTUNITIES.
Washington, D.C.: American Enterprise Institute for
Public Policy Research, 1967. 133pp.

CA 40.   Shinjo, Hiroshi. HISTORY OF THE YEN: 100
YEARS OF JAPANESE MONEY-ECONOMY. Kobe: Research
Institute for Economics and Business Administration,
Kobe University, 1962. 205pp.

CA 41.   Shinohara, Miyohei. GROWTH AND CYCLES IN
THE JAPANESE ECONOMY. Tokyo: Kinokuniya Bookstore,
1962. 349pp.

CA 42.   Takahashi, Masao. MODERN JAPANESE ECONOMY
SINCE 1868. Tokyo: Kokusai Bunka Shinkokai, 1968.
170pp.

CA 43.   Thrush, John C., and Smith, Philip R.
JAPAN'S ECONOMIC GROWTH AND EDUCATIONAL CHANGE: 1950-
1970. London: EBHA Press, 1980. 90pp.

CA 44.   Tsuru, Shigeto. ESSAYS ON JAPANESE ECONOMY.
Tokyo: Kinokuniya, 1958. 241pp.

CA 45.   Tsunoyama, S. A CONCISE ECONOMIC HISTORY OF
MODERN JAPAN. Bombay: Vora, 1965. 132pp.

CA 46.   Tsurumi, Hiroki. A COMPARISON OF
ECONOMETRIC MACRO MODELS IN THE UNITED STATES, CANADA,
AND JAPAN. Kingston, Ont.: Institute of Economic
Research, Queen's University , 1972. 17pp.

CA 47.   Tsurumi, Yoshi. JAPANESE BUSINESS: A
RESEARCH GUIDE WITH ANNOTATED BIBLIOGRAPHY. New York:
Praeger, 1978. 163pp.

CA 48.   Tung, Rosalie Lam. KEY TO JAPAN'S ECONOMIC
STRENGTH: HUMAN POWER. Lexington, Mass.: Lexington
books, D. C. Heath, 1984. 219pp.

CA. General Works

CA 49.   Uchino, Tatsuro. JAPAN'S POSTWAR ECONOMY:
AN INSIDER'S VIEW OF ITS HISTORY AND ITS FUTURE. Trans.
by Harbison, Mark A. Tokyo; New York: Kodansha
International; dist.   by Harper & Row, 1983. 286pp.

CA 50.   Yoshihara, Kunio. JAPANESE ECONOMIC
DEVELOPMENT; A SHORT INTRODUCTION. 2nd ed.   Tokyo; New
York: Oxford University Press, 1986. 205pp.

CA 51.   Yoshitake, Kiyohiko. AN INTRODUCTION TO
PUBLIC ENTERPRISE IN JAPAN. Beverly Hills, Calif.:
Sage, 1973. 367pp.

CA 52.   Zepke, Nick. THE HUNDRED YEAR MIRACLE;
ECONOMIC DEVELOPMENT IN JAPAN 1918-1970. Auckland,
N.Z.: Heinemann, 1977. 43pp.

Articles

CA 53.   Allen, George Cyrill. "The Concentration of
Economic Control in Japan." ECONOMIC JOURNAL v.47 June
1937 pp.271-286.

CA 54.   Bell, John Fred. "Origins of Japanese
Academic Economics." MONUMENTA NIPPONICA v.16 no.2-4
1960-1961 pp.43-68.

CA 55.   Darraugh, Masako N. "A Model of Consumption
and Leisure in an Intertemporal Framework: A Systematic
Treatment Using Japanese Data." INTERNATIONAL ECONOMIC
REVIEW v.18 Oct. 1977 pp.677-696.

CA 56.   Emi, Koichi. "An Approach to the
Measurement of National Saving in Japan, 1878-1940."
HITOTSUBASHI JOURNAL OF ECONOMICS v.6 June 1965
pp.1-19.

CA 57. Fairbank, John K., et al. "The Influence of Modern Western Science and Technology on Japan and China." EXPLORATIONS IN ENTREPRENEURIAL HISTORY v.7 Apr. 1955. pp.189-204.

CA 58. Harris, Chauncy D. "Urban and Industrial Transformation of Japan." GEOGRAPHICAL REVIEW v.72 Jan. 1982 pp.50-89.

CA 59. Hirschmeier, J. "The Japanese Spirit of Enterprise, 1967-1970." BUSINESS HISTORY REVIEW v.44 no.1 1970 pp.13-38.

CA 60. Imai, Kenichi. "Japan's Industrial Society: Technical Innovation and Formation of a Network Society." JOURNAL OF JAPANESE TRADE AND INDUSTRY July/Aug. 1983 pp.43-48. (Summarized translation of the first chapter of his book JAPAN'S INDUSTRIAL SOCIETY.)

CA 61. Marshall, Byron K. "Japanese Business Ideology and Labor Policy." COLUMBIA JOURNAL OF WORLD BUSINESS v.12 Spring 1977 pp.22-29.

CA 62. Miyazawa, Kenichi. "The Dual Structure of the Japanese Economy and Its Growth Pattern." THE DEVELOPING ECONOMIES v.2 June 1964 pp.147-170.

CA 63. Okita, Saburo, and Kuroda, Toshio. "Japan's Three Transitions." POPULI (United Nations) v.8 no.3 1981 pp.44-54.

CA 64. Ott, David Jackson. "The Financial Development of Japan, 1878-1958." JOURNAL OF POLITICAL ECONOMY v.69 Apr. 1961 pp.121-141.

CA 65. Park, Yung Ho. "Big Business and Education Policy in Japan." ASIAN SURVEY v.22 Mar. 1982 pp.315-336.

CA. General Works

CA 66.   Ranis, Gustav. "The Capital-Output Ratio in
Japanese Economic Development." REVIEW OF ECONOMIC
STUDIES v. 26 Oct. 1958 pp. 23-32.

CA 67.   Ranis, Gustav. "The Community-Centered
Entrepreneurships in Japanese Development."
EXPLORATIONS IN ENTREPRENEURIAL HISTORY v. 3 Dec. 1955
p. 80-98.

CA 68.   Ranis, Gustav. "Factor Proportions in
Japanese Economic Development." AMERICAN ECONOMIC
REVIEW v. 47 Sep. 1957 pp. 594+.

CA 69.   Rosovsky, Henry. "The Statistical
Measurement of Japanese Economic Growth." ECONOMIC
DEVELOPMENT AND CULTURAL CHANGE v. 7 Oct. 1985 pp. 75-84.

CA 70.   Rosovsky, Henry, and Ohkawa, Kazushi. "The
Indigenous Components in the Modern Japanese Economy."
ECONOMIC DEVELOPMENT AND CULTURAL CHANGE v. 9 Apr. 1961
pp. 476-501.

CA 71.   Rosovsky, Henry, and Yamamura, K.
"Entrepreneurial Studies in Japan: An Introduction."
BUSINESS HISTORY REVIEW v. 44 no. 1 1970 pp. 1-12.

CA 72.   Sayle, M. "Japan Victorious." NEW YORK
REVIEW OF BOOKS v. 32 Mar. 28, 1985 pp. 33-40.

CA 73.   Shinohara, Miyohei. "Factors in Japan's
Economic Growth." HITOTSUBASHI JOURNAL OF ECONOMICS v. 4
Feb. 1964 pp. 21-36.

CA 74.   Shinohara, Miyohei. "Growth and the Long
Swing in the Japanese Economy." HITOTSUBASHI JOURNAL OF
ECONOMICS v. 1 Oct 1960 pp. 58-83.

CA 75.   Smith, Thomas C. "Old Values and New
Techniques in the Modernization of Japan." FAR EASTERN
QUARTERLY v. 45 no. 3 1955 pp. 355-363.

CA 76.   Taeuber, Irene Barnes. "Population Growth
and Economic Development in Japan." JOURNAL OF ECONOMIC
HISTORY v.11 Fall 1951 pp.417-428.

CA 77.   Tsuchiya, M. "The Japanese Business as a
Capsule."JAPANESE ECONOMIC STUDIES v.8 no.1 1979
pp.8-41.

CA 78.   Tsuru, Shigeto. "Business Cycles in Postwar
Japan." in Lundberg, Erik, ed.   THE BUSINESS CYCLE IN
THE POSTWAR WORLD. London: Macmillan, 1955. pp.178-200.

CA 79.   Tsuru, Shigeto. "Growth and Stability of
the Postwar Japanese Economy." AMERICAN ECONOMIC
ASSOCIATION PAPERS AND PROCEEDINGS v.51 May 1961
pp.400-411.

CA 80.   Tsuru, Shigeto. "A Survey of Economic
Research in Japan, 1960-1983." THE ECONOMIC REVIEW v.35
Oct. 1984 pp.289-306.

CA 81.   Tsuru, Shigeto. "A Survey of Economic
Research in Postwar Japan." AMERICAN ECONOMIC REVIEW
v.54 June 1964 pp.79-101.

CA 82.   Veblen, T. "The Opportunity of Japan." in
Addzooni, L. ESSAYS IN OUR CHANGING ORDER. New York:
Viking Press, 1954. pp.248-266.

CB. Emergence of Japanese Business and Industry

Monographic Works

CB 1.   Bisson, Thomas A. ZAIBATSU DISSOLUTION IN
JAPAN. Berkeley: University of California Press, 1954.
314pp.

CB. Emergence of Business/Industry

CB 2. Denison, Edward F., and Chung, Wiliam K. HOW JAPAN'S ECONOMY GREW SO FAST: THE SOURCES OF POSTWAR EXPANSION. Washington: Brookings Institution, 1976. 267pp.

CB 3. Fruin, W. Mark. KIKKOMAN: COMPANY, CLAN, AND COMMUNITY. Harvard Studies in Business History, v.35. Boston: Harvard University Press, 1983. 358pp.

CB 4. Ginsburg, Norton S. JAPANESE PREWAR TRADE AND SHIPPING IN THE ORIENTAL TRIANGLE. Chicago: University of Chicago Press, 1949. 308pp.

CB 5. Hirschmeier, Johannes, and Yui, Tsunehiko. THE DEVELOPMENT OF JAPANESE BUSINESS, 1600-1980. 2nd ed. London; Boston: Allen & Unwin, 1981. 406pp.

CB 6. Hirschmeier, Johannes. THE ORIGINS OF ENTREPRENEURSHIP IN MEIJI JAPAN. Cambridge, Mass.: Harvard University Press, 1964. 354pp.

CB 7. Ho, Alfred Kuo-liang. THE FAR EAST IN WORLD TRADE, DEVELOPMENT AND GROWTH SINCE 1945. New York: Praeger, 1967.

CB 8. Kitamura, Hiroshi. CHOICES FOR THE JAPANESE ECONOMY: NATIONAL AND INTERNATIONAL IMPLICATIONS OF ECONOMIC GROWTH. London: Royal Institute of International Affairs, 1976. 211pp.

CB 9. Komiya, Ryutaro, ed. POSTWAR ECONOMIC GROWTH IN JAPAN. Berkeley and Los Angeles: University of California Press, 1966. 260pp.

CB 10. Kosai, Yutaka. THE ERA OF HIGH-SPEED GROWTH: NOTES ON THE MODERN JAPANESE ECONOMY. Kaminski, Jacqueline, trans. New York: Columbia University Press, 1984. 250pp.

CB 11. Kosai, Yutaka, and Ogino, Yoshitaro. THE CONTEMPORARY JAPANESE ECONOMY. Thompson, Ralph, trans. Armonk, N.Y.: M. E. Sharpe, 1984. 160pp.

CB 12.   Lebra, Joyce C., ed.   JAPAN'S GREATER EAST
ASIA CO-PROSPERITY SPHERE IN WORLD WAR II: SELECTED
READINGS AND DOCUMENTS. New York: Oxford University
Press, 1975. 212pp.

CB 13.   Lockwood, William W. THE ECONOMIC
DEVELOPMENT OF JAPAN: GROWTH AND STRUCTURAL CHANGE,
1868-1938. Princeton, N.J.: Princeton University Press,
1954. 603pp.

CB 14.   Marshall, Byron K. CAPITALISM AND
NATIONALISM IN PREWAR JAPAN: THE IDEOLOGY OF THE
BUSINESS ELITE, 1868--1941. Stanford: Stanford
University Press, 1967. 163pp.

CB 15.   Marubeni Corporation. THE JAPANESE EDGE:
THE REAL STORY BEHIND A SOGO SHOSHA--ONE OF JAPAN'S
UNIQUE NEW CLASS OF GLOBAL CORPORATIONS. Tokyo:
Marubeni, 1981. 199pp.

CB 16.   Marubeni Corporation. THE UNIQUE WORLD OF
THE SOGO SHOSHA. Tokyo: Marubeni Corp., 1978. 117pp.

CB 17.   Nakamura, Takefusa. ECONOMIC GROWTH IN
PREWAR JAPAN. Feldman, Robert A., trans.   New Haven:
Yale University Press, 1983. 326pp.

CB 18.   Nakayama, Ichiro. INDUSTRIALIZATION OF
JAPAN. Honolulu: East-West Center Press, 1964. 73pp.

CB 19.   Ohkawa, Kazushi, and Rosovsky, Henry.
JAPANESE ECONOMIC GROWTH; TREND ACCELERATION IN THE
TWENTIETH CENTURY. Palo Alto, Calif.: Stanford
University Press, 1973. 325pp.

CB 20.   Ohkawa, Kazushi, and Shinohara, Miyohei.
PATTERNS OF JAPANESE ECONOMIC DEVELOPMENT. New Haven:
Yale University Press, 1979. 411pp.

CB. Emergence of Business/Industry

CB 21. Okimoto, Daniel I. JAPAN'S ECONOMY: COPING WITH CHANGE IN THE INTERNATIONAL ENVIRONMENT. Boulder, Colo.: Westview Press, 1982. 304pp.

CB 22. Patrick, Hugh Talbot. JAPANESE INDUSTRIALIZATION AND ITS SOCIAL CONSEQUENCES. Berkeley: University of California Press, 1976. 505pp.

CB 23. Roberts, John G. MITSUI: THREE CENTURIES OF JAPANESE BUSINESS. New York: Weatherhill, 1973. 564pp.

CB 24. Rosovsky, Henry. CAPITAL FORMATION IN JAPAN: 1868-1940. New York: Free Press of Glencoe, 1961. 358pp.

CB 25. Russell, Oland D. THE HOUSE OF MITSUI. Boston: Little, Brown & Co., 1939. 328pp.

CB 26. Schumpeter, Elizabeth B., ed. THE INDUSTRIALIZATION OF JAPAN AND MANCHUKUO: 1930-1940: POPULATION, RAW MATERIALS AND INDUSTRY. New York: Macmillan, 1940. 944pp.

CB 27. Sheldon, Charles David. THE RISE OF THE MERCHANT CLASS IN TOKUGAWA JAPAN, 1600-1868: AN INTRODUCTORY SURVEY. Locust Valley, N.Y.: J. J. Augustin, 1958. 206pp.

CB 28. Tanaka, Kakuei. BUILDING A NEW JAPAN: A PLAN FOR REMODELING THE JAPANESE ARCHIPELAGO. Tokyo: Simul Press; dist. by International Scholarly Books Services, 1973, c1972. 228pp.

CB 29. Tsurumi, Yoshi, and Tsurumi, Rebecca. SOGOSOSHA: ENGINES OF EXPORT-BASED GROWTH. Rev. ed. Montreal: Institute for Research on Public Policy, 1984. 128pp.

CB 30. Tsuru, Shigeto. THE MAINSPRINGS OF JAPANESE GROWTH; A TURNING POINT? Atlantic Papers: 1976/3. Paris: Atlantic Institute for International Affairs, 1977. 76pp.

CB 31. Yamamura, Kozo. A STUDY OF SAMURAI INCOME AND ENTREPRENEURSHIP: QUANTITATIVE ANALYSES OF ECONOMIC ANS SOCIAL ASPECTS OF THE SAMURAI IN TOKUGAWA AND MEIJI, JAPAN. Cambridge, Mass.: Harvard University Press, 1974. 243pp.

CB 32. Yoshihara, Kunio. SOGO SHOSHA: THE VANGUARD OF THE JAPANESE ECONOMY. New York: Oxford University Press, 1982. 358pp.

Articles

CB 33. Baba, Keinosuke. "Japanese Gains From Trade, 1878-1932." ANNALS OF THE HITOTSUBASHI ACADEMY v.8 Apr. 1958 pp.127-142.

CB 34. Bronfenbrenner, Martin. "Some Lessons of Japan's Economic Development, 1853-1938." PACIFIC AFFAIRS v.34 Spring 1961 pp.2-27.

CB 35. Chenery, Hollis B.; Shishido, Shuntaro; and Watanabe, Tsunehiko. "The Pattern of Japanese Growth, 1914-1954." ECONOMETRICA v.30 Jan. 1962 pp.98-139.

CB 36. Crawcour, E. Sydney. "Development of a Credit System in Japan." JOURNAL OF ECONOMIC HISTORY v.21 Sep. 1961 pp.342-360.

CB 37. Emi, Koichi. "The Growth of the Japanese Economy in the First Half of the Meiji Period--In Terms of Problems of Underdeveloped Nations." HITOTSUBASHI JOURNAL OF ECONOMICS v.3 June 1963 pp.6-15.

CB 38. Grusky, D. B. "Industrialization and the Status Attainment Process: the Thesis of Industrialism Reconsidered." AMERICAN SOCIOLOGICAL REVIEW v.48 Aug. 1983 pp.494-506.

CB. Emergence of Business/Industry

CB 39.   Hall, John Whitney. "Foundations of the Modern Japanese Daimyo." JOURNAL OF ASIAN STUDIES v. 20 Nay 1961 pp. 317-329.

CB 40.   Horie, Yasuzo. "An Outline of the Rise of Modern Capitalism in Japan." KYO v. 11 July 1936 pp. 99-115.

CB 41.   Horie, Yasuzo. "Government Industries in the Early Years of the Meiji Era." KYO v. 14 July 1939 pp. 67-87.

CB 42.   Horie, Yasuzo. "Foreign Trade Policy in the Early Meiji Era." KYO v. 22 Oct. 1952 pp. 1-21.

CB 43.   Klein, L. R., and Shinkai, Y. "An Econometric Model of Japan, 1930-1959." INTERNATIONAL ECONOMIC REVIEW v. 4 1963 no. 1 pp. 1-28.

CB 44.   Nagahara, Keiji. "The Historical Premises of the Modernization of Japan: On the Structure of the Tokugawa Shogunate." HITOTSUBASHI JOURNAL OF ECONOMICS v. 3 Oct. 1962 pp. 61-72.

CB 45.   Obelsky, Alvan J. "Japan's Transition: A Socio-Economic Interpretation." KOBE UNIVERSITY ECONOMIC REVIEW no. 9 1963 pp. 1-12.

CB 46.   Ohkawa, Kazushi, and Rosovsky, Henry. "Recent Japanese Growth in Historical Perspective." AMERICAN ECONOMIC REVIEW v. 53 no. 2 1963 pp. 578-588.

CB 47.   Okita, Saburo. "Economic Growth of Postwar Japan." THE DEVELOPING ECONOMIES no. 2 Sep./Dec. 1962 pp. 1-12.

CB 48.   Okita, Saburo. "A Japanese Viewpoint." OECD OBSERVER no. 127 Mar. 1984 pp. 17-18.

CB 49. Rosovsky, Henry. "Japan's Transition to Modern Economic Growth: 1868-1885." in Rosovsky, Henry, ed. INDUSTRIALIZATION IN TWO SYSTEMS: ESSAYS IN HONOR OF ALEXANDER GERSCHENKRON. New York: Wiley, 1966. pp. 91-139.

CB 50. Smith, Thomas Carlyle. "The Introduction of Western Industry to Japan During the Last Years of the Tokugawa Period." HARVARD JOURNAL OF ASIATIC STUDIES June 1948 pp. 130-152.

CB 51. Smith, Thomas Carlyle. "Landlords and Rural Capitalists in the Modernization of Japan." JOURNAL OF ECONOMIC HISTORY v. 16 June 1956 pp. 165-181.

CB 52. Wilkins, M. "Japanese Multinational Enterprise Before 1914." BUSINESS HISTORY REVIEW v. 60 Summer 1986 pp. 199-231.

CB 53. Yamamura, Kozo. "Zaibatsu, Prewar and Zaibatsu, Postwar." JOURNAL OF ASIAN STUDIES v. 23 Aug. 1964 pp. 539-554.

CB 54. Yamanaka, Tokutaro. "Japanese Small Industries During the Industrial Revolution." ANNALS OF HITOTSUBASHI ACADEMY v. 2 Oct. 1951 pp. 15-36.

CB 55. Yasunaga, Takemi "Changing Values Transform Industrial Society; Employee Opinion of Business also Changing." ORIENTAL ECONOMIST v. 50 Sep. 1982 pp. 38-42.

CC. Land and Agriculture

Monographic Works

CC 1. Dore, Ronald Phillips. LAND REFORM IN JAPAN. London; New York: Oxford University Press, 1959. 510pp.

CC. Land and Agriculture

CC 2. Fukutake, Tadashi. JAPANESE RURAL SOCIETY. Dore, R. P., trans. New York: Oxford University Press, 1967. 230pp.

CC 3. Fukutake, Tadashi. RURAL SOCIETY: CHINA, INDIA, JAPAN. Seattle: University of Washington Press, 1967. 207pp.

CC 4. Grad, Andrew J. LAND AND PEASANT IN JAPAN: AN INTRODUCTORY SURVEY. New York: Institute of Pacific Relations, 1952. 262pp.

CC 5. Kada, Ryohei. PART-TIME FAMILY FARMING; OFF-FARM EMPLOYMENT AND FARM ADJUSTMENTS IN THE U.S. AND JAPAN. Tokyo: Center for Academic Publications Japan, 1980. 264pp.

CC 6. Nakamura, James I. AGRICULTURAL PRODUCTION AND THE ECONOMIC DEVELOPMENT OF JAPAN, 1873-1922. Princeton: Princeton University Press, 1966. 257pp.

CC 7. Nasu, Shiroshi. LAND UTILIZATION IN JAPAN. New York: Institute of Public Relations, 1929. 275pp.

CC 8. Saxon, Eric, and Anderson, Kym. JAPANESE AGRICULTURAL PROTECTION IN HISTORIC PERSPECTIVE. Pacific Economic Papers no. 92. Canberra, Australia: Australia-Japan Research Centre, Australian National University, 1982. 42pp.

Articles

CC 9. Dore, Ronald Phillips. "Agricultural Improvement in Japan, 1870-1900." ECONOMIC DEVELOPMENT AND CULTURAL CHANGE v.9 no.1, part 2 Oct. 1960 pp.69-92.

CC 10.   Dore, Ronald Phillips. "Beyond Land Reform: Japan's Agricultural Prospect." PACIFIC AFFAIRS v. 36 Fall 1963 pp. 265-276.

CC 11.   Evans, Richard. "The Revolution in International Real Estate: Tokyo's Toughest, London's Dearest for Office Space." EUROMONEY Sep. 1984 pp. 51+.

CC 12.   Frost, Peter. "Land Reform of 1946." KODANSHA ENCYCLOPEDIA OF JAPAN (see item A 28) v. 4 pp. 364-365.

CC 13.   Ginsburg, Norton S. "Japanese Agriculture: The Land and the People." ECONOMIC DEVELOPMENT AND CULTURAL CHANGE v. 1 Dec. 1952 pp. 315-319.

CC 14.   Grabowski, Richard., and Sivan, David. "The Direction of Technological Change in Japanese Agriculture, 1874-1981." THE DEVELOPING ECONOMIES v. 21 Sep. 1983 pp. 234-243.

CC 15.   Ito, Akira. "The Decline of Sericulture and Related Shifts in Japan's Dryland Field Agriculture Since 1930." RURAL ECONOMIC PROBLEMS v. 1 May 1964 pp. 25-44.

CC 16.   Johnston, Bruce F. "Agricultural Productivity and Economic Development in Japan." JOURNAL OF POLITICAL ECONOMY v. 59 Dec. 1951 pp. 498-513.

CC 17.   Johnston, Bruce F. "Agricultural Development and Economic Transformation: A Comparative Study of the Japanese Experience." FOOD RESEARCH INSTITUTE STUDIES v. 3 Nov. 1962 pp. 223-276.

CC 18.   Kaneda, Hiromitsu. "Structural Change and Policy Response in Japanese Agriculture After Land Reform." ECONOMIC DEVELOPMENT AND CULTURAL CHANGE v. 28 Apr. 1980 pp. 469-486.

CC. Land and Agriculture

CC 19. Kaneda, Hiromitsu. "Substitution of Labor and Non-Labor Inputs and Technical Change in Japanese Agriculture. "REVIEW OF ECONOMICS AND STATISTICS v. 47 May 1965 pp. 163-171.

CC 20. Kawano, Shigeto. "Economic Significance of the Land Reform in Japan." THE DEVELOPING ECONOMIES v. 3 June 1965 pp. 139-157.

CC 21. Ohkawa, Kazushi. "The Role of Agriculture in Early Economic Development, A Study of the Japanese Case." in Berril, Kenneth, ed. ECONOMIC DEVELOPMENT WITH SPECIAL REFERENCE TO EAST ASIA. New York: St. Martin's Press, 1964. pp. 322-335.

CC 22. Ohkawa, Kazushi, and Rosovsky, Henry. "The Role of Agriculture in Modern Japanese Economic Development." ECONOMIC DEVELOPMENT AND CULTURAL CHANGE v. 9 no. 1, part 2 Oct. 1960 pp. 43-68.

CC 23. Ouchi, T. "The Influence of Japan's Rapid Economic Growth on Agriculture." SECOND INTERNATIONAL CONFERENCE OF ECONOMIC HISTORY. Paris: Mouton, 1962 pp. 343-352.

CC 24. Sauvez, Marc. "Villes du Japon: un Pays sans Intéret Public." URBANISME v. 52 Feb. 1983 pp. 47-51. (Summary in English).

CC 25. Tanaka, Usami. "The Japanese Landlord-Tenant Tenure System in the Meiji Era." KOBE UNIVERSITY ECONOMIC REVIEW v. 27 1981 pp. 1-13.

CC 26. Yamada, Hiroyuki. "Cross-Section Analysis of Urbanization in the Tokyo Metropolitan Region." KYOTO UNIVERSITY ECONOMIC REVIEW v. 52 Apr. /Oct 1982 pp. 1-29.

CC 27. Zetter, John. "Japan: The Urban Challenge." OECD OBSERVER June 1986 pp. 4-8.

CD. Traditions of Business

Monographic Works

CD 1.   Ballon, Robert J., ed.   DOING BUSINESS IN JAPAN. Tokyo: Sophia University Press, 1967. 215pp.

CD 2.   Ballon, Robert J.; Tomita, Iwao; and Usami, Hajime. FINANCIAL REPORTING IN JAPAN. Tokyo: Kodansha International, 1976. 305pp.

CD 3.   De Mente, Boye. JAPANESE ETIQUETTE AND ETHICS IN BUSINESS. 5th ed.   (Published in 1981 as: The Japanese Way of Doing Business.) Lincolnwood, Ill.: Passport Books, 1987. 182pp.

CD 4.   De Mente, Boye. JAPANESE MANNERS AND ETHICS IN BUSINESS. Tokyo: East Asia Press, 1961. 179pp.

CD 5.   De Mente, Boye. THE JAPANESE WAY OF DOING BUSINESS: A PRACTICAL GUIDE TO MOTIVATIONS, TECHNIQUES, AND GOALS OF JAPANESE BUSINESS. Rev. ed. of Japanese Manners and Ethics in Business, 1961. Englewood Cliffs, N.J.: Prentice-Hall, 1981. 156pp.

CD 6.   Hunsburger, Warren S. JAPAN, LESSONS IN ENTERPRISE. Chicago: Scott, Foresman & Co., 1963. 72pp.

CD 7.   Ohmae, Kenichi. THE MIND OF THE STRATEGIST: THE ART OF JAPANESE BUSINESS. New York: McGraw-Hill, 1982. 283 pp.

CD 8.   Rebischung, James. JAPAN: THE FACTS OF MODERN BUSINESS AND SOCIAL LIFE. Rutland, Vt.: C.E. Tuttle, 1975. 130pp.

CD. Traditions of Business

Articles

CD 9.   Ballon, Robert J. "A Lesson from Japan:
Contract, Control and Authority." JOURNAL OF
CONTEMPORARY BUSINESS v. 8 no. 2 1979 pp. 27-35.

CD 10.   Hahn, E. "Negotiating Contracts with the
Japanese." CASE WESTERN RESERVE JOURNAL OF
INTERNATIONAL LAW v. 14 1982 pp. 377-385.

CD 11.   "The Japanese Business Viewpoint." NATION'S
BUSINESS v. 72 Jan. 1984 pp. 36+.

CD 12.   Kuttner, R. "Zen and the Art of Trade
Negotiation." NEW REPUBLIC v. 193 Aug 12/19, 1985
pp. 20-23.

CE. Japanese Economy and Business from a Western Viewpoint (Comparative Treatments)

Monographic Works

CE 1.   De Mente, Boye. HOW TO DO BUSINESS IN JAPAN:
A GUIDE FOR INTERNATIONAL BUSINESSMEN. Phoenix: Phoenix
Books, 1983. 230pp.

CE 2.   Deutsch, Mitchell F. DOING BUSINESS WITH THE
JAPANESE. New York: New American Library, 1983. 197pp.

CE 3.   Dore, Ronald Phillips. JAPAN AND WORLD
DEPRESSION: THEN AND NOW. Essays in Memory of E. F.
Penrose. New York: St. Martin's Press, 1986. 224pp.

CE 4.   Ehrlich, Eva. ESTABLISHMENT AND ENTERPRISE
SIZE IN MANUFACTURING: AN EAST--WEST INTERNATIONAL
COMPARISON. Vienna: Wiener Institut für Internationale

CE. Business: Western Viewpoint

Wirtschaftsvergleiche, 1982. 139pp.

CE 5.   Ehrlich, Eva. JAPAN: A CASE OF CATCHING UP.
Budapest: Akademiai Kiado, 1984. 268pp.

CE 6.   Frank, Isaiah, ed.   THE JAPANESE ECONOMY IN
INTERNATIONAL PERSPECTIVE. New York: Johns Hopkins
University Press, 1975. 314pp.

CE 7.   Furstenberg, Friedrich. WHY THE JAPANESE
HAVE BEEN SO SUCCESSFUL IN BUSINESS. London: Leviathon
House, 1974. 107pp.

CE 8.   Goldsmith, Raymond W. THE FINANCIAL
DEVELOPMENT OF INDIA, JAPAN, AND THE UNITED STATES: A
TRILATERAL INSTITUTIONAL, STATISTICAL, AND ANALYTIC
COMPARISON. New Haven: Yale University Press, 1983.
120pp.

CE 9.   Graham, John L., and Sano, Yoshihiro. SMART
BARGAINING: DOING BUSINESS WITH THE JAPANESE.
Cambridge, Mass.: Ballinger, 1984. 164pp.

CE 10.   Imai, Masaaki. NEVER TAKE YES FOR AN
ANSWER: AN INSIDE LOOK AT JAPANESE BUSINESS FOR FOREIGN
BUSINESSMEN. Tokyo: Simul Press, 1975. 138pp.

CE 11.   Kojima, Kiyoshi. JAPAN AND A NEW WORLD
ECONOMIC ORDER. Boulder, Colo.: Westview Press, 1977.
190pp.

CE 12.   Komuta, Kensaburo. JAPAN'S ECONOMY IN WORLD
PERSPECTIVE. ed. by Matsumura, Molleen. Berkeley,
Calif.: Alin Foundation Press, 1983. 70pp.

CE 13.   Kuznets, Simon S; Moore, Wilbert E.;
Spengler, Joseph J. ECONOMIC GROWTH, BRAZIL, INDIA,
JAPAN. Durham: Duke University Press, 1955. 613pp.

CE 14.   Norbury, Paul, and Bownas, Geoffrey, eds.
BUSINESS IN JAPAN: A GUIDE TO JAPANESE BUSINESS
PRACTICE AND PROCEDURE. Boulder, Colo.: Westview Press,

159

CE. Business: Western Viewpoint

1980. 210pp.

CE 15.   Richardson, Bradley M., and Ueda, Taizo, eds. BUSINESS AND SOCIETY IN JAPAN: FUNDAMENTALS FOR BUSINESSMEN. New York: Praeger, 1981. 334pp.

CE 16.   Rowland, Diana. JAPANESE BUSINESS ETIQUETTE: A PRACTICAL GUIDE TO BUSINESS AND SOCIAL SUCCESS WITH THE JAPANESE. New York: Warner Books, 1985. 208pp.

CE 17.   Seward, Jack, and Van Zandt, Howard. JAPAN: THE HUNGRY GUEST; JAPANESE BUSINESS ETHICS vs. THOSE OF THE U.S. Tokyo: Lotus Press, 1985. 292pp.

CE 18.   Tung, Rosalie Lam. BUSINESS NEGOTIATIONS WITH THE JAPANESE. Lexington, Mass.: Lexington Books, D. C. Heath, 1984. 250pp.

CE 19.   Zimmerman, Mark. HOW TO DO BUSINESS WITH THE JAPANESE: A STRATEGY FOR SUCCESS. New York: Random House, 1985. 320pp.

Articles

CE 20.   Alster, N. "Strategic Shift: Japan Searches for New Formula." ELECTRONIC BUSINESS v. 12 Nov. 1, 1986 pp. 76-8+.

CE 21.   Ballon, Robert J. "Understanding the Japanese: Preparation for International Business." BUSINESS HORIZONS v. 13 no. 3 1970 pp. 21-30.

CE 22.   Barrett, M. E., and Gehrke, J. A. "Significant Differences Between Japanese and American Business." MSU BUSINESS TOPICS v. 22 no. 1 1974 pp. 41-50.

CE 23.   Bartels, R. "National Culture--Business
Relations: United States and Japan Contrasted."
MANAGEMENT INTERNATIONAL REVIEW v.22 no.2 1982 pp.4-12.

CE 24.   Birnbaum, P. "Humoring the Japanese."
ACROSS THE BOARD v.23 Oct. 1986 pp.10-12.

CE 25.   Braham, J. "Trade: the Culture Gap."
INDUSTRY WEEK v.225 Apr. 29, 1985 pp.19-20.

CE 26.   Eckhouse, J. "Bring Your Visa Card, but
Leave Your Lawyer at Home." ELECTRONIC BUSINESS v.11
Feb. 15, 1985 pp.88-89.

CE 27.   Kuwayama, Patricia Hagan. "Success Story."
WILSON QUARTERLY v.6 Winter 1982 pp.133-144.

CE 28.   Nishikata, Masumi. "Japanese and American
Business Practices; a Study of Cultural Differences."
JAPANESE TRADE AND INDUSTRY v.1 July 1982 pp.40-44.

CE 29.   O'Neill, John. "Japan to Pose More Problems
for European Business." VISION Sep. 1980 pp.24-29.

CE 30.   Saunders, J., and Chong, T. K. "Trade with
China and Japan." MANAGEMENT DECISIONS v.24 no.3 1986
pp.7-12.

CE 31.   Tung, Rosalie L. "How To Negotiate with the
Japanese." CALIFORNIA MANAGEMENT REVIEW v.26 Summer
1984 pp.62-77.

CE 32.   Van Zandt, H. F. "How To Negotiate in
Japan." HARVARD BUSINESS REVIEW v.48 no.6 1970
pp.45-56.

CE 33.   Van Zandt, H. F. "Learning To Do Business
with 'Japan Inc.'" HARVARD BUSINESS REVIEW v.50 no.4
1972 pp.83-92.

CE. Business: Western Viewpoint

CE 34. "Why Japanese Business Is Losing Its Halo." BUSINESS AND SOCIETY REVIEW no. 12 Winter 1974/1975 pp. 35-43.

CE 35. Zimmerman, M. "Getting On the Japanese Wavelength." ACROSS THE BOARD v. 22 Apr. 1985 pp. 30-37. (Excerpt from HOW TO DO BUSINESS WITH THE JAPANESE, see item CE 19.)

CF. Contemporary Conditions and Broad Issues

Monographic Works

CF 1. Hidaka, Rokuro. THE PRICE OF AFFLUENCE: DILEMMAS OF CONTEMPORARY JAPAN. McCormack, Gavan, trans. Tokyo: Kodansha International, 1984. 176pp.

CF 2. INDUSTRIAL REVIEW OF JAPAN, 1956-- . (AN ANNUAL IN-DEPTH REPORT ON THE STATE OF THE JAPANESE ECONOMY.) Tokyo: Japan Economic Journal, annual.

CF 3. Ishizuka, Shunjiro, ed. WHITE PAPERS OF JAPAN, 1969-- . (ANNUAL ABSTRACT OF OFFICIAL REPORTS AND STATISTICS OF THE JAPANESE GOVERNMENT). Tokyo: Japan Institute of International Affairs, annual.

CF 4. JAPAN ECONOMIC ALMANAC. Tokyo: Japan Economic Journal, 1985- . Annual.

CF 5. Japan. Office of the Prime Minister. Statistical Bureau. JAPAN STATISTICAL YEARBOOK, 1980. Tokyo, 1980. 732pp.

CF 6. Kahn, Herman, and Pepper, Thomas. THE JAPANESE CHALLENGE: THE SUCCESS AND FAILURE OF ECONOMIC SUCCESS. New York: Thomas Y. Crowell, 1979. 162 pp.

CF 7.   Kanamori, Hisao, et al.   THE FUTURE OF THE
JAPANESE ECONOMY AND ITS PRIMARY COMMODITY
REQUIREMENTS. JERC Center Paper no.   26. Tokyo:
Japanese Economic Research Center, 1975. 39pp.

CF 8.   Kaplan, Morton A., ed..   JAPAN AT THE
TURNING POINT: PROSPECTS FOR THE COMING DECADE. The
Professors World Peace Acadamy of Japan. Tokyo:
Riverfield, 1981. 123pp.

CF 9.   Kaplan, Morton A., and Mushakoji, Kinhide.
JAPAN, AMERICA, AND THE FUTURE WORLD ORDER. New York:
Free Press, 1976. 369pp.

CF 10.   Katz, Joshua D., and Friedman-Lichtschein,
Tilly C., eds.   JAPAN'S NEW WORLD ROLE. Boulder, Colo.:
Westview Press, 1984. 190pp. Reprint of the June 1982
issue of the JOURNAL OF INTERNATIONAL AFFAIRS v.37
no.1.

CF 11.   Liesner, Thelma. ECONOMIC STATISTICS, 1900-
1983. New York: Facts on File Pubs., 1985. 142pp.

CF 12.   Lin, Ching-Yuan. JAPANESE AND U.S.
INFLATION: A COMPARATIVE ANALYSIS. Lexington, Mass.:
Lexington, D.C. Heath, 1984. 192pp.

CF 13.   Nihon Keizai Kenkyu Senta. JAPAN'S ECONOMY
IN 1980 IN THE GLOBAL CONTEXT: THE NATION'S ROLE IN A
POLYCENTRIC WORLD. Abridged translation.   Tokyo: Japan
Economic Research Center, 1972. 101pp.

CF 14.   THE POLITICS OF JAPAN'S ENERGY STRATEGY:
RESOURCES--DIPLOMACY--SECURITY. Berkeley: Institute of
East Asian Studies, University of California, 1981.
166pp.

CF 15.   Saso, Mary, and Kirby, Stuart. JAPANESE
INDUSTRIAL COMPETITION TO 1990. Cambridge, Mass.: Abt
Books, 1982. 203pp.

CF. Contemporary Conditions

CF 16. Shinohara, Miyohei. STRUCTURAL CHANGES IN JAPAN'S ECONOMIC DEVELOPMENT. Economic Research Series no. 11. The Institute of Economic Research, Hitotsubashi University. Tokyo: Kinokuniya Bookstore, 1970. 445pp.

CF 17. Sinha, Manos Radha. JAPAN'S OPTIONS FOR THE 1980s. New York: St. Martin's Press, 1982. 269pp.

CF 18. WHITE PAPER ON INTERNATIONAL TRADE: JAPAN 1983; SUMMARY. New York: Elsevier Science Publishers, 1984. 426pp.

CF 19. Woronoff, Jon. JAPAN, THE COMING ECONOMIC CRISES. 5th ed. Tokyo: Lotus Press, 1979. 316 pp.

CF 20. Yamamura, Kozo, ed. POLICY AND TRADE ISSUES OF THE JAPANESE ECONOMY: AMERICAN AND JAPANESE PERSPECTIVES. Publications of the School of International Studies on Asia: no. 36. Seattle: University of Washington Press, 1983. 348pp.

CF 21. Yamazawa, Ippei. TRADE FRICTION AND THE COMPETITIVENESS OF JAPANESE INDUSTRIES. Tokyo: Japan Foundation, Office for the Japanese Studies Center, 1982. 13pp.

Articles

CF 22. Abegglen, James C. "The Economic Growth of Japan." SCIENTIFIC AMERICAN v.222 Mar. 1970 pp.30-37.

CF 23. Abi, K. "Industrial Development and Technological Progress in Japan." ASIAN AFFAIRS v.1 1956 pp.176-188.

CF 24. Allen, George Cyrill. "Japan's Economic Prospects." WORLD TODAY v.19 Oct. 1963 pp.439-447.

CF 25.   Ambirajan, S. "Japanese Economic Recovery
and Its Lessons for India." INDIAN JOURNAL OF ECONOMICS
v. 39 Jan. 1959 pp. 283-293.

CF 26.   Araki, Y. "Toward Japanese Recovery." U. S.
BANKER v. 94 May 1983 pp. 42+.

CF 27.   Ariki, Soichiro. "Japan's Economy at the
Crossroads: An Analysis of Conditions for Her
Survival." RIVISTA INTERNAZIONALE DI SCIENZE ECONOMICHE
E COMMERCIALI v. 28 July-Aug. 1981 pp. 644-660.

CF 28.   Armstrong, L. "Is Japan Finally Ready to
Pump Up Its Economy." BUSINESS WEEK Feb. 17, 1986
pp. 48-49.

CF 29.   Armstrong, L. "Now Japan Inc. Has to Do
Some Belt-Tightening." BUSINESS WEEK Dec. 23, 1985
p. 39.

CF 30.   Bronfenbrenner, Martin. "Economic Thought
and Its Application and Methodology in the East: State
of Japanese Economics." AMERICAN ECONOMIC ASSOCIATION
PAPERS AND PROCEEDINGS v. 46 May 1956 pp. 389-398.

CF 31.   Bronfenbrenner, Martin. "The Japanese
Economy Faces Independence." KEIZAI KENKYU v. 4 Oct.
1953 pp. 330-343.

CF 32.   Buell, B. "Japan Looks for a Brighter New
Year." BUSINESS WEEK Jan. 12, 1987 pp. 58-59.

CF 33.   Bunke, H. C. "A Japanese Pilgrimage."
BUSINESS HORIZONS v. 24 no. 3 1981 pp. 2-9.

CF 34.   Crawcour, E. Sydney. "Progress and
Structural Change in the Japanese Economy." ASIAN
SURVEY v. 1 no. 6 1961 pp. 3-9.

CF. Contemporary Conditions

CF 35.   Cullison, A. E. "Has Growth in Japan
Plateaued? Too Early To Tell, But Data Suggest a
Definite Slowing." JOURNAL OF COMMERCE AND COMMERCIAL
Mar. 3, 1986 pp. 1A+.

CF 36.   Dahlby, T. "The Economics of Relaxation."
NEWSWEEK v. 107 Feb. 10, 1986 pp. 58-59.

CF 37.   Davies, D. "Japan '81." FAR EASTERN
ECONOMIC REVIEW v. 112 June 12-18, 1981 pp. 43-76.

CF 38.   Drucker, Peter F. "Behind Japan's Success."
HARVARD BUSINESS REVIEW v. 59 Jan./Feb. 1981 pp. 83-90.
also in McKINSEY QUARTERLY Winter 1983 p. 45-57.

CF 39.   Drucker, Peter F. "Japan: The Problem of
Success." FOREIGN AFFAIRS v. 56 1978 pp. 564-578.

CF 40.   Drucker, Peter F. "Japan Tries for a Second
Miracle." HARPER'S MAGAZINE no. 226 Mar. 1963 pp. 72-78.

CF 41.   Drucker, Peter F. "The Price of Success,
Japan Revisited." ACROSS THE BOARD v. 15 Aug. 1978
pp. 28-35.

CF 42.   "Economic Structure of Japan." ORIENTAL
ECONOMIST v. 32 no. 641 Mar. 1964 p. 44.

CF 43.   Fisher, M. H. "Dismantling Japan's Two-Tier
Economy." BANKER v. 3 no. 425 July 1961 pp. 489-497.

CF 44.   "Focus Japan." COLUMBIA JOURNAL OF WORLD
BUSINESS v. 16 Summer 1981 pp. 5-35.

CF 45.   Fujii, J. "1982 Roads Will Be Bumpy for the
Japanese." FAR EASTERN ECONOMIC REVIEW v. 115 Feb. 26-Mar.
4 1982 pp. 37-38.

CF 46.   Fujii, Motohide. "Economic Diplomacy Makes
Headway." ASIA SCENE v. 8 Oct 1963 pp. 6-9.

CF 47. Gall, N. "The Rise and Fall of Industrial Japan." COMMENTARY v.76 Oct. 1983 pp.27-34.

CF 48. Gregory, G., et al. "Industrial Japan '81." FAR EASTERN ECONOMIC REVIEW v.114 Dec. 4-10, 1981 pp.43-78.

CF 49. Henriksen, O. "Explaining the Japanese Miracle." INTERNATIONAL MANAGEMENT v.37 Jan. 1982 p.23.

CF 50. "The Heretic Who's a Hero to Japanese Business." BUSINESS WEEK Apr. 16, 1984 pp.190+.

CF 51. Hollerman, Leon. "Japan's Foreign Trade Dependence and the Five Year Economic Plan." REVIEW OF ECONOMICS AND STATISTICS v.40 Nov. 1958 pp.416-419.

CF 52. Hollerman, Leon. "Japan's Place in the Scale of Economic Development." ECONOMIC DEVELOPMENT AND CULTURAL CHANGE v.12 Jan. 1964 pp.139-157.

CF 53. Ichimura, Shinichi, et al. "A Quarterly Econometric Model of Japan, 1952-1959." OSAKA ECONOMIC PAPERS v.12 Mar. 1964 p.19-44.

CF 54. Iida, Tsuneo. "What is Unique About the Japanese Economy?" ORIENTAL ECONOMIST v.49 July 1981 pp.8-11.

CF 55. "Industrial Japan '79: Casting Off the Old." FAR EASTERN ECONOMIC REVIEW Dec. 14, 1979 pp.45-90.

CF 56. "Industrial Japan '81." FAR EASTERN ECONOMIC REVIEW Dec. 4, 1981 pp.43-82.

CF 57. Ito, Taikichi. "The High Growth of the Japanese Economy and the Problems of Small Enterprises." THE DEVELOPING ECONOMIES v.1 July/Dec 1963 pp.3-34.

CF. Contemporary Conditions

CF 58.   Itoh, Makoto. "The Great World Crisis and Japanese Capitalism." CAPITAL AND CLASS v.21 Winter 1983 pp.49-60.

CF 59.   Jacobs, Norman. "Modern Capitalism and Japanese Development." in Cahnman, Werner J., and Boskoff, Alvin. SOCIOLOGY AND HISTORY: THEORY AND RESEARCH. New York: Free Press of Glencoe, 1964. pp.191-196.

CF 60.   "Japan." LEVIATHAN v.12 no.4 1984 pp.445-549.

CF 61.   "Japan: a Survey." ECONOMIST v.288 July 9, 1983 (25 page section following page 50).

CF 62.   "Japan '80." FAR EASTERN ECONOMIC REVIEW June 13, 1980 pp.45-88.

CF 63.   "Japan, Inc. For Sale." ECONOMIST v.288 Nov. 13-19, 1982 p.82.

CF 64.   "Japan Moves Off the Sidelines of World Politics." BUSINESS WEEK June 25, 1985 pp.28-29.

CF 65.   "Japan Shoots For No. 1." BUSINESS WEEK May 5, 1980 pp.100-103.

CF 66.   "Japan: the Bath that Does Not Cleanse." ECONOMIST v.293 Nov. 17, 1984 pp.39-40.

CF 67.   "Japan: What's Happening Out There?" ECONOMIST v.293 Oct. 6, 1984 p.44.

CF 68.   "The Japanese Challenge." WORLD PRESS REVIEW v.27 Oct. 1980 pp.43-48.

CF 69.   "The Japanese Economy." EUROMONEY Sep. 1982 pp.169-207.

CF 70. "The Japanese Economy: Its Present State and Outlook; Trends in Major Industries." FUJI BANK BULLETIN v.34 Nov./Dec 1983 pp.1-28.

CF 71. "The Japanese Economy, 1985: Special Issue." JOURNAL OF JAPANESE TRADE AND INDUSTRY v.4 Jan./Feb. 1985 pp.12-39+.

CF 72. "The Japanese Economy--Present Condition and Outlook." SUMITOMO BANK REVIEW May 1981 v.22 May 1981 pp.1-6.

CF 73. "Japan's Economic Outlook for 1983." JAPAN QUARTERLY v.30 Mar. 1983 pp.13-27.

CF 74. Kagami, N. "Maturing of the Japanese Economy in the 1980s." NATIONAL WESTMINSTER BANK QUARTERLY REPORT Nov. 1983 pp.18-28.

CF 75. Katsumura, Yasuo. "The View from the 1983 Economic White Paper." ECONOMIC EYE v.4 Dec. 1983 pp.19-23.

CF 76. Kawata, F. "A Note on the Recent Trends of Japanese Foreign Trade." KOBE ECONOMIC AND BUSINESS REVIEW v.11 1964 pp.83-91.

CF 77. Kawata, F. "Recent Trends in the Balance of Payments of Japan." KOBE ECONOMIC AND BUSINESS REVIEW v.11 1964 pp.83-91.

CF 78. Krauss, Ellis S. "Japan in 1983: Altering the Status Quo?" ASIAN SURVEY v.24 Jan. 1984 pp.81-99.

CF 79. "Land of Rising Unemployment." FORTUNE v.115 Feb. 2, 1987 pp.10+.

CF 80. Lee, Tim. "The Changing Composition of Economic Growth (1967-1984)." ASIAN MONETARY MONITOR (Hong Kong) v.7 Nov./Dec. 1983 pp.38-47.

CF. Contemporary Conditions

CF 81.   Mead, Christopher A. "Second Japanese
Miracle on the Horizon. " CREATIVE COMPUTING v. 10 Aug.
1984 pp. 120-123.

CF 82.   Miyazaki, Isamu. "Taking Stock of the
Japanese Economy. " JOURNAL OF JAPANESE TRADE AND
INDUSTRY v. 4 Jan. /Feb. 1985 pp. 12-15.

CF 83.   Nakamura, Hideichiro. "Is Japan's Economic
Strength Fortuitous?" JAPANESE ECONOMIC STUDIES v. 11
Spring 1983 pp. 48-74.

CF 84.   Nanto, D K. "Japan's Economy. " CURRENT
HISTORY v. 84 Dec. 1985 pp. 414-417+.

CF 85.   "Pacific Century, 1975-2075. " ECONOMIST
Jan. 4, 1975 pp. 15-35.

CF 86.   Patrick, Hugh Talbot. "Growth and Cycles in
the Japanese Economy. " PACIFIC AFFAIRS v. 36 Fall 1963
pp. 276-283.

CF 87.   Prasad, S. B. "Emerging Forces Against
Paternalism in Japanese Industry. " MSU BUSINESS TOPICS
v. 17 no. 1 1969 pp. 31-36.

CF 88.   Reddy, Allan C. , et al.   "A Macro
Behavioral Model of the Japanese Economic Miracle"
AKRON BUSINESS AND ECONOMIC REVIEW v. 15 Spring 1984
pp. 40-45.

CF 89.   Saito, Takeshi. "The Japanese Economy:
Clouds on the Horizon?" FUJI BANK BULLETIN v. 36
Mar. /Apr. 1985 pp. 1-4.

CF 90.   Sayle, M. , et al.   "Japan '82. " FAR EASTERN
ECONOMIC REVIEW v. 116 June 11/17, 1981 pp. 45-82.

CF 91.   Shinohara, Miyohei. "International
Comparison of the Levels of Industrial Production in
1958. " THE DEVELOPING ECONOMIES v. 3 Mar. 1965 pp. 3-17.

CF 92.   Sweezy, Paul M. "Japan in Perspective."
MONTHLY REVIEW Feb. 1980 pp. 1-14.

CF 93.   Tachi, Ryuichiro. "The 'Softization' of the
Japanese Economy." JAPANESE ECONOMIC STUDIES v. 13
Spring 1985 pp. 67-104.

CF 94.   Takahashi, Takeo. "Japan as a Supply-Side
Economy." ECONOMIC EYE v. 2 Dec. 1981 pp. 4-9.

CF 95.   "Toward a Techno-Society." JAPAN QUARTERLY
v. 29 Dec. 1982 pp. 426-447.

CF 96.   Uchida, Tadao. "The Reform of Japan's
Public Administration and Finance: A Critical
Assessment." JAPANESE ECONOMIC STUDIES v. 10 Spring 1982
pp. 3-52.

CF 97.   Wallace, James. "As Japan Starts to Feel
Its Oats: Already an Economic Power, Tokyo Now Seeks to
Make Its Weight Felt in Other Arenas." U. S. NEWS AND
WORLD REPORT v. 91 Sep. 7, 1981 pp. 31-32.

CF 98.   "Where Growth Still Works." ECONOMIST v. 280
July 18, 1981 pp. survey 3-7.

CF 99.   Woronoff, Jon. "Japan: Economic Report."
ASIAN BUSINESS v. 19 June 1983 pp. 41+.   (22 page
section)

CG. Perspectives on U.S.-Japan Economic Relations

Monographic Works

CG 1.   Bergsten, C. Fred. THE UNITED STATES--JAPAN
ECONOMIC PROBLEM. Washington, D.C.: Institute for
International Economics, 1985. 164pp.

CG. U.S.-Japan Economic Relations

CG 2.   Clapp, Priscilla, and Halperin, Morton H.,
eds.   UNITED STATES--JAPANESE RELATIONS: THE 1970s.
Cambridge, Mass.: Harvard University Press, 1974.
256pp.

CG 3.   Hellmann, Donald C. JAPANESE-AMERICAN
RELATIONS. Washington, D.C.: American Enterprise for
Public Policy Research, 1975. 27pp.

CG 4.   McCraw, Thomas K., ed.   AMERICA vs. JAPAN: A
COMPARATIVE STUDY OF BUSINESS--GOVERNMENT RELATIONS
CONDUCTED AT HARVARD BUSINESS SCHOOL. Boston: Harvard
Business School Press, 1986. 463pp.

CG 5.   Morley, James William, ed.   PROLOGUE TO THE
FUTURE: THE UNITED STATES AND JAPAN IN THE POST-
INDUSTRIAL AGE. Lexington, Mass.: Lexington Books, D.
C. Heath, 1974. 232pp.

CG 6.   Seward, Jack. AMERICA AND JAPAN: THE TWAIN
MEET. Tokyo: Lotus Press, 1981. 190pp.

CG 7.   Tasca, Diane, ed.   U.S.--JAPANESE ECONOMIC
RELATIONS: COOPERATION, COMPETITION, AND CONFRONTATION.
New York: Pergamon, 1980. 135pp.

CG 8.   Vernon, Raymond. TWO HUNGRY GIANTS: THE
UNITED STATES AND JAPAN IN THE QUEST FOR OIL AND ORES.
Cambridge, Mass: Harvard University Press, 1983. 161pp.

Articles

CG 9.   Bere, J. F. "New Realism in Japanese-
American Relations." (Address given March 9, 1982)
VITAL SPEECHES OF THE DAY v.48 Apr. 15, 1982
pp.398-401.

CG 10.   Blumenthal, W. M. "The Issues in Japan-U.S. Economic Relations." JOURNAL OF BUSINESS STATEGY v.4 Summer 1983 pp.70-73.

CG 11.   Dam, Kenneth W. "U.S.--Japan Relations in Perspective." DEPARTMENT OF STATE BULLETIN v.84 Mar. 1984 pp.11-15.

CG 12.   "Dangerous Drift of US--Japanese Relations." BUSINESS WEEK June 15, 1981 pp.57+.

CG 13.   Grapp, Henry F. "The Early Impact of Japan Upon American Agriculture." AGRICULTURAL HISTORY v.23 Apr. 1949 pp.110-116.

CG 14.   Jorgenson, Dale W., and Nishimizu, Nieko. "U.S. and the Japanese Economic Growth, 1952-1974: An International Comparison." THE ECONOMIC JOURNAL Dec. 1978 pp.707-726.

CG 15.   Naoki, Tanaka. "The Changing Japan--U.S. Economic Relationship: From Friction to Integration." JAPAN QUARTERLY v.32 Jan./Mar. 1984 pp.2-8.

CG 16.   Ozaki, Robert S. "United States--Japanese Economic Relations." CURRENT HISTORY v.82 Nov. 1983 pp.357-61.

CG 17.   Sayle, M. "Samurai Meets Cowboy." FAR EASTERN ECONOMIC REVIEW v.112 May 8/14, 1981 pp.21-22.

CG 18.   Shinkai, Yoichi. "Patterns of American and Japanese Growth and Productivity: A Japanese Perspective." JAPAN QUARTERLY v.27 July/Sep. 1980 pp.357-375.

CG 19.   Wilkins, M. "American-Japanese Direct Foreign Investment Relationships, 1930-1952." BUSINESS HISTORY REVIEW v.56 Winter 1982 pp.497-518.

CG 20.   "Yen Agreed, Taxes Forgotten." ECONOMIST v.301 Nov. 8, 1986 pp.14-15.

CH. Foreign Economic Relations

CH. Perspectives on Japan's
Foreign Economic Relations

Monographic Works

CH 1. Allen, George C. JAPAN'S PLACE IN TRADE
STRATEGY: LARGER ROLE IN THE PACIFIC REGION. London:
Moor House, 1968. 62pp.

CH 2. Armour, J. L., ed. ASIA AND JAPAN: THE
SEARCH FOR MODERNIZATION AND IDENTITY. London; Dover,
N.H.: Athlone Press, 1985. 169pp.

CH 3. ASEAN--JAPAN INDUSTRIAL CO-OPERATION.
Singapore: Institute of Southeast Asian Studies, 1984.
125pp.

CH 4. ASEAN--JAPAN RELATIONS. Singapore: Institute
of Southeast Asian Studies, 1983. 274pp.

CH 5. Fan, Kok Sim, comp., JAPAN, SOUTH KOREA, AND
MALAYSIA'S "LOOK EAST" POLICY: A BIBLIOGRAPHY OF RECENT
MATERIALS. Kuala Lumpur, Malaysia: Library, Institute
of Advanced Studies, University of Malaysia, Pantai
Valley, Kuala Lumpur, July 1983. 41pp.

CH 6. Hellman, Donald C. JAPAN AND EAST ASIA, THE
NEW INTERNATIONAL ORDER. New York: Praeger, 1972.
243pp.

CH 7. Hofheinz, Roy, and Calder, Kent E. THE EAST-
ASIA EDGE. New York: Basic Books, 1982. 296p.

CH 8. Hori, Takeaki. THE JAPANESE AND THE
AUSTRALIANS: BUSINESS AND CULTURAL EXCHANGE. New York:
Pergamon, 1982. 142pp.

CH 9.   Huh, Kung-Mo. JAPAN'S TRADE IN ASIA:
DEVELOPMENTS SINCE 1926, PROSPECTS FOR 1970. New York:
Praeger, 1966. 283pp.

CH 10.   Japan Committee for Economic Development
(Keizai Doyukai). JAPAN IN THE WORLD ECONOMY.
Washington, D.C.: Committee on Economic Development,
April 1963. 45pp.

CH 11.   Jones, Francis Clifford. JAPAN'S NEW ORDER
IN EAST ASIA, ITS RISE AND FALL, 1937-45. London:
Oxford University Press, 1954. 498pp.

CH 12.   Langdon, Frank. THE POLITICS OF CANADIAN-
JAPANESE ECONOMIC RELATIONS, 1952-1983. Vancouver :
University of British Columbia Press, 1983. 180pp.

CH 13.   Lincoln, Edward J. JAPAN'S ECONOMIC ROLE IN
NORTHEAST ASIA. Lanham, Md.: University Press of North
America; New York: Asia Society, 1987. 65pp.

CH 14.   Moss, Joanna, and Ravenhill, John. EMERGING
JAPANESE ECONOMIC INFLUENCE IN AFRICA: IMPLICATIONS FOR
THE UNITED STATES. Berkeley: Institute of International
Studies, University of California, 1985. 150pp.

CH 15.   Ohkawa, Kazushi; Ranis, Gustav; and
Meissner, Larry, eds. JAPAN AND THE DEVELOPING
COUNTRIES: A COMPARATIVE ANALYSIS. Oxford; New York:
Basil Blackwell, 1984. 456pp.

CH 16.   Okita, Saburo. THE DEVELOPING ECONOMIES AND
JAPAN: LESSONS IN GROWTH. Tokyo: University of Tokyo,
1980. 284pp.

CH 17.   Ozaki, Robert S., and Arnold, Walter, eds.
JAPAN'S FOREIGN RELATIONS: A GLOBAL SEARCH FOR ECONOMIC
SECURITY. Boulder, Colo.: Westview Press, 1984. 225pp.

CH. Foreign Economic Relations

CH 18. Paarlberg, P. L., and Sharples, Jerry A.
JAPANESE AND EUROPEAN COMMUNITY AGRICULTURAL TRADE
POLICIES: SOME U.S. STRATEGIES. Washington, D.C.: U.S.
Dept. of Agriculture, 1984. 16pp.

CH 19. Sigur, Gaston, and Kim, Young C. JAPANESE
AND U.S. POLICY IN ASIA. New York: Praeger, 1982.
208pp.

CH 20. Wilkinson, Endymion. JAPAN VERSUS EUROPE.
(Former title: MISUNDERSTANDING: EUROPE VERSUS JAPAN.)
New York: Penguin Books, 1983. 288pp.

CH 21. Wilkinson, Endymion. MISUNDERSTANDING:
EUROPE VERSUS JAPAN. Tokyo: Chuokoron: 1980. 293pp.

CH 22. Woronoff, Jon. WORLD TRADE WAR. New York:
Praeger, 1984. 320pp.

CH 23. Yasutomo, Dennis T. JAPAN AND THE ASIAN
DEVELOPMENT BANK. New York: Praeger, 1983. 210pp.

Articles

CH 24. Almond, H. H. Jr. "The Anglo-Japanese
Commercial Treaty of 1963." INTERNATIONAL AND
COMPARATIVE LAW QUARTERLY v.13 July 1964 pp.925-968.

CH 25. "Americans' Confidence in Japan Shows
Slight Drop." BUSINESS JAPAN v.28 Jun. 1983 pp.12-13.

CH 26. Bobrow, Davis B. "Playing for Safety:
Japan's Security Practices." JAPAN QUARTERLY v.31
Jan./Mar. 1984 pp.33-43.

CH 27. Drifte, Reinhard. "The European Community
and Japan; Beyond the Economic Dimensions." JOURNAL OF
INTERNATIONAL AFFAIRS v.37 Summer 1983 pp.147-161.

CH 28.   Elsbree, Willard H. "Japan and the ASEAN in the 1980's; Problems and Prospects." SOUTHEAST ASIAN AFFAIRS v.8 1981 pp.49-61.

CH 29.   Fukai, Shigeko N. "Japan's North South Dialogue at the United Nations." WORLD POLITICS v.35 Oct. 1982 pp.73-105.

CH 30.   Hills, Jill. "Foreign Policy and Technology: The Japan--U.S., Japan--Britain and Japan--EEC Technology Agreement." POLITICAL STUDIES v.31 June 1983 pp.205-222.

CH 31.   "Japan: Trouble With the Neighbours." ECONOMIST v.292 Sept. 22, 1984 pp.80+.

CH 32.   Kassem, M. S. "A Tale of Two Countries--Japan and Britain." COLUMBIA JOURNAL OF WORLD BUSINESS v.9 no.2 1974 pp.35-48.

CH 33.   Kim, K. I., et al.   "An Empirical Study of the Transnational Production Sharing of the Asian NICs (Newly Industrializing Countries) with Japan." JOURNAL OF INTERNATIONAL BUSINESS STUDIES v.17 Summer 1986 pp.117-130.

CH 34.   Lewis, J. "Stemming the Tide." FAR EASTERN ECONOMIC REVIEW v.113 July 3/9, 1981 pp.40-41.

CH 35.   Patrick, Hugh Talbot. "Lessons for Under-Developed Countries from the Japanese Experience of Economic Development." INDIAN ECONOMIC JOURNAL v.9 Oct. 1961 pp.150-166.

CH 36.   "Profile: Japan." ASIAN FINANCIER v.9 Feb. 1983 pp.41-44+.

CH 37.   Qadir, Shahid. "Japanese Economic Stake in the Third World." PAKISTAN HORIZON v.35 no.2 1982 pp.51-60.

CH. Foreign Economic Relations

CH 38.   Smith, L. "Japan Wants to Make Friends."
FORTUNE v. 112 Sep. 2, 1985 pp. 84-88.

CH 39.   Trezise, Philip H. "The Place of Japan in
the Network of World Trade." AMERICAN ECONOMIC REVIEW
v. 53 May 1963 pp. 589-598.

CH 40.   Yoshida, I. "Types and Scale of Japan's
Economic and Technical Help." ASIAN AFFAIRS v. 4 1959
pp. 61-72.

VII.

CHAPTER 4

D. INDUSTRIAL POLICY

DA. Planning, Policies, Strategies;
General Treatments

Monographic Works

DA 1.   Dore, Ronald Phillips. FLEXIBLE RIGIDITIES:
INDUSTRIAL POLICY AND STRUCTURAL ADJUSTMENT IN THE
JAPANESE ECONOMY, 1970-1980. Stanford, Calif.: Stanford
University Press, 1986. 220pp.

DA 2.   Fine, Sherwood M. JAPAN'S POSTWAR INDUSTRIAL
RECOVERY. Tokyo: Foreign Affairs Association of Japan,
1953. 52pp.

DA 3.   Gibney, Frank. MIRACLE BY DESIGN: THE REAL
REASONS BEHIND JAPAN'S ECONOMIC SUCCESS. New York:
Times Books, 1982. 239pp.

DA. Planning Strategies

DA 4.   Japan Economic Institute of America. JAPAN'S
INDUSTRIAL POLICIES: WHAT ARE THEY, DO THEY MATTER, AND
ARE THEY DIFFERENT FROM THOSE IN THE UNITED STATES?
Washington, D. C. : The Institute, 1984. 56pp.

DA 5.   JAPAN'S INDUSTRIAL POLICIES: WHAT ARE THEY,
DO THEY MATTER, AND ARE THEY DIFFERENT FROM THOSE IN
THE UNITED STATES? Washington, D.C. : Japan Economic
Institute of America, 1984. 56pp. (Same as item DA 4)

DA 6.   Komiya, Ryutaro, ed.   INDUSTRIAL POLICY OF
JAPAN. Tokyo; Orlando, Fla. : Academic Press, 1986.

DA 7.   Magaziner, Ira C. , and Hout, Thomas M.
JAPANESE INDUSTRIAL POLICY. Berkeley: Institute of
International Studies, University of California, 1981,
c1980.   111pp.

DA 8.   Mitsubishi Economic Research Institute.
CAPITAL PROCUREMENT IN POST-WAR JAPANESE INDUSTRY.
Tokyo: The Institute, 1957. 20pp.

DA 9.   Nagamine, Haruo, ed.   JAPAN--A COMPENDIUM:
FACTS AND FIGURES ON DEVELOPMENT, ADMINISTRATION, AND
PLANNING. New York: UNIPUB, 1982. 55pp.

DA 10.   Shinohara, Miyohei. INDUSTRIAL GROWTH,
TRADE, AND DYNAMIC PATTERNS IN THE JAPANESE ECONOMY.
Tokyo: University of Tokyo Press, 1982. 243pp.

DA 11.   Shishido, Toshiio, and Sato, Ryuzo.
ECONOMIC POLICY AND DEVELOPMENT: NEW PERSPECTIVES.
Dover, Mass. : Auburn House, 1985.

DA 12.   Takahashi, Chotaro. DYNAMIC CHANGES OF
INCOME AND ITS DISTRIBUTION IN JAPAN. Tokyo:
Kinokuniya, 1961. 182pp.

DA 13.   Trevor, Malcolm. JAPANESE INDUSTRIAL
KNOWLEDGE: CAN IT HELP BRITISH INDUSTRY? Brookfield,
Vt. : Gower, 1985. 122pp.

DA 14. Wilson, John Oliver. THE POWER ECONOMY: BUILDING AN ECONOMY THAT WORKS. Boston: Little, Brown, 1985. 302pp.

DA 15. Yamamura, Kozo. ECONOMIC POLICY IN POSTWAR JAPAN: GROWTH VERSUS ECONOMIC DEMOCRACY. Berkeley: University of California Press, 1967. 226pp.

Articles

DA 16. Aghevli, Bijan B., and Rodriguez, Carlos A. "Trade, Prices and Output in Japan: A Simple Monetary Model." INTERNATIONAL MONETARY FUND STAFF PAPERS v.26 Mar. 1979 pp.38-54.

DA 17. Aliber, Robert Z. "Planning, Growth, and Competition in the Japanese Economy." ASIAN SURVEY v.3 Dec. 1963 pp.596-608.

DA 18. Barang, Marcel. "Vaulting into the Fifth Generation: Japan Goes For No. 1." SOUTH Sep. 1983 pp.21-27.

DA 19. Bilgin, B. "Japan's Changing Industrial Strategy and Its Implications for Japanese Investment in Canada." PACIFIC AFFAIRS v.55 Summer 1982 pp.267-272.

DA 20. Boyer, E. "How Japan Manages Declining Industries." FORTUNE v.107 Jan. 10, 1983 pp.58-63.

DA 21. Byron, Christopher. "How Japan Does It." TIME Mar. 30, 1981 pp.54-60.

DA 22. Davies, D. "Making Things First, Money Later." FAR EASTERN ECONOMIC REVIEW June 12-18, 1981 p.65.

DA. Planning Strategies

DA 23.   Davies, D. "Modernising Despite Feeble
Corporate Leaders." FAR EASTERN ECONOMIC REVIEW June
12-18, 1981.

DA 24.   "The Factory of Japan's Future." MANAGEMENT
TODAY April 1984 pp.66-71.

DA 25.   Garzony, L. G. "A Perspective on Japanese
Manufacturing Success, 1950--1985. INDUSTRIAL
MANAGEMENT v.23 Sep./Oct. 1981 pp.16-20.

DA 26.   Hagen, Everett Einar. "How Economic Growth
Begins: A General Theory Applied to Japan." PUBLIC
OPINION QUARTERLY v.22 Fall 1958 pp.373-390.

DA 27.   Hazama, H. "Industrialization and
Groupism." in International Conference on Business
History (2nd: 1976: Fuji Education Center) SOCIAL ORDER
AND ENTREPRENEURSHIP: PROCEEDINGS OF THE SECOND FUJI
CONFERENCE. Tokyo: University of Tokyo Press, 1977.
pp.119-223.

DA 28.   Hills, Jill. "The Industrial Policy Of
Japan." PUBLIC POLICY v.3 Feb. 1983 pp.63-80.

DA 29.   Horvath, Dezso, and McMillan, Charles.
"Industrial Planning in Japan." CALIFORNIA MANAGEMENT
REVIEW v.23 Fall 1980 pp.11-21.

DA 30.   Hoshino, Yasuo. "The Performance of
Corporate Mergers in Japan." JOURNAL OF BUSINESS
FINANCE AND ACCOUNTING v.9 Summer 1982 pp.153-165.

DA 31.   Ikeda, Katsuhiko. "The Performance of
Merging Firms in Japanese Manufacturing Industry:
1964-75." JOURNAL OF INDUSTRIAL ECONOMICS v.31 Mar.
1982 pp.257-265.

DA 32.   Imai, Kenichi. "Japanese Industrial
Organization." JAPANESE ECONOMIC STUDIES v.6 no.3-4
1978 pp.3-67.

DA 33. "Japan's Economy: Enough Puff to Reflate?" CONOMIST v. 295 Apr. 27, 1985 pp. 80+.

DA 34. "Japan's Industrial Policy--Four Articles." OURNAL OF JAPANESE TRADE AND INDUSTRY July/Aug. 1983 p. 18-37.

DA 35. "Japan's New Bid to Outdo U.S." U.S. NEWS ND WORLD REPORT v. 89 Oct. 17, 1980 pp. 41-44.

DA 36. "Japan's Strategy for the '80s." BUSINESS EEK Dec. 14, 1981 pp. 39-114.

DA 37. Johnson, Chalmers. "The Institutional ormulation of Japanese Industrial Policies." ALIFORNIA MANAGEMENT REVIEW v. 27 no. 4 1985 pp. 59-69.

DA 38. Johnson, Chalmers. "The Internationalization' of the Japanese Economy." ALIFORNIA MANAGEMENT REVIEW v. 25 Spring 1983 pp. 5-26.

DA 39. Kabashima, Ikuo. "Supportive Participation ith Economic Growth: the Case of Japan." WORLD OLITICS v. 36 Apr. 1984 pp. 309-338.

DA 40. Kajinishi, Mitsuhaya. "Industrialization in apan." FIRST INTERNATIONAL CONFERENCE ON ECONOMIC ISTORY. Stockholm, 1960. pp. 251-259.

DA 41. Karsh, Bernard, and Cole, Robert E. Industrialization and the Convergence Hypothesis: Some spects of Contemporary Japan." JOURNAL OF SOCIAL SSUES v. 24 1968 pp. 45-64.

DA 42. Kato, Hiroshi. "Administrative Reform is apan's Only Option." ECONOMIC EYE v. 3 Mar. 1982 p. 8-12.

DA 43. Kazuo, Tomiyama. "General Aspects of ost-War Reconstruction and High Economic Growth." APAN QUARTERLY v. 28 Jan./Mar. 1981 pp. 65-72.

DA. Planning Strategies

DA 44. Kojima, Kiyoshi. "Economic Development and Import Dependence in Japan." ANNALS OF THE HITOTSUBASHI ACADEMY v.1 Oct. 1960 pp.29-51.

DA 45. Kosai, Yutaka. "Ongoing Change in the Japanese Economic System." ECONOMIC EYE v.5 Dec. 1984 pp.16-19.

DA 46. Levy, Marion J., Jr. "Contrasting Factors in the Modernization in China And Japan." ECONOMIC DEVELOPMENT AND CULTURAL CHANGE v.2 Oct. 1953 pp. 161-197.

DA 47. Liu, Yuan-zhang. "Japanese Experience in Industrial Development." REGIONAL DEVELOPMENT DIALOGUE Special Issue 1984 pp.1-39.

DA 48. Matsukawa, S. "Dualistic Economic Development: An Econometric Model of Japan, 1953-1968." EMPIRICAL ECONOMICS v.7 1982 no.3/4 pp.191-211.

DA 49. Moriguchi, Chikashi. "Japan's Recent Experiences of Qualitative Economic Planning." REVUE ECONOMIQUE v.31 Sep. 1980 pp.853-856.

DA 50. Murray, Alan. "Industrial Policy: an Unfair Trade Practice?" CONGRESSIONAL QUARTERLY WEEKLY REPORT v.41 Jan. 29, 1983 pp.211-214.

DA 51. Nishikawa, Jun. "Possibilities for Another Development; the Case for Japan." JAPAN QUARTERLY v.27 Apr./June 1980 pp.180-192.

DA 52. Noguchi, Yuichiro. "Trends in Thought Among Structural Reformists in Japanese Industry." JOURNAL OF SOCIAL AND POLITICAL IDEAS IN JAPAN v.5 Apr. 1967 pp.11-26.

DA 53. Nozawa, Massanori. "The Alternative Economic Strategy in Japan." KYOTO UNIVERSITY ECONOMIC REVIEW v.52 no. 1-2 Apr./Oct. 1982 pp.38-63.

DA 54. Ohmae, Kenichi. "The Long and Short of Japanese Planning." WALL STREET JOURNAL v. 203 Jan. 18, 1982 p. 22.

DA 55. Oshima, Harry T. "Reinterpreting Japan's Postwar Growth." ECONOMIC DEVELOPMENT AND CULTURAL CHANGE v. 31 Oct. 1982 pp. 1-43.

DA 56. Ovans, A. "Japan's Success Derives from Strategy, Not Culture." ELECTRONIC BUSINESS v. 12 Sep. 15, 1986 pp. 150-151.

DA 57. "A Power Shift in Japanese Industry." BUSINESS WEEK Oct. 1, 1984 p. 71.

DA 58. Pugel, Thomas A. "Japan's Industry Policy: Instruments, Trends, and Effects." JOURNAL OF COMPARATIVE ECONOMICS v. 8 Dec. 1984 pp. 420-435.

DA 59. Puri, Tino, and Bhide, Amar. "The Crucial Weakness of Japan Inc." WALL STREET JOURNAL v. 197 June 8, 1981 p. 20.

DA 60. Ranis, Gustav. "The Financing of Japanese Economic Development." ECONOMIC HISTORY REVIEW v. 11 Apr. 1959 pp. 440-454.

DA 61. Sakisaka, Masao. "Economic Planning in Japan." THE DEVELOPING ECONOMIES v. 1 July/Dec. 1963 pp. 68-83.

DA 62. Sakoh, Katsuro. "Japanese Economic Success: Industrial Policy for Free Market?" CATO JOURNAL v. 4 Fall 1984 pp. 521-548.

DA 63. Samuels, Richard J. "Looking Behind Japan, Inc." TECHNOLOGY REVIEW v. 83 July 1981 pp. 42-47.

DA 64. Sandeman, Hugh. "The Best at the Game: A Survey of Japanese Industry." ECONOMIST (London) v. 280 July 18, 1981 pp. 50+.

DA. Planning Strategies

DA 65. Sawada, Jim. "Government Industrial Policy for a Healthy World Economy." TECHNOLOGICAL FORCASTING AND SOCIAL CHANGE v.24 Oct. 1983 pp.93-105.

DA 66. Saxonhouse, Gary R. "Industrial Restructuring in Japan." JOURNAL OF JAPANESE STUDIES v.5 no.2 1979 pp.272-320.

DA 67. "Scale of Industrial Equipment Undergoing Swift Expansion in Japan." JAPAN ECONOMIC JOURNAL Oct. 18, 1966 p.10+.

DA 68. Schmiegelow, Michele. "Cutting Across Doctrines: Positive Adjustment in Japan." INTERNATIONAL ORGANIZATION v.39 Spring 1985 pp.261-296.

DA 69. Schmookler, Andrew B. "An Overview of Japan's Economic Success: Its Sources and Its Implications for the U.S." JOURNAL OF EAST ASIAN AFFAIRS v.3 Fall/Winter 1983 pp.356-377.

DA 70. Sekiguchi, Sueo, and Horiuchi, Toshihiro. "Myth and Reality of Japan's Industrial Policies." THE WORLD ECONOMY v.8 Dec. 1985 pp.373-391.

DA 71. Sen, A. "Lessons for Development from the Japanese Experience." JOURNAL OF ECONOMIC ISSUES v.17 June 1983 pp.415-22.

DA 72. Strier, F. D. "On Economic Planning, Japan and West Germany Have a Better Idea." CENTER MAGAZINE v.17 Jan./Feb. 1984 pp.35-40.

DA 73. Struthers, J. E. "Why Can't We Do What Japan Does?" CANADIAN BUSINESS REVIEW v.8 Summer 1981 pp.24-26.

DA 74. Sumiyo, Mikio. "Capital Formation and Industrialization in Japan." SECOND INTERNATIONAL CONFERENCE OF ECONOMIC HISTORY. Paris: Mouton, 1962. pp.673-681.

DA 75.   Tharp, M. "Japan's Locomotive Force." FAR EASTERN ECONOMIC REVIEW v. 122 Nov. 3, 1983 pp. 62-63.

DA 76.   Thomas, Barbara S. "Capital Formation in Japan and the United States: A Comparative Assessment." COLUMBIA JOURNAL OF TRANSNATIONAL LAW v. 21 no. 2 1983 pp. 227-242.

DA 77.   Tsuru, Shigeto. "The Take-off in Japan." in Rostow, W. W., ed.   THE ECONOMICS OF TAKE-OFF INTO SUSTAINED GROWTH. London: Macmillan, 1963.

DA 78.   Tsurumi, Yoshi. "Japan's Challenge to the U.S.: Industrial Policies and Corporate Strategies." COLUMBIA JOURNAL OF WORLD BUSINESS v. 17 Summer 1982 pp. 87-95.

DA 79.   Uriu, Robert M. "The Declining Industries of Japan: Adjustment and Reallocation." JOURNAL OF INTERNATIONAL AFFAIRS v. 38 Summer 1984 pp. 99-111.

DA 80.   Watanabe, Tsunehiko. "Economic Aspects of Dualism in the Industrial Development of Japan." ECONOMIC DEVELOPMENT AND CULTURAL CHANGE v. 12 Apr. 1965 pp. 293-312.

DA 81.   "Who's Best for the West." ECONOMIST v. 285 Oct. 23/29, 1982 pp. 13-14.

DA 82.   Woronoff, Jon. "Industrial Japan." ASIAN BUSINESS v. 21 Apr. 1985 pp. 70+.

DA 83.   Yokoyama, Taizo. "The Japanese Industrial Policy." RIVISTA INTERNAZIONALE DI SCIENZE ECONOMICHE E COMMERCIALI (Milan) v. 31 Sep. 1984 pp. 812-818.

DA 84.   Yoshida, M. "New Momentum Generated for Financial Liberation." BUSINESS JAPAN v. 30 Jan. 1985 pp. 37+.

DA 85.   Young, L. H. "A Debate that Holds a Key to Japan's Future." BUSINESS WEEK Nov. 15, 1982 pp. 16+.

DA. Planning Strategies

DA 86.   Young, Michael K.   "Economic Security; Japan
Reviews Its Options." JOURNAL OF JAPANESE TRADE AND
INDUSTRY v. 2 no. 1 1983 pp. 31-33.

DB. Structural Aspects; The Corporate Environment

Monographic Works

DB 1.   Broadbridge, Seymour A. INDUSTRIAL DUALISM
IN JAPAN. London: F. Cass, 1966. 105pp.

DB 2.   Bronte, Stephen. JAPANESE FINANCE. London:
Euromoney Pubs., 1982. 259p.

DB 3.   Caves, Richard E. and Uekusa, Masu.
INDUSTRIAL ORGANIZATION IN JAPAN. Washington: Brookings
Institution, 1976. 169pp.

DB 4.   Czinkota, Michael R., and Woronoff, Jon.
JAPAN'S MARKET: THE DISTRIBUTION SYSTEM. New York:
Praeger, 1986. 145pp.

DB 5.   Dodwell Marketing Consultants. INDUSTRIAL
GROUPINGS IN JAPAN. Rev. ed.   Tokyo, 1984/85. 527pp.

DB 6.   Fuji Bank, Ltd. BANKING IN MODERN JAPAN. 2nd
ed.   Tokyo: Research Division, Fuji Bank, Ltd., 1967.
299pp.

DB 7.   Glazer, Herbert. JAPANESE TRADING COMPANIES.
Washington, D.C.: Center for Asian Studies, American
University, 1981. 21pp.

DB 8.   Hadley, Eleanor M. ANTITRUST IN JAPAN.
Princeton, N.J.: Princeton University Press, 1970.
528pp.

DB 9.   INNOVATIONS IN JAPAN'S COMMUNITY-BASED
INDUSTRIES: A CASE STUDY. New York: Unipub, 1981. 51pp.

DB 10.   Iyori, Hiroshi. ANTIMONOPOLY LEGISLATION IN
JAPAN. New York: Federal Legal Publications, 1969.
265pp.

DB 11.   JAPAN'S COMMUNITY-BASED INDUSTRIES: A CASE
STUDY OF SMALL INDUSTRY. New York: Unipub, 1980. 300pp.

DB 12.   Johnson, Chalmers. JAPAN'S PUBLIC POLICY
COMPANIES. Washington, D.C.: American Enterprise
Institute for Public Policy, 1978.

DB 13.   Kojima, Kiyoshi. JAPAN'S GENERAL TRADING
COMPANIES. Washington, D. C.: OECD Publications and
Development Center, 1984. 119pp.

DB 14.   Leggatt, Timothy W. THE EVOLUTION OF
INDUSTRIAL SYSTEMS: THE FORKING PATHS. London; Dover,
N.H.: Croom Helm, 1985. 258pp.

DB 15.   McMillan, Charles J. THE JAPANESE
INDUSTRIAL SYSTEM. Berlin; New York: W. de Gruyter,
1984. 356pp.

DB 16.   Sasaki, Naoto. MANAGEMENT AND INDUSTRIAL
STRUCTURE IN JAPAN. London: Pergamon Press, 1981.
141pp.

DB 17.   Woronoff, Jon. JAPAN'S COMMERCIAL EMPIRE.
Armonk, N.Y.: M. E. Sharpe, 1984. 415pp.

DB 18.   Yamanaka, Tokutaro, ed.   SMALL BUSINESS IN
JAPAN'S ECONOMIC PROGRESS. Tokyo: Asahi Evening News,
1971. 140pp.

DB 19.   Yamanaka, Tokutaro, and Kobayashi, Yoshio.
THE HISTORY AND STRUCTURE OF JAPAN'S SMALL AND MEDIUM
INDUSTRIES. Tokyo: Science Council of Japan, 1957.
89pp.

DB. Corporate Environment

DB 20. Yoshino, Michael Y. THE JAPANESE MARKETING SYSTEM: ADAPTATIONS AND INNOVATIONS. Cambridge, Mass.: M. I. T. Press, 1971. 319pp.

DB 21. Young, Alexander. THE SOGO SHOSHA: JAPAN'S MULTINATIONAL TRADING COMPANIES. Boulder, Colo.: Westview Press, 1979.

Articles

DB 22. Amaya, Naohiro. "Reflections and Outlook on Japan's Industrial Structure." ASIA PACIFIC COMMUNITY Fall 1978 pp. 7-23.

DB 23. Anthony, David F. "The Japanese General Trading Company: Model for the United States." ASIAN FORUM v. 4 June/Sep. 1972 pp. 61-66.

DB 24. Boreham, G. F. "Financial System: One Reason for Japan's Success." CANADIAN BANKER AND ICB REVIEW v. 88 Dec. 1981 pp. 12-17.

DB 25. Emmott, Bill. "Limbering Up: A Survey of Japanese Finance and Banking." ECONOMIST (London) v. 293 Dec. 8, 1984 pp. 28 page section following p.   56.

DB 26. Froomkin, J. N. "Management and Organization in Japanese Industry." ACADEMY OF MANAGEMENT JOURNAL v. 7 no. 1 1964 pp. 71-76.

DB 27. Hadley, Eleanor M. "Trust Busting in Japan." HARVARD BUSINESS REVIEW v. 26 July 1948 pp. 425-440.

DB 28. Ishida, Hideto. "Anticompetitive Practices in the Distribution of Goods and Services in Japan: The Problem of Distribution Keiretsu." JOURNAL OF JAPANESE STUDIES v. 9 Summer 1983 pp. 319-334.

DB 29. Kerns, H. "Japan's Slow-Go-Shosha." FAR EAST ECONOMIC REVIEW v.118 Nov. 12-18, 1982 pp.88+.

DB 30. Kerns, H. "Tokyo's Monopoly Game." FAR EAST ECONOMIC REVIEW v.122 Nov. 24, 1983 pp.72+.

DB 31. Kogiku, K. C. "Japan's Industrial Structure Policy." RIVISTA INTERNAZIONALE DI SCIENZE ECONOMICHE E COMMERCIALI v.25 Aug./Sep. 1978 pp.677-711.

DB 32. Kotabe, Masaaki. "Changing Roles of the Sogo Shoshas, the Manufacturing Firms, and the MITI in the Context of the Japanese Trade or Die Mentality." COLUMBIA JOURNAL OF WORLD BUSINESS v.19 Fall 1984 pp.33-42.

DB 33. Langdon, Frank C. "Big Business Lobbying in Japan: The Case of the Central Bank Reform." AMERICAN POLITICAL SCIENCE REVIEW v.55 Sep. 1961 pp.527-538.

DB 34. McAbee, Michael. "'Pebbles' Support Japan's Monolith." INDUSTRY WEEK v.197 May 1. 1978 pp.40-44.

DB 35. Monti, Mario. "Financial Structure and Capital Accumulation: A Comparative Note on Japan and Italy." RIVISTA INTERNAZIONALE DI SCIENZE ECONOMICHE E COMMERCIALE v.27 1980 pp.934-941.

DB 36. "New Look, Old Dominance." FAR EAST ECONOMIC REVIEW v.112 May 8/14, 1981.

DB 37. Ouchi, William G. "Organizational Paradigms: a Commentary on Japanese Management and Theory Z Organizations." ORGANIZATIONAL DYNAMICS v.9 Spring 1981 pp.36-43.

DB 38. Ozawa, Terutomo. "International Investment of Industrial Structure; New Theoretical Implications from the Japanese Experience." OXFORD ECONOMIC PAPERS Mar. 1979 pp.72-92.

DB. Corporate Environment

DB 39.   Ozawa, Terutomo. "Japan's Industrial
Groups." MSU BUSINESS TOPICS v.28 Autumn 1980
pp.33-41.

DB 40.   Rehder, R. R. "Japan's Synergistic Society:
How It Works and Its Implications for the United
States." MANAGEMENT REVIEW v.70 Oct. 1981 pp.64-66.

DB 41.   Rotwein, Eugene. "Economic Concentration
and Monopoly in Japan." JOURNAL OF POLITICAL ECONOMY
v.72 June 1964 pp.262-277.

DB 42.   Sakakibara, Eisuke, and Feldman, Robert A.
"The Japanese Financial System in Comparative
Perspective." JOURNAL OF COMPARATIVE ECONOMICS v.7 Mar.
1983 pp.1-24.

DB 43.   "The Samurai Bond Market." EUROMONEY Mar.
1979 pp.18-63.

DB 44.   "Sogo Shoshas: Total Business Development
Not Just Passive Investment." FAR EAST ECONOMIC REVIEW
v.118 Dec. 3-9, 1982 pp.74-75+.

DB 45.   Tsuji, Shinji. "Organizational and Legal
Development of Japan's Financial System in the Last
Hundred Years." FUJI BANK BULLETIN v.31 Nov. 1980
pp.220-229.

DB 46.   Tsurumi, Yoshi. "Managing Consumer and
Industrial Marketing Systems in Japan." SLOAN
MANAGEMENT REVIEW v.24 Fall 1982 pp.41-50.

DB 47.   Watanabe, S. "Entrepreneurship in Small
Enterprises in Japanese Manufacturing." INTERNATIONAL
LABOR REVIEW v.102 no.6 1970 pp.531-576.

DB 48.   Yamamura, Kozo. "Wage Structure and
Economic Growth in Postwar Japan." INDUSTRIAL AND
LABOR RELATIONS REVIEW v.19 Oct. 1965 pp.58-69.

DC. Role of Government; Administrative Guidance;
     Linkages with Business and Industry

Monographic Works

DC 1.   Bryant, William E. JAPANESE PRIVATE ECONOMIC
DIPLOMACY: AN ANALYSIS OF BUSINESS-GOVERNMENT LINKAGES.
New York: Praeger, 1975. 138pp.

DC 2.   Faure, Guy. LE ROLE DU MITI DANS LES
PROCESSUS DE PRISE DE DECISION INDUSTRIELLE AU JAPON.
Tokyo: Maison Fanco-Japonaise, 1984. 396pp.

DC 3.   JAPANESE INDUSTRIAL COLLUSION AND TRADE: A
STUDY. PREPARED FOR THE USE OF THE SUBCOMMITTEE ON
ECONOMIC GOALS AND INTERGOVERNMENTAL POLICY OF THE
JOINT ECONOMIC COMMITTEE, CONGRESS OF THE U.S. Senate
Print 99-123. Washington, D.C.: Government Printing
Office, 1986. 14pp.

DC 4.   Johnson, Chalmers. MITI AND THE JAPANESE
MIRACLE: THE GROWTH OF INDUSTRIAL POLICY, 1925-1975.
Stanford, Calif.: Stanford University Press, 1982.
393pp.

DC 5.   Kaplan, Eugene J. JAPAN: THE
GOVERNMENT--BUSINESS RELATIONSHIP: A GUIDE FOR THE
AMERICAN BUSINESSMAN. Washington, D.C.: U.S. Department
of Commerce, Bureau of International Commerce, 1972.

DC 6.   Lockwood, William W., ed.   THE STATE AND
ECONOMIC ENTERPRISE IN JAPAN: ESSAYS IN THE POLITICAL
ECONOMY OF GROWTH. Princeton, N.J.: Princeton
University Press, 1965. 753pp.

DC 7.   Murakami, Hyoe and Hirschmeier, Johannes.
POLITICS AND ECONOMICS IN CONTEMPORARY JAPAN. Tokyo;
New York: Kodansha, 1983, c1979.   232pp.

DC. Role of Government

DC 8.   Tsurumi, Yoshi. MULTINATIONAL MANAGEMENT:
BUSINESS STRATEGY AND GOVERNMENT POLICY. 2nd ed.
Cambridge, Mass.: Ballinger, 1977. 490pp.

DC 9.   Yanaga, Chitoshi. BIG BUSINESS IN JAPANESE
POLITICS. New Haven, Yale University Press, 1968.

Articles

DC 10.   Calder, Kent E. "Japan's Minimalist
Government." WALL STREET JOURNAL v.197 Feb. 13, 1981
p.16.

DC 11.   Chinn, Dennis L. "Staple Food Control and
Industrial Development in Post War Japan 1950-57; The
Role of the Black Market." JOURNAL OF DEVELOPMENT
ECONOMICS v.4 June 1977 pp.179-190.

DC 12.   Doe, P. "MITI's Specialty: Cheap and
Abundant Capital." ELECTRONIC BUSINESS v.10 Aug 1, 1984
pp.70+.

DC 13.   Doe, P. "Playing It Cool with Japan Inc.'s
Red-Hot Education Mama." ELECTRONIC BUSINESS v.9 Aug.
1983 pp.70+.

DC 14.   Dore, Ronald Phillips. "The Modernizer as a
Special Case: Japanese Factory Legislation, 1882-1911.
COMPARATIVE STUDIES IN SOCIETY AND HISTORY v.5 no.11
pp.433-450.

DC 15.   Etzioni, Amitai. "MITIzation of America?"
PUBLIC INTEREST no.72 Summer 1983 pp.44-51.

DC 16.   Farnsworth, L. W. "Japan in 1981: Meeting
the Challenges." ASIAN SURVEY v.22 Jan. 1982 pp.56-68.

DC 17.   Henderson, D. R. "The Myth of MITI."
FORTUNE v. 108 Aug. 8, 1983 pp. 113-114+.

DC 18.   "How MITI Minds Japan's Business."
SCHOLASTIC UPDATE v. 116 Nov. 11, 1983 pp. 23-24.

DC 19.   "Hudson Institute Analyzes Japan's
Policies." BUSINESS AMERICA v. 5 Nov. 1, 1982 p. 36.

DC 20.   Ishi, Hiromitsu. "Reforming Japan's
Government-backed Financing." ECONOMIC EYE v. 5 Mar.
1984 pp. 18-22.   (Translated from EKONOMISUTO, Oct.
1983.)

DC 21.   "Japan's Gentle Persuaders." ECONOMIST
v. 278 Jan. 17, 1981 pp. 70-71.

DC 22.   Koyima, R., and Yamamoto, K. "Japan: the
Officer In Charge of Economic Affairs." HISTORY OF
POLITICAL ECONOMY v. 13 Fall 1981 pp. 600-628.

DC 23.   Noguchi, Yukio. "The Failure of Government
to Perform Its Proper Task--A Case Study of Japan."
ORDO v. 34 1983 pp. 59-70.

DC 24.   Onoe, Hisao. "Indicative Type Plan as an
Investment of Governmental Intervention in Japan."
REVISTA INTERNAZIONALE DI SCIENZE ECONOMICHE E
COMMERCIALI v. 33 Jan 1986 pp. 23-40.

DC 25.   Oudiz, G., and Sachs, J. "Macroeconomic
Policy Coordination Among the Industrial Economies."
BROOKINGS PAPERS ON ECONOMIC ACTIVITY no. 1 1984
pp. 1-75.

DC 26.   Ozawa, Terutomo. "Government Control Over
Technology Acquisition and Firms' Entry into New
Sectors: The Experience of Japan's Synthetic Fiber
Industry." CAMBRIDGE JOURNAL OF ECONOMICS v. 4 June 1980
pp. 133-146.

DC. Role of Government

DC 27.   Pearlstine, N. "Hanging Together: Japan's
Establishment Rushes, More or Less, to Aid Mazda's
Maker." WALL STREET JOURNAL v. 189 Mar. 24, 1975 pp. 1+.

DC 28.   Rapp, William V. "Unbundling Japan, Inc."
CREATIVE COMPUTING v. 10 Aug. 1984 pp. 43-48.

DC 29.   Reich, Robert B. "High-Tech Industrial
Policy: Comparing the United States with Other Advanced
Nations." JOURNAL OF JAPANESE TRADE AND INDUSTRY
July/Aug. 1983 pp. 31-33.

DC 30.   Rubenstein, A. H. et al.   "Management
Perceptions of Government Incentives to Technological
Innovation in England, France, West Germany and Japan."
RESEARCH POLICY v. 6 no. 4 1977 PP. 324-357.

DC 31.   Sayle, M. "Bureaucracy and the Barriers
That Do Not Exist." FAR EASTERN ECONOMIC REVIEW v. 116 Ap
16/22, 1982 pp. 64-65.

DC 32.   "Says High Productivity, Not Government
Policy is Key to Japan's Success." ELECTRONIC NEWS Sep.
15, 1980 p. x.

DC 33.   Shinohara, Miyohei. "MITI's Industrial
Policy and Japanese Industrial Organization--A
Retrospective Evaluation." THE DEVELOPING ECONOMIES
v. 14 no. 4 1976 pp. 366-380.

DC 34.   Smith, A. "Is the Japanese Empire
Returning?" ESQUIRE v. 103 Mar. 1985 pp. 92-93.

DC 35.   Soukup, James R. "Business Political
Participation in Japan: Continuity and Change." in
Sakai, Robert K., ed.   STUDIES ON ASIA. Lincoln:
University of Nebraska Press, 1965 v. 6 pp. 163-178.

DC 36.   Trezise, Philip H. "Japanese Miracles
Revisited." SOCIETY v. 22 Nov. /Dec 1984.

DC 37. "Trustbusting in Japan: Cartels and Government--Business Cooperation." HARVARD LAW REVIEW v. 94 Mar. 1981 pp. 1064-1084."

DC 38. Tsunoyama, S. "Government and Business: An Introductory Essay." in International Conference on Business History (5th; 1978; Fuji Education Center). GOVERNMENT AND BUSINESS: PROCEEDINGS OF THE FIFTH FUJI CONFERENCE. Tokyo: University of Tokyo Press, 1980. pp. 1-18.

DC 39. Tsuruta, Toshimasa. "The Myth of Japan, Inc. : in Japan, Government Controls All Industrial Development, or Does it? Some of Her Most Prosperous Industries Owe their Very Success to the Government's Failure in Achieving Total Control." TECHNOLOGY REVIEW v. 86 July 1983 pp. 42-48.

DC 40. Udagawa, M., and S. Nakamura. "Japanese Business and Government in the Inter-War Period: Heavy Industrialization and the Industrial Rationalization Movement." in International Conference on Business History (5th; 1978; Fuji Conference Center). GOVERNMENT AND BUSINESS: PROCEEDINGS OF THE FIFTH FUJI CONFERENCE. Tokyo: University of Tokyo Press, 1980. pp. 83-100.

DC 41. Valery, N. "Planning for Obsolescence." ECONOMIST v. 288 Jul. 9-15, 1983 pp. survey 17-18.

DC 42. Vogel, Ezra F. "Guided Free Enterprise in Japan." HARVARD BUSINESS REVIEW v. 56 May/June 1978 pp. 161-170.

DC 43. Yamauchi, Ichizo. "Long-Range Strategic Planning in Japanese R and D." FUTURES v. 15 Oct. 1983 pp. 328-341.

DD. Targeting Key Industries

Monographic Works

DD 1.   Gresser, Julian. HIGH TECHNOLOGY AND
JAPANESE INDUSTRIAL POLICY: A STRATEGY FOR U.S.
POLICYMAKERS. Subcommittee on Ways and Means, U. S.
House of Representatives. Washington, D.C.: U. S.
Government Printing Office, 1980. 73pp.

DD 2.   Gresser, Julian. PARTNERS IN PROSPERITY:
STRATEGIC INDUSTRIES IN THE UNITED STATES AND JAPAN.
New York: McGraw-Hill, 1984. 432pp.

DD 3.   Okimoto, Daniel I. PIONEER AND PURSUER: THE
ROLE OF THE STATE IN THE EVOLUTION OF THE JAPANESE AND
AMERICAN SEMICONDUCTOR INDUSTRIES. Stanford, Calif.:
Stanford University Press, 1983. 93pp.

DD 4.   Organization for Economic Cooperation and
Development. THE INDUSTRIAL POLICY OF JAPAN. Paris,
OECD, 1972. 195pp.

DD 5.   Patrick, Hugh Talbot, and Meissner, Larry,
eds.   JAPAN'S HIGH TECHNOLOGY INDUSTRIES AND INDUSTRIAL
POLICY. Seattle: University of Washington Press, 1986.
277pp.

Articles

DD 6.   Doe, P. "MITI's 1983 Budget: What's 27
Billion Yen?" ELECTRONIC BUSINESS v.9 Oct. 1983
pp.79-80.

DD 7.   Gold, Bela. "Factors Stimulating Technological Progress in Japanese Industries: The Case of Computerization in Steel." QUARTERLY REVIEW OF ECONOMICS AND BUSINESS v.4 Winter 1978 pp.47-57.

DD 8.   "ITA Report Analyzes Japan's Approach to Development of Two Key Industries." BUSINESS AMERICA v.6 Mar. 7, 1983 p.5.

DD 9.   "Japan in the Third Industrial Revolution." SUMITOMO QUARTERLY Winter 1984 pp.4-9. (re: Interview with Toshio Sanuki)

DD 10.   Kawatani, Yukimaro. "Japan in the Computer Age." INDUSTRIAL MANAGEMENT & DATA SYSTEMS Jan./Feb. 1982 pp.24-28.

DD 11.   "MITI Plans Fixing Specific Goals for Various Industries." JAPAN ECONOMIC JOURNAL Oct. 25, 1966 p.1.

DD 12.   "MITI Plans to Bolster Technology." JAPAN ECONOMIC JOURNAL June 20, 1967 p.1.

DD 13.   Ouchi, William G. "Political and Economic Teamwork: The Development of the Microelectronics Industry of Japan." CALIFORNIA MANAGEMENT REVIEW v.26 Summer 1984 pp.8-34.

DD 14.   Saxonhouse, Gary R. "What is All This About 'Industrial Targeting' in Japan?" WORLD ECONOMY v.6 Sep. 1983 pp.253-273.

DD 15.   Schlossstein, Steven. "Winning Isn't Everything...Or is It? CREATIVE COMPUTING v.10 Aug. 1984 pp.16-30.

DD 16.   Sease, Douglas R., and Lehner, Urban C. "Steel Success: Japanese Steelmakers Thrive with the Aid of Government Body." WALL STREET JOURNAL v.197 Apr. 10, 1981 pp.1+.

DD. Targeting Key Industries

DD 17.   Shuichi, Miyoshi. "Steel: A Prime Pacemaker for Economic Growth." JAPAN QUARTERLY v.28 Apr./June 1981 pp.245-255.

DD 18.   "Technopolis Envisages Ideal Union of Technology and Region Development." BUSINESS JAPAN v.29 Aug. 1984 pp.17-18+.

DD 19.   Tran, Van Tho. "Industrial Policy and the Textile Industry: the Japanese Experience." JOURNAL OF CONTEMPORARY BUSINESS v.11 no.1 1982 pp.113-128.

DD 20.   "A U.S. Turn to Native Talent in Japan." BUSINESS WEEK Dec. 8, 1980 pp.56+.

DD 21.   Yonezawa, Y., and Kon-ya, F. "The Japanese Market and the Economic Environment." JOURNAL OF PORTFOLIO MANAGEMENT v.9 Fall 1982 pp.36-45.

DE. Energy Policy

Monographic Works

DE 1.   Blaker, Michael. OIL AND THE ATOM: ISSUES IN U.S.--JAPAN ENERGY RELATIONS. New York: Columbia University East Asian Institute, 1981. 100pp.

DE 2.   Goodman, Herbert I. JAPAN AND THE WORLD ENERGY PROBLEM. Stanford, Calif.: Northeast Asia--United States Forum on International Policy, Stanford University, 1980. 66pp.

DE 3.   Imai, Ryukichi, and Rowen, Henry S. NUCLEAR ENERGY AND NUCLEAR PROLIFERATIONS, JAPANESE AND AMERICAN VIEWS. Boulder, Colo.: Westview Press, 1980. 194pp.

DE 4.   Samuels, Richard J. THE BUSINESS OF THE
JAPANESE STATE. Cornell, N.Y.: Cornell University
Press, 1987. 376pp.

Articles

DE 5.   Eguchi, Yujiro. "Japanese Energy Policy."
INTERNATIONAL AFFAIRS v.56 Spring 1980 pp.263-279.

DE 6.   Ginsburg, Norton S. "Natural Resources and
Economic Development: Case Studies: Japan." ANNALS OF
THE ASSOCIATION OF AMERICAN GEOGRAPHERS v.47 Sep. 1957
pp.197-212.

DE 7.   Goto, Kunio. "Energy and Scenario and
Japan's Option." RIVISTA INTERNAZIONALE DI SCIENZE
ECONOMICHE E COMMERCIALI v.27 July-Aug. 1980
pp.690-708.

DE 8.   Ishimatsu, Tohru. "Energy Imputs and
Economic Growth in Japan." KOBE UNIVERSITY ECONOMIC
REVIEW v.10 1964 pp.29-62.

DE 9.   Mack, T. "A Historic Moment." FORBES v.138
Nov. 3, 1986 pp.54+.

DE 10.   MacKean, Margaret A. "Japan's Energy
Policies." CURRENT HISTORY v.82 Nov. 1983 pp.385-389+.

DE 11.   Mahler, Walter R. "Japan's Adjustment to
the Increased Cost of Energy." FINANCE AND DEVELOPMENT
v.18 Dec. 1981 pp.26-29.

DE 12.   Nemetz, P. W., et al. "Japan's Energy
Strategy at the Crossroads." PACIFIC AFFAIRS v.57
Winter 1985 pp.553-576.

DE. Energy Policy

DE 13.   Sakisaka, Masao. "Japan's Energy
Supply/Demand Structure and its Trade Relationship with
the United States and the Middle East." JOURNAL OF
ENERGY AND DEVELOPMENT v.10 Autumn 1984 pp.1-11.

DE 14.   Samuels, Richard J. "Public Energy
Corporations in Industrial Democracies; Japan in
Comparative Perspective." JOURNAL OF COMMONWEALTH AND
COMPARATIVE POLITICS v.22 Mar. 1984 pp.53-101.

DE 15.   Shigehara, K. "Absorption of the Two Oil
Shocks: The Japanese Case." EUROPEAN ECONOMIC REVIEW
v.18 May/June 1982 pp.249-261.

DF. Environmental Policy

Monographic Works

DF 1.   Gresser, Julian; Fujikura, Koichiro; and
Morishima, Akio. ENVIRONMENTAL LAW IN JAPAN. Cambridge,
Mass.: M.I.T. Press, 1981.

Articles

DF 2.   Meyerson, Adam. "Japan: Environmentalism
with Growth." WALL STREET JOURNAL v.196 Sep. 5, 1980
P.18.

DG. Fiscal Policy

Monographic Works

DG 1.   Bigman, David, and Taya, Teizo, eds.
EXCHANGE RATES AND TRADE INSTABILITY; CAUSES,
CONSEQUENCES AND REMEDIES. Cambridge, Mass.: Harper &
Row, 1983. 340pp.

DG 2.   Campbell, John Creighton. CONTEMPORARY
JAPANESE BUDGET POLITICS. Berkeley, Calif.: University
of California Press, 1977. 308pp.

DG 3.   Emi, Koichi. GOVERNMENT FISCAL ACTIVITY AND
ECONOMIC GROWTH IN JAPAN: 1868-1960. Tokyo: Kinokuniya
Book Store, 1963. 186pp.

DG 4.   Michaely, Michael. BALANCE OF PAYMENTS
ADJUSTMENT POLICIES, JAPAN, GERMANY, AND THE
NETHERLANDS. New York: Columbia University Press, 1968.
112pp.

Articles

DG 5.   Akhtar, M. A., and Putnam, Bluford H.
"Recent Experience with Monetary Growth and Inflation
in Germany, Japan, and the United States." JOURNAL OF
POST KEYNESIAN ECONOMICS v.2 no.4 Summer 1980
pp.585-92.

DG 6.   Bhandari, Dharmendra. "Taxing for
Development; Corporate Taxation in Japan." BULLETIN FOR
INTERNATIONAL FISCAL DOCUMENTATION v.36 Mar. 1982
pp.99-110.

DG. Fiscal Policy

DG 7.   Cullison, A. E. "Japanese Growth Tied to
Public Works Funds." JOURNAL OF COMMERCE AND COMMERCIAL
Jan. 2, 1986 p. 3A.

DG 8.   "Deregulation of Finance and
Internationalization of the Yen." FUJI BANK BULLETIN
v. 35 Sep./Oct. 1984 pp. 5-12.

DG 9.   Evans, Robert, Jr. "Lessons from Japan's
Incomes Policy." CHALLENGE v. 27 Jan./Feb 1985
pp. 33-39.

DG 10.   Hamilton, Adrian D. "Financial Decontrol in
Japan: a Case of When not Whether." BANKER v. 134 Aug.
1984 pp. 29-33.

DG 11.   Ichimura, Shinichi. "Economic Growth,
Savings and Housing Finance in Japan." JOURNAL OF
ECONOMIC STUDIES v. 8 no. 3 1981 pp. 41-64.

DG 12.   Ikeda, Kotaro. "The Establishment of the
Income Tax in Japan: A Historical and Sociological
Study." PUBLIC FINANCE v. 12 no. 2 1957 pp. 145-170.

DG 13.   Ikegami, Jun. "Fiscal Policy for Promoting
Growth in Japanese Economy in the Post-War Period."
KYOTO UNIVERSITY ECONOMIC REVIEW v. 52 Apr./Oct. 1982
pp. 30-37.

DG 14.   Ikemoto, K. "The Balance of Trade and
Economic Fluctuations." KOBE UNIVERSITY ECONOMIC REVIEW
v. 10 1964 pp. 63-68.

DG 15.   "Is Japan Holding the Yen Down?" BUSINESS
WEEK Mar. 8, 1982 pp. 89-90.

DG 16.   Ishi, Hiromitsu. "Effects of Taxation on
the Distribution of Income and Wealth in Japan."
HITOTSUBASHI JOURNAL OF ECONOMICS v. 21 June 1980
pp. 27-47.

DG 17. Ishi, Hiromitsu. "An Overview of Postwar Tax Policies in Japan." HITOSUBASHI JOURNAL OF ECONOMICS v. 23 Feb. 1983 pp. 21-39.

DG 18. Itagaki, Yoichi. "A Review of the Concept of the Dual Economy." THE DEVELOPING ECONOMIES v. 6 1968 pp. 143-157.

DG 19. Kashiwagi, Yusuke. "The Yen's Future as a World Currency." EUROMONEY Sep. 1982 pp. 169-170+.

DG 20. Koizumi, A. "Foreign Exchange Reserves as a Buffer in Japan's Counter-Cyclical Policy." ANNALS OF THE HITOTSUBASHI ACADEMY v. 9 1959 pp. 255-266.

DG 21. Meade, J. "Japan and the General Agreement on Tariffs and Trade." THREE BANKS REVIEW (Edinburgh) v. 34 1957 pp. 3-32.

DG 22. Miyamoto, Kunio. "Japan's Massive Current Account Surplus." ECONOMIC EYE v. 5 Dec. 1984 pp. 4-7.

DG 23. Moore, Geoffrey H. "Will the 'Real' Trade Balance Please Stand Up?" JOURNAL OF INTERNATIONAL BUSINESS STUDIES v. 14 Spring/Summer 1983 pp. 155-159.

DG 24. Nakamura, Takafusa. "Domestic Policy, Exchange Rate and Balance of Payments in Japan." INTERNAZIONALE DI SCIENZE ECONOMICHE E COMMERCIALI v. 27 Oct. /Nov. 1980 pp. 968-967.

DG 25. Narvekar, P. R. "The 1954-1955 Improvement in Japan's Balanace of Payments." INTERNATIONAL MONETARY FUND STAFF PAPERS v. 6 1957 pp. 143-169.

DG 26. Pigott, Charles. "Wringing Out Inflation: Japan's Experience." FEDERAL RESERVE BOARD OF SAN FRANCISCO ECONOMIC REVIEW Summer 1980 pp. 24-42.

DG 27. Rosovsky, Henry. "Japanese Capital Formation, the Role of the Public Sector." JOURNAL OF ECONOMIC HISTORY v. 19 Sep. 1959 pp. 350-375.

DG. Fiscal Policy

DG 28. Rowley, A. "Tokyo's Tidal Wave Builds." FAR
EASTERN ECONOMIC REVIEW v.119 Fe. 3, 1983 pp.42-45.

DG 29. Shinohara, Miyohei. "The Structure of
Saving and the Consumption Function in Postwar Japan."
JOURNAL OF POLITICAL ECONOMY v.67 Dec. 1959
pp.589-603.

DG 30. Soukup, James R. "Comparative Studies in
Political Finance: Japan." JOURNAL OF POLITICS v.25
Nov. 1963 pp.737-756.

DG 31. Tokoyama, Tsunesaburo. "Economic Recovery
and Public Finance in Post-War Japan." PUBLIC FINANCE
v.8 no.3 1953 pp.282-316.

DG 32. Ueda, Kazuo. "Trade Balance Adjustment with
Imported Intermediate Goods: the Japanese Case." REVIEW
OF ECONOMICS AND STATISTICS v.65 Nov. 1983 pp.618-625.

DG 33. Vasoff, J. D. "Fighting Inflation Japanese
Style." CA MAGAZINE v.115 Jul. 1982 pp.29-30.

DG 34. Yamaguchi, M. "Prudent Monetary and
Budgetary Policies Sustain Economic Expansion."
BUSINESS JAPAN v.30 Jan. 1985 p.33.

DH. Monetary Policy, Banking, Financial Operations

Monographic Works

DH 1. Arai, Masao. DEVELOPMENT OF LOCAL BANKING IN
JAPAN: PERIOD OF DEVELOPMENT OF INDUSTRIAL CAPITALISM.
Tokyo: Science Council of Japan, 1958. 45pp.

DH 2. Emery, Robert F. THE JAPANESE MONEY MARKET:
Lexington, Mass.: Lexington Books, 1984. 143pp.

DH 3.   Frankel, Jeffrey A. THE YEN/DOLLAR
AGREEMENT, LIBERALIZING JAPANESE CAPITAL MARKETS.
Cambridge, Mass: MIT Press, 1984. 76pp.

DH 4.   Furuya, Seikow Y. JAPAN'S FOREIGN EXCHANGE
AND HER BALANCE OF INTERNATIONAL PAYMENTS, WITH SPECIAL
REFERENCE TO RECENT THEORIES OF FOREIGN EXCHANGE.
Columbia University Studies in the Social Sciences, No.
299. New York: AMS Press, 1968, c1928.   208pp.

DH 5.   Hayden, Eric W. INTERNATIONALIZING JAPAN'S
FINANCIAL SYSTEM. Stanford, Calif.: Stanford
University, 1980. 29pp.

DH 6.   Horne, James. JAPAN'S FINANCIAL MARKETS:
CONFLICT AND CONSENSUS IN POLICYMAKING. Boston:
Allen-Unwin, 1985. 272pp.

DH 7.   Japanese Economic Federation. THE CAPITAL
MARKET OF JAPAN. Tokyo: The Federation, 1940. 72pp.

DH 8.   Kluge, Holger. FINANCIAL REPORTING IN JAPAN:
CASE STUDY. Sophia University Socio-Economic Research
Institute Bulletin no.   67. Tokyo: Kodansha
International; New York: Harper & Row, 1976. 305pp.

DH 9.   McRae, Hamish. JAPAN'S ROLE IN THE EMERGING
GLOBAL SECURITIES MARKETS. New York: Group of Thirty,
1985. 30pp.

DH 10.   Ouchi, Hyoye. FINANCIAL AND MONETARY SYSTEM
IN POSTWAR JAPAN. New York: Institute of Pacific
relations, 1947. 23pp.

DH 11.   Patrick, Hugh Talbot. THE BANK OF JAPAN: A
CASE STUDY IN THE EFFECTIVENESS OF CENTRAL BANK
TECHNIQUES OF MONETARY CONTROL. Ann Arbor: University
Microfilms, 1960. 324pp.

DH. Monetary Policy

DH 12.   Patrick, Hugh Talbot. MONETARY POLICY AND CENTRAL BANKING IN CONTEMPORARY JAPAN. Bombay: Bombay University Press, 1962. 219pp.

DH 13.   Pressnell, L. S., ed.   MONEY AND BANKING IN JAPAN. New York: St. Martin's Press, 1973. 456pp.

DH 14.   Prindl, Andreas R. JAPANESE FINANCE. New York: Wiley, 1981. 137pp.

DH 15.   Sarasas, Phra. MONEY AND BANKING IN JAPAN. London: HeathcGranton Ltd., 1940. 544pp.

DH 16.   Schiffer, Hubert F. THE MODERN JAPANESE BANKING SYSTEM. New York: University Publishers, 1962. 240pp.

DH 17.   Spindler, J. Andrew. THE POLITICS OF INTERNATIONAL CREDIT: PRIVATE FINANCE AND FOREIGN POLICY IN GERMANY AND JAPAN. Washington: Brookings Institution, 1984. 220pp.

DH 18.   Suzuki, Yoshio. MONEY AND BANKING IN CONTEMPORARY JAPAN: THE THEORETICAL SETTING AND ITS APPLICATIONS. New Haven, Conn.: Yale University Press, 1980. 256pp.

DH 19.   Tatuta, Misao. SECURITIES REGULATIONS IN JAPAN. Tokyo: University of Tokyo Press, 1970. 127pp.

DH 20.   Terasawa, Yoshio. JAPAN'S SECURITIES MARKET. Tokyo: Sophia University, 1980. 33pp.

DH 21.   United States. Congress. Joint Economic Committee. THE JAPANESE FINANCIAL SYSTEM IN COMPARATIVE PERSPECTIVE: A STUDY. 97th Congress, 2nd Session. Washington: Government Printing Office, 1982. 61p.

DH 22.   Yonehara, Junshichiro. LOCAL PUBLIC FINANCE IN JAPAN. Centre for Research on Federal Financial Relations Monograph, No. 36. Canberra: Australia National University, 1981. 112pp.

Articles

DH 23.   "Banks Buying More Stocks of Companies."
JAPAN ECONOMIC JOURNAL July 11, 1967 p.1.

DH 24.   Castro, J. "Land of the Rising Yen." TIME
v.127 Mar. 31, 1986 p.53.

DH 25.   "Corporate Finance: Turning to Japan for
Cut-rate Loans." BUSINESS WEEK Nov. 23, 1981 p.114.

DH 26.   Curtin, Donal. "Japanese Banking--The
International Retreat." EUROMONEY Mar. 1983
pp.122-154.

DH 27.   Dornbusch, Rudiger. "Monetary Policy under
Exchange-Rate Flexibility." FEDERAL RESERVE BANK OF
BOSTON 1979 pp.90-122.

DH 28.   Ehrlich, Edna E. "Note on Postwar Credit
Policies in Japan." REVIEW OF ECONOMICS AND STATISTICS
v.39 Nov. 1957 pp.469-471.

DH 29.   Eken, Sena. "Integration of Domestic and
International Financial Markets: The Japanese
Experience." INTERNATIONAL MONETARY FUND STAFF PAPERS
v.31 Sep. 1984 pp.499-548.

DH 30.   Ezekiel, Hannan. "The Call Money Market in
Japan." INTERNATIONAL MONETARY FUND STAFF PAPERS v.8
1966.

DH 31.   Friedman, M. "Monetary Variability: United
States and Japan." JOURNAL OF MONEY, CREDIT AND BANKING
v.15 Aug.1983 pp.339-343.

DH. Monetary Policy

DH 32. Fujino, Shozaburo. "Behavior of Commercial Banks and the Supply of Money." HITOTSUBASHI JOURNAL OF ECONOMICS v.2 Sep. 1961 pp.42-55.

DH 33. Fujioka, M. "Appraisal of Japan's Plan to Double Income." INTERNATIONAL MONETARY FUND STAFF PAPERS v.10 1963 pp.150-185.

DH 34. Greenwood, John. "Japan: Monetary Base Control in Action." ASIAN MONETARY MONITOR (Hong Kong) v.7 Jul./Aug. 1983 pp.13-24.

DH 35. Grossman, R. "Why Venture Capital Won't Work for the Japanese." BUSINESS WEEK Nov. 29, 1982 p.97.

DH 36. Isobe, A. "The Japanese Foreign Exchange Market." INTERNATIONAL MONETARY FUND STAFF PAPERS v.8 1966 p.257+.

DH 37. "Japan and America: Uncle Sam Knows Best." ECONOMIST v.300 Sep. 20, 1986 p.95.

DH 38. "Japanese Financial Markets: Berated." ECONOMIST v.290 Mar. 31, 1984 pp.85-86.

DH 39. "Japanese International Finance." EUROMONEY Mar. 1983 pp.122-155.

DH 40. "Japanese International Finance." EUROMONEY Mar. 1984 pp.156-192.

DH 41. "Limbering Up: a Survey of Japanese Finance and Banking." ECONOMIST v.293 Dec. 8, 1984 pp.survey 1-28.

DH 42. Mayekawa, Haruo. "Monetary Policy in Japan; Review of Its Conduct During the Past Ten Years." KREDIT KAPITAL v.12 1979 no.4 pp.441-456.

DH 43.   "The Men from the Ministry: Financial
Innovators and Traditional Die-hards Clash." ECONOMIST
v. 293 Dec. 8, 1984 pp. survey 22+.

DH 44.   Nakamae, Tadashi. "The Coming World Role of
the Yen." EUROMONEY (London) Sep. 1980 pp. 17+.

DH 45.   Noritake, Yasuo. "The Development of
Monetary and Banking System in Japan, 1932-1945. KOBE
UNIVERSITY ECONOMIC REVIEW no. 2 1956 pp. 69-77.

DH 46.   Nukazawa, Kazuo. "Political Arithmetics of
Yen for Dollars." THE WORLD ECONOMY v. 6 Sep. 1983
pp. 272-289.

DH 47.   Oates, D. "Samurai Shareholders."
INTERNATIONAL MANAGEMENT v. 29 May 1974 pp. 49-50.

DH 48.   Ohkawa, Kazushi. "The Use of National
Income Accounts for Long-Range Planning in Japan." in
Clark, Colin, and Stuvel, Geer, eds.. INCOME
REDISTRIBUTION AND THE STATISTICAL FOUNDATIONS OF
ECONOMIC POLICY. London: Bowes & Bowes, 1964.
pp. 51-69.

DH 49.   Okita, Saburo. "Savings and Economic Growth
in Postwar Japan." ASIAN STUDIES v. 6 Feb. 1964
pp. 16-61.

DH 50.   Ouchi, William G. "Stability Amidst
Mobility." CREDIT AND FINANCIAL MANAGEMENT v. 86
pp. 18-19 Jan. 1984.

DH 51.   Pigott, Charles. "Financial Reform in Japan
(since 1970)." FEDERAL RESERVE OF SAN FRANCISCO Winter
1983 pp. 25-46.

DH 52.   Shioda, Nagahide. "Changes in the Yen
Valuation and Japan's Distributive Mechanism." JAPANESE
ECONOMIC STUDIES v. 9 Fall 1980 v. 45-67.

DH. Monetary Policy

DH 53.   Thomas, Barbara S. "Easing Access to
Japanese Capital." BUSINESS WEEK Aug. 30, 1982
pp. 10-11.

DH 54.   Tsuji, Shinji. "Effectiveness of Credit
Restraints." FUJI BANK BULLETIN v.31 Sep. 1980
pp. 179-180.

DH 55.   Yoshimura, Kanbei. "Japanese Capital
Market." REVISTA INTERNAZIONALE DI SCIENZE ECONOMICHE E
COMMERCIALE v.27 1980 no.10-11 pp.942-949.

DH 56.   Yoshitomi, Masaru. "An Appraisal of
Japanese Financial Policies." WORLD ECONOMY v.6 Mar.
1983 pp.27-38.

DI. Investing in Japan -- American Business

Monographic Works

DI 1.   Alexander, Arthur J. BARRIERS TO U.S.
SERVICE TRADE IN JAPAN. Santa Monica, Calif.: Rand,
1984. 50pp.

DI 2.   American Chamber of Commerce in Japan.
REPORT ON TRADE/INVESTMENT BARRIERS: MEMBERSHIP SURVEY.
Tokyo: The Association, 1982.

DH 3.   American Chamber of Commerce in Japan.
UNITED STATES MANUFACTURING INVESTMENT IN JAPAN, WHITE
PAPER. Tokyo: The Association, 1980.

DJ. Investing in Japan -- Foreign Business

Monographic Works

DJ 1.   Ballon, Robert J., and Lee, Eugene A., eds.
FOREIGN INVESTMENT AND JAPAN. Tokyo: Sophia University
and Kodansha International, 1972. 340pp.

DJ 2.   Boston Consulting Group. THE FOREIGN COMPANY
IN JAPAN. Boston: Boston Consulting Group, 1977.

DJ 3.   Henderson, Dan Fenno. FOREIGN ENTERPRISE IN
JAPAN: LAWS AND POLICIES. Chapel Hill: University of
North Carolina Press, 1973. 574pp.

DJ 4.   Islam, Nurul. FOREIGN CAPITAL AND ECONOMIC
DEVELOPMENT: JAPAN, INDIA, AND CANADA; STUDIES IN SOME
ASPECTS OF ABSORPTION OF FOREIGN CAPITAL. Rutland, Vt.:
C. E. Tuttle, 1960. 251pp.

DJ 5.   Keizai Koho Center. WHICH FOREIGN COMPANIES
HAVE BEEN SUCCESSFUL IN JAPAN AND WHY? A SURVEY BY THE
SOGO SHOSHA (Committee, Japan Foreign Trade Council).
KKC Brief no.2. Tokyo: Keizai Koho Center, 1982. 4pp.

DJ 6.   Ozaki, Robert S. THE CONTROL OF IMPORTS AND
FOREIGN CAPITAL IN JAPAN. New York: Praeger, 1972.
309pp.

DJ 7.   Sadamoto, Kuni, ed.   BREAKING THE BARRIERS.
Tokyo: International Scholarly Book Services, 1982.
264pp.

DJ. Foreign Business in Japan

Articles

DJ 8.   Dobrzynski, J. H., and Treece, J. B. "If You
Can't Beat 'Em, Buy 'Em: Takeovers Arrive in Japan."
BUSINESS WEEK Sep. 29, 1986 pp. 80-82.

DJ 9.   Hasegawa, K. "Japan as a Capital Market."
JAPAN QUARTERLY v. 30 Jan./Mar. 1983 pp. 24-27.

DJ 10.   Helm, L. "The 'Four Tigers' Are Pouncing On
Japan's Markets." BUSINESS WEEK Mar. 24, 1986
pp. 48-49.   (re: South Korea, Singapore, Taiwan, Hong
Kong)

DJ 11.   "Investing in Japan." Eight articles.
JAPANESE JOURNAL OF TRADE AND INDUSTRY v. 3 Sep./Oct.
1984 pp. 12-27.

DJ 12.   Kato, Shuji. "Irasshai! Japan Opens its
Doors to Foreign Firms." JOURNAL OF JAPANESE TRADE AND
INDUSTRY v. 2 Jan./Feb. 1983 pp. 11-14.

DJ 13.   "The Lure of Japan's Open Door." EUROMONEY
Mar. 1986 pp. 70-128.

DJ 14.   March, Robert M. "Foreign Firms in Japan."
CALIFORNIA MANAGEMENT REVIEW v. 22 Spring 1980
pp. 42-50.

DJ 15.   Misawa, Mitsuru. "A Japanese Perspective:
Is Worldwide Unitary Taxation Fair?" SLOAN MANAGEMENT
REVIEW v. 26 Winter 1985 pp. 51-55.

DJ 16.   Phalon, R. A. "Letting Go." FORBES v. 135
May 6, 1985 pp. 46-48.

DJ 17.   "Plant Investment: Foreign Firms step up
Activities." BUSINESS JAPAN v. 29 Dec. 1984 p. 19.

DJ 18. Saso, Mary. "The Roots of Japanese Manufacturing's Competitive Edge." MULTINATIONAL BUSINESS no.3 1984 pp.1-13.

DJ 19. Smith, Lee. "Want to Buy a Japanese Company?" FORTUNE v.107 Jun. 27, 1983 pp.106-109. (Includes table: The Foreign Stake in Japan's Top Ten Industrials".)

DJ 20. Tharp, M. "Goodbye, Japan Inc." FAR EASTERN ECONOMIC REVIEW v.120 May 26, 1983 pp.84+.

DJ 21. Tharp, M. "On Second Thoughts." FAR EAST ECONOMIC REVIEW v.122 Nov. 3, 1983 pp.63-64.

DJ 22. Woronoff, Jon. "Japanese Business Ties Close the Door to Foreign Interests." ASIAN BUSINESS v.18 Sep. 1982 pp.82-83+.

DK. Japan as Market

Monographic Works

DK 1. Ballon, Robert J. JAPAN'S MARKET AND FOREIGN BUSINESS. Tokyo: Sophia University Press, 1971. 304pp.

DK 2. THE JAPANESE MARKET IN FIGURES: A HANDBOOK OF BASIC MARKETING INFORMATION. Tokyo: JETRO; New York: Japan Trade Center, 1983. 52pp.

DK 3. Shimaguchi, Mitsuaki. MARKETING CHANNELS IN JAPAN. Edited by Dufey, Gunter. Research for Business Decisions Series: no. 7. Ann Arbor, Mich.: UMI Research Press, 1978. 192pp.

DK 4. Yoshino, Michael Y. MARKETING IN JAPAN: A MANAGEMENT GUIDE. New York: Praeger, 1975. 156pp.

DK. Japan as Market

Articles

DK 5.   Alden, V. R. "Who Says You Can't Crack Japanese Markets?" HARVARD BUSINESS REVIEW v.65 Jan./Feb. 1987 pp.52-56.

DK 6.   Barbour, A. "Can Japanese Trading Companies Do Battle for U.S. Manufacturers in the Land of the Rising Sun" AMERICAN IMPORT/EXPORT MANAGEMENT v.100 June 1984 p.18+.

DK 7.   Dowd, Laurence P. "Wholesale Marketing in Japan." JOURNAL OF MARKETING v.23 Jan. 1959 pp.257-262.

DK 8.   "Is Japan an Open Market." INC v.6 Dec. 1984 pp.183-184.

DK 9.   "Japan: the Left-hand-drive Barrier to US Sales." BUSINESS WEEK Feb. 15, 1982 pp.60+.

DK 10.   Kraar, Louis. "Inside Japan's Open Market." FORTUNE v.104 Oct. 5, 1981 pp.118-120+.

DK 11.   Maratos, W. "How Can You Sell to Japan? Let Us Count the Ways." AMERICAN IMPORT/EXPORT MANAGEMENT v.101 Dec. 1984 pp.20-21.

DK 12.   "Marketing in a Maze: Japan's Complicated Distribution System hinders Foreign Companies' Efforts to sell Goods There." WALL STREET JOURNAL v.191 May 3, 1978 p.44.

DK 13.   Miyakawa, T. A. "Most Japanese Retailers Begin Direct Importing to Satisfy the Demand for Foreign Consumer Goods." BUSINESS AMERICA v.4 Nov. 16, 1981 pp.13-14.

DK 14.   "More Delay in Opening Up Japan's Markets."
BUSINESS WEEK Aug. 20, 1984 p. 40.

DK 15.   Mutakami, Atsushi. "The Underlying Factors
of Successful Penetration of the East Asian Countries'
Products into Japanese Market." KOBE UNIVERSITY
ECONOMIC REVIEW v. 26 1980 pp. 1-28.

DK 16.   Nielson, Hal G. "Business Opportunities in
Japan." HASTINGS INTERNATIONAL AND COMPARATIVE LAW
REVIEW v. 7 Winter 1984 pp. 13-34.

DK 17.   Strenski, J. B. "Understanding of Culture
Essential to Success in Japanese Market." PUBLIC
RELATIONS QUARTERLY v. 31 Summer 1986 p. 9.

DK 18.   Tsuruoka, D. "A Tough Market to Crack."
NEWSWEEK v. 106 Dec. 16, 1985 p. 54.

DL. Joint Ventures

Monographic Works

DL 1.   Ballon, Robert J., ed.   JOINT VENTURES AND
JAPAN. Tokyo: Sophia University Press, 1968. 138pp.

DL 2.   Tsuda, Mamoru. A PRELIMINARY STUDY OF
JAPANESE--FILIPINO JOINT VENTURES. Quezon City:
Foundation for Nationalist Studies, 1978. 174pp.

Articles

DL 3.   Anand, V. "A Wave of Joint Ventures."
GLOBAL TRADE EXECUTIVE v. 105 Oct. 1986 pp. 22-23.

DL 4.   Beauchamp, M. "Use a Long Spoon." FORBES v. 138 Dec. 15, 1986 p. 122.

DL 5.   Burton, F. N., and Saelens, F. H. "Linkage Characteristics of International Joint Ventures in Japan." MANAGEMENT INTERNATIONAL REVIEW v. 22 no. 2 1982 pp. 20-29.

DL 6.   Sullivan, J., and Peterson, R. B. "Factors Associated with Trust in Japanese-American Joint Ventures." MANAGEMENT INTERNATIONAL REVIEW v. 22 no. 2 1982 pp. 30-40.

DL 7.   Sullivan, J., and Peterson, R. B. "Trust in Japanese-American Joint Ventures." MANAGEMENT INTERNATIONAL REVIEW v. 22 no. 2 1982 pp. 30-40.

DL 8.   Wright, Richard W. "Canadian Joint Ventures in Japan." BUSINESS QUARTERLY v. 42 no. 3 1977 pp. 42-53.

DL 9.   Wright, Richard W. "Joint Venture Problems in Japan." COLUMBIA JOURNAL OF WORLD BUSINESS v. 14 no. 1 pp. 25-31.

VIII.

CHAPTER 5

E. TRADE AND TRADE RELATIONS

EA. Trade Policies and Practices

Monographic Works

EA 1.   Allen, George C. HOW JAPAN COMPETES: AN
ASSESSMENT OF INTERNATIONAL TRADING WITH SPECIAL
REFERENCE TO "DUMPING". Institute of Economic Affairs
Series: Hobart Paper 81. London: The Institute, 1978.
74pp.

EA 2.   Farley, Miriam Southwell. THE PROBLEMS OF
JAPANESE TRADE EXPANSION IN THE POST-WAR SITUATION. New
York: Institute of Pacific Relations, 1940. 93pp.

EA 3.   Higashi, Chikara. JAPANESE TRADE POLICY
FORMULATION. New York: Praeger, 1983. 179pp.

EA 4.   Ho, Alfred Kuo-liang. JAPAN'S TRADE
LIBERALIZATION IN THE 1960s. White Plains, N.Y.:
International Arts & Sciences Press, 1973. 118pp.

EA 5.   Ilgen, Thomas L., and Pempel, T. J. TRADING
TECHNOLOGY: EUROPE AND JAPAN IN THE MIDDLE EAST. New
York: Praeger, 1986. 215pp.

EA. Trade Policies and Practices

EA 6.   Japan. Ministerial Conference for Economic Measures. ON THE PROMOTION OF EXTERNAL ECONOMIC MEASURES. Tokyo, Jan. 13, 1983. 39pp.

EA 7.   JAPAN TRADE DIRECTORY 1987-88. Tokyo: Japan External Trade Organization, 1987. 1400pp.

EA 8.   JAPAN'S ECONOMIC EXPANSION AND FOREIGN TRADE, 1955 TO 1970. GATT Studies in International Trade, No. 2. New York: Unipub, 1971.

EA 9.   Kershner, Thomas R. JAPANESE FOREIGN TRADE. Lexington, Mass.: Lexington Books, D.C. Heath, 1975. 204pp.

EA 10.   Sethi, S. Prakash. JAPANESE BUSINESS AND SOCIAL CONFLICT: A COMPARTATIVE ANALYSIS OF RESPONSE PATTERNS WITH AMERICAN BUSINESS. Cambridge, Mass.: Ballinger Pub. Co., 1975.

EA 11.   United States Tariff Commission. POSTWAR DEVELOPMENTS IN JAPAN'S FOREIGN TRADE. New York: Greenwood Press, 1969, c1958.   242pp.

Articles

EA 12.   Abernathy, W. J., et al.   "New Industrial Competition." HARVARD BUSINESS REVIEW v.59 Sep./Oct. 1981 pp.68-81.   Same article: MCKINSEY QUARTERLY Summer 1982 pp.2-25.

EA 13.   Alm, Richard. "Is Japan Really Opening Door to Trade?" U.S. NEWS AND WORLD REPORT v.99 Aug. 12, 1985 p.24.

EA 14.   Armstrong, L. "The Big Guns Aimed at Small Retailers." BUSINESS WEEK July 1, 1985 p.35.

EA. Trade Policies and Practices

EA 15. Austen, I. "A U.S. Attack on Tokyo."
MACLEANS v.98 Apr. 15 1985 p.38.

EA 16. Bartholomew, J. "Not So Much a Decision,
More a Way of Life." FAR EASTERN ECONOMIC REVIEW v.114
Nov. 13-19, 1981 pp.58-60.

EA 17. Burton, J. "Japan Trade Door Opens a Bit
More." INDUSTRIAL MARKETING v.68 Mar. 1983 pp.8+.

EA 18. Byron, Christopher. "Tempers Rising Over
Trade." TIME v.119 Feb. 1, 1982 p.58.

EA 19. Calder, Kent E. "Opening Japan." FOREIGN
POLICY v.47 Summer 1982 pp.82-97.

EA 20. Caplan, B. "Japan: a Question of Economic
Capability." BANKER v.132 May 1982 pp.39-43.

EA 21. "Changing Trade Structures: the United
States, West Germany, and Japan." FUJI BANK BULLETIN
Jan./Feb. 1983 pp.5-14.

EA 22. Curran, Timothy J. "Politics of Trade
Liberalization in Japan." JOURNAL OF INTERNATIONAL
AFFAIRS v.37 Summer 1983 pp.105-122.

EA 23. Davies, D. "Western Media are Japan's Best
Agents." FAR EASTERN ECONOMIC REVIEW v.112 June 12-18,
1981 pp.53-54.

EA 24. Dreyfuss, J. "Japan's Comeback Plan."
FORTUNE v.114 Sep. 29, 1986 pp.136-138+.

EA 25. Duncan, T. "Thorny Nationalist Questions."
WORLD PRESS REVIEW v.33 Mar. 1986 pp.35-36.

EA 26. Eisenstein, P. "Yenflation Forces Japanese
to Court U.S. Suppliers." AUTOMOTIVE INDUSTRIES v.166
Sep. 1986 pp.25+.

EA. Trade Policies and Practices

EA 27. Fairlamb, D. "Why the Yen is Weak." DUN'S BUSINESS MONTHLY v. 125 Mar. 1985 pp. 38-40.

EA 28. Flint, J. "Welcome to Hard Times." FORBES v. 137 Mar. 24, 1986 p. 144.

EA 29. Forbes, M. S., Jr. "On the Subject of Japan..." FORBES v. 132 Oct. 10, 1983 p. 23.

EA 30. Fukushima, K. "Japan's Real Trade Policy." FOREIGN POLICY v. 59 Summer 1985 pp. 22-39.

EA 31. Gergen, D. "Japan: the New OPEC?" U.S. NEWS AND WORLD REPORT v. 98 Apr. 1, 1985 p. 78.

EA 32. Hamilton, A. "Japan's New Game." MANAGEMENT TODAY Mar. 1984 pp. 76-79+.

EA 33. Helm, L., and Treece, J. B. "As the Crossfire grows Heavier, Nakasone looks Weaker." BUSINESS WEEK May 6, 1985 pp. 60-61.

EA 34. Hollerman, Leon. "Liberalization and Japanese Trade in the 1970's." ASIAN SURVEY v. 10 no. 5 1970 pp. 427-437.

EA 35. "How the US and Japan Hope to Mint a Stronger Yen." BUSINESS WEEK Nov. 28, 1983 p. 64.

EA 36. Hsieh, D. A. "Determination of the Real Exchange Rate: The Productivity Approach." JOURNAL OF INTERNATIONAL ECONOMICS v. 12 May 1982 pp. 355-362.

EA 37. "Is Free Trade Dead?" ECONOMIST Dec. 25, 1982 pp. 75-78+.

EA 38. Jackson, J. H.; Louis, J. V.; Matsushita, M. "Implementing the Tokyo Round: Legal Aspects of Changing Economic Rules." MICHIGAN LAW REVIEW v. 81 Dec. 1982 pp. 267+.

EA 39. Jackson, S., et al. "Japan's Overture Falls Flat." BUSINESS WEEK Apr. 22, 1985 pp. 32-33.

EA 40. "Japan." NATION'S BUSINESS v. 73 Jan. 1985 pp. 28-30+. (special section)

EA 41. "Japan: Then and Now." OECD OBSERVER no. 127 Mar. 1984 pp. 3-15.

EA 42. "Japan's Bid to Out-Design the U.S." BUSINESS WEEK Apr. 13, 1981 pp. 123-124.

EA 43. Jones, P. M. "Japan's New Trade Policy." SENIOR SCHOLASTIC v. 115 Nov. 12, 1982 pp. 5-8.

EA 44. Kilpatrick, J. J. "Japan's Hard Work." NATION'S BUSINESS v. 73 Dec. 1985 p. 6.

EA 45. Kirkland, R. I., Jr. "Are the Japanese Rigging the Yen?" FORTUNE v. 105 May 31, 1982 pp. 91-92+.

EA 46. Kojima, Kiyoshi. "Japanese Foreign Trade and Economic Growth--With Special Reference to Terms of Trade." ANNALS OF THE HITOTSUBASHI ACADEMY v. 8 Apr. 1958 pp. 143-168.

EA 47. Kojima, Kiyoshi. "Japan's Trade Policy." ECONOMIC RECORD v. 41 1965 pp. 54-77.

EA 48. Kragenau, Henry. "Successes and Dangers of Japanese Foreign Trade Strategy." INTER-ECONOMICS v. 19 Jan./Feb. 1984 pp. 39-44.

EA 49. Kubota, Akira. "Japan's Economic Relations: Trade Barriers vs. Perception Barriers." ASIA PACIFIC COMMUNITY v. 30 Aug. 1985 pp. 119-134.

EA 50. Lehner, Urban C., and Kanabayashi, Masayoshi. "Japan Working on Another Plan to Open Market." WALL STREET JOURNAL v. 201 Jan. 12, 1983 p. 33.

EA. Trade Policies and Practices

EA 51. Lehner, Urban C. "Strong Premier: Nakasone Stirs Pride of the Japanese as He Firms Up Ties to West." WALL STREET JOURNAL v. 202 Sep. 1, 1983 pp. 1+.

EA 52. Leontiades, J. "Market Share and Corporate Strategy in International Industries." JOURNAL OF BUSINESS STRATEGY v. 5 Summer 1984 pp. 30-37.

EA 53. McAbee, Michael. "Japan: Land of the Setting Sun?" INDUSTRY WEEK v. 225 Apr. 29, 1985 pp. 50-53.

EA 54. Manning, R. "Numbers Game." FAR EASTERN ECONOMIC REVIEW v. 122 Oct. 13, 1983 pp. 81-82.

EA 55. Marshall, R. R. "Japan and Germany: Recovery with Policy Stability." BANKER v. 135 Jan. 1985 pp. 53-55.

EA 56. Matsui, K. "Some Notes on Japan's Foreign Trade." KYOTO UNIVERSITY ECONOMIC REVIEW v. 27 1957 no. 2 pp. 19-55.

EA 57. Matthews, Ron G. "A European View on the Relationship Between Japan's Economic Development and her Export-led Growth Strategy." ASIAN PROFILE v. 10 Dec. 1982 pp. 523-534.

EA 58. (not used)

EA 59. Narkevar, P. R. "The Role of Competitiveness in Japan's Export Performance, 1954-1958." INTERNATIONAL MONETARY FUND STAFF PAPERS v. 8 1960 pp. 65-90.

EA 60. Newman, P. C. "Trading on the Japanese Model." MACLEAN'S v. 96 Nov. 21, 1983 p. 46.

EA 61. Noguchi, Yuichiro. "Economic Nationalism." JOURNAL OF SOCIAL AND POLITICAL IDEAS IN JAPAN v. 4 Apr. 1966 pp. 94-99.

EA 62.   Okamoto, Yasuo. "The Grand Strategy of Japanese Business." JAPANESE ECONOMIC STUDIES v.10 Summer 1982 pp.3-52.

EA 63.   Okita, Saburo. "Role of the Trade Ombudsman in Liberalising Japan's Market." WORLD ECONOMY (London) v.7 Sep. 1984 pp.241-256.   (re: Headquarters for the Promotion of Settlements of Grievances Related to the Openess of the Japanese Market, established Jan. 1982)

EA 64.   Pfeiffer, J. E. "Striking the Right Trade Posture." SCIENCE '85 v.6 Sep. 1985 pp.80-81.

EA 65.   Pine, Art. "At a Crossroad: Japan Nears a Choice of Easing Trade Curbs or Facing West's Ire." WALL STREET JOURNAL v.199 Jan. 26, 1982 pp.1+.

EA 66.   Rafferty, Kevin. "Shifting into Overdrive: Japan; Economists are Now Forecasting Faster Growth and Even Bigger Trade Surpluses for Japan." INSTITUTIONAL INVESTOR v.18 Nov. 1984 pp.231+.

EA 67.   Shapiro, Irving. "Second Thoughts about Japan." WALL STREET JOURNAL v.197 June 5, 1981 p.24.

EA 68.   Smith, Allan D. "The Japanese Foreign Exchange and Foreign Trade Control Law and Administrative Guidance: The Labyrinth and the Castle." LAW AND POLICY IN INTERNATIONAL BUSINESS v.16 no.2 1984 pp.417-476.

EA 69.   "Sometimes a Problem is Overexaggerated." U.S. NEWS AND WORLD REPORT v.99 July 29, 1985 pp.51-52. (Interview with A. Morita.)

EA 70.   Stone, Merlin. "Competing with Japan--the Rules of the Game." LONG RANGE PLANNING v.17 Apr. 1984 pp.33-46.

EA. Trade Policies and Practices

EA 71. Tatemoto, M., and Ichimura, S. "Factor Proportions and Foreign Trade, the Case of Japan." REVIEW OF ECONOMICS AND STATISTICS v.41 1959 pp.442-446.

EA 72. Tharp, M. "Chasm Widens." FAR EAST ECONOMIC REVIEW v.118 Dec. 17-23, 1982 pp.55-57.

EA 73. Tharp, M. "Few Steps Further." FAR EASTERN ECONOMIC REVIEW v.119 Mar. 31, 1983 pp.56+.

EA 74. Tharp, M. "Japanese Stalemate." FAR EASTERN ECONOMIC REVIEW v.117 July 16/22, 1982 pp.44-46.

EA 75. Tharp, M. "Japanese Technique of Killing with Silence." FAR EASTERN ECONOMIC REVIEW v.116 June 11/17, 1982 pp.57-62.

EA 76. Tharp, M. "Threat of the Rising Sun." FAR EASTERN ECONOMIC REVIEW v.117 Sep. 10/16, 1982 pp.66+.

EA 77. Thompson, Donald B. "How Japan, Inc. Undercuts U.S. Steelmakers." INDUSTRY WEEK v.195 Oct. 10, 1977 pp.17-25.

EA 78. "Three Myths about Japan." NATIONAL REVIEW v.37 Sep. 6, 1985 p.19.

EA 79. "A Tough Choice on Yen Controls." BUSINESS WEEK Nov. 8, 1982 p.99.

EA 80. Urata, Masutaro. "Japan's Open Trade Policy." HARVARD INTERNATIONAL REVIEW v.7 Sep./Oct. 1984 pp.143-45.

EA 81. Werner, Roy A. "Is Japan an Open Market?" ASIAN AFFAIRS v.9 Jan./Feb. 1982 pp.147-162.

EA 82. White, T. H. "The Danger from Japan." NEW YORK TIMES MAGAZINE July 28, 1985 pp.18-23+.

EA 83. Wilson, Dick. "Japan: the Trade Challenge."
BANKER v.132 May 1982 v.27-29+.

EA 84. Woronoff, Jon. "Advice On Avoiding Even
Worse Trade Conflicts: Double Standard in Trade can be
Dangerous." ORIENTAL ECONOMIST v.50 Mar. 1982
pp.18-21.

EA 85. Yeutter, C. K. "Improved Market Access to
Japan." DEPARTMENT OF STATE BULLETIN v.85 Oct. 1985
pp.27-29.

EB. Export--Import

Monographic Works

EB 1. Hadley, Eleanor M. JAPAN'S EXPORT
COMPETITIVENESS IN THIRD WORLD MARKETS. Washington,
D.C.: Center for Strategic and International Studies,
1981.

Articles

EB 2. Alm, Richard. "Japan Acts to Buy American,
but How Much?" U.S. NEWS AND WORLD REPORT v.99 Oct. 21,
1985 p.49.

EB 3. "And in Japan, Retailers Say Imports are
Booming." MANAGEMENT REVIEW v.71 Apr. 1982 pp.5-6.

EB 4. Ball, Robert. "The Japanese Juggernaut Lands
in Europe." FORTUNE v.104 Nov.30, 1981 pp.108-122.

EB. Export--Import

EB 5.   "Behind the Export Explosion, a Battered Home Market." BUSINESS WEEK July 2, 1984 pp. 36-37.

EB 6.   Bomster, M. "High Court Won't Review Dumping Duties." ELECTRONICS NEWS v. 29 Oct. 10, 1983 p. 60.

EB 7.   "Cheaper Imports--At Last!" BUSINESS JAPAN v. 31 July 1986 pp. 15-16.

EB 8.   Citrin, Daniel. "Exchange Rate Changes and Exports of Selected Japanese Industries." STAFFF PAPERS v. 32 Sep. 1985 pp. 404-429.

EB 9.   Cullison, A. E. "Export Data Worry Japanese Officials." JOURNAL OF COMMERCE AND COMMERCIAL July 22, 1985 p. 3A.

EB 10.   Doan, Michael. "How Four U.S. Industries are Hurt by Dumping: From Steel Mills to Rose Gardens, American Firms Claim They're Losing Out to Cheap Imports Illegally Promoted by Foreign Governments." U.S. NEWS AND WORLD REPORT v. 93 July 5, 1982 pp. 45-46.

EB 11.   Doerner, W. R. "Swamped by Japan." TIME v. 125 Apr. 15, 1985 pp. 62-64.

EB 12.   Ethier, W. J. "Dumping." JOURNAL OF POLITICAL ECONOMY v. 114 Nov. 13-19, 1981 p. 56.

EB 13.   Greene, R. "One to Watch." FORBES v. 133 Feb. 13, 1984 p. 14.

EB 14.   Helm, L. "Nakasone's Import Drive could be Headed for a Dead End." BUSINESS WEEK Oct. 21, 1985 pp. 54-55.

EB 15.   Jacquemin, Alexis, et al.   "A Dynamic Analysis of Export Cartels; the Japanese Case." THE ECONOMIC JOURNAL Sep. 1981 pp. 685-696.

EB 16.   "Japanese Exports: Still Soaring." ECONOMIST v. 280 Sep. 5, 1981 pp. 62-63.

EB 17.   Kawata, F. "World Trade and Japan's
Exports." KOBE ECONOMIC AND BUSINESS REVIEW v.6 1959
pp.41-48.

EB 18.   Krisher, Bernard. "Japan Opens Some Doors
to Imports." FORTUNE v.105 Jan. 25, 1982 pp.47-48.

EB 19.   Kurokawa, N. "Liberalizing Beef and Orange
Imports; Why It's So Hard." JAPAN QUARTERLY v.30
Jul./Sep. 1983 pp.261-265.

EB 20.   "More Dumped Upon than Dumping; Japan's
Imports." ECONOMIST v.284 Sep. 25/Oct. 1, 1982
pp.88-89.

EB 21.   Moriguchi, C. "Japan; Exports Should Keep
It Ahead of the Pack." BUSINESS WEEK Feb. 15, 1982
pp.102-103.

EB 22.   Ozaki, Robert S. "Postwar Expansion of
Japanese Exports." WESTERN ECONOMIC JOURNAL v.1 no.2
1963 pp.140-155.

EB 23.   Rose, Sanford. "The Secret of Japan's
Export Prowess." FORTUNE Jan. 30, 1978 pp.56-62.

EB 24.   Smith, C. "After the Export Boom." WORLD
PRESS REVIEW v.33 Mar. 1986 p.40.

EC. U.S.--Japan Trade

Monographic Works

EC 1.   American Chamber of Commerce in Japan.
UNITED STATES--JAPAN TRADE: WHITE PAPER, MAY 1979.
Tokyo: The Association, 1979. 27pp.

EC 2.   Blaker, Michael, ed.   THE POLITICS OF TRADE:
U.S. AND JAPANESE POLICYMAKING FOR THE GATT
NEGOTIATIONS. New York: Columbia University Press,
1979. 184pp.

EC 3.   Castle, Emery N., and Hemmi, Kenzo, eds.
UNITED STATES-JAPANESE AGRICULTURE TRADE RELATIONS.
Baltimore: Johns Hopkins University Press, 1982. 416pp.

EC 4.   Cohen, Jerome B., ed.   PACIFIC PARTNERSHIP:
UNITED STATES-JAPAN TRADE: PROSPECTS AND
RECOMMENDATIONS FOR THE SEVENTIES. Lexington, Mass.:
Lexington Books, D. C. Heath, 1972. 270pp.

EC 5.   Hallerman, Leon. JAPAN AND THE UNITED
STATES: ECONOMIC AND POLITICAL ADVERSARIES. Boulder,
Colo.: Westview Press, 1980. 224pp.

EC 6.   Harris, A. W. U.S. TRADE PROBLEMS IN STEEL:
JAPAN, WEST GERMANY, AND ITALY. New York: Praeger,
1983. 276pp.

EC 7.   HAWAII'S TRADE WITH JAPAN, 1974--1983.
Honolulu: Hawaii Department of Planning and Economic
Development, 1984. 19pp.

EC 8.   Hunsberger, Warren S. JAPAN AND THE UNITED
STATES IN WORLD TRADE. New York: Harper & Row, 1964.
492pp.

EC 9.   Japan--U.S. Economic Relations Group.
REPORT: PREPARED FOR THE PRESIDENT OF THE UNITED STATES
AND THE PRIME MINISTER OF JAPAN. Sponsored by the U.S.
Executive Office of the President. Washington, D.C.:
National Technical Information Service, 1981. 107 pp.

EC 10.   "Japan vs. USA, the High Tech Shoot Out."
(videorecording) NBC News: NBC Report. Wilmette, Ill.:
Films, Inc., 1982. 52mins.

EC 11. THE JAPANESE NON-TARIFF BARRIER ISSUES:
AMERICAN VIEWS AND THE IMPLICATIONS FOR JAPAN--U.S.
TRADE RELATIONS. Arthur D. Little, Inc. Tokyo: National
Institute for Research Advancement, 1979. 169pp.

EC 12. JAPAN'S ECONOMY AND TRADE WITH THE UNITED
STATES: SELECTED PAPERS SUBMITTED TO THE SUBCOMMITTEE
ON ECONOMIC GOALS AND INTERNATIONAL POLICY OF THE JOINT
ECONOMIC COMMITTEE, CONGRESS OF THE UNITED STATES.
Committee Print 99-103. Washington, D.C.: U. S.
Government Printing Office, 1985. 245pp.

EC 13. Monroe, Wilbur F. JAPANESE EXPORTS TO THE
UNITED STATES: ANALYSIS OF "IMPORT-PULL" AND
"EXPORT-PUSH" FACTORS. Washington: United States-Japan
Trade Council, 1978. 217pp.

EC 14. Moran, Robert T. GETTING YOUR YEN'S WORTH.
Houston: Gulf Pub. Co., 1984. 181pp.

EC 15. Petri, Peter A. MODELING JAPANESE-AMERICAN
TRADE: A STUDY OF ASYMMETRIC INTERDEPENDENCE. (Harvard
Economic Studies, v.156). Cambridge, Mass.: Harvard
University Press, 1984. 232pp.

EC 16. Pugel, Thomas A., ed., with Hawkins, Robert
G. THE FRAGILE INTERDEPENDENCE: ECONOMIC ISSUES IN
U.S.--JAPANESE TRADE AND INVESTMENT. Lexington, Mass.:
Lexington Books, 1986. 276pp.

Articles

EC 17. Abegglen, James C., and Hout, Thomas.
"Facing up to the Trade Gap with Japan." FOREIGN
AFFAIRS v.57 Fall 1978 pp.146-168.

EC 18. Alden, V. R. "The Trade Deficit: Stop
looking for Scapegoats." BUSINESS WEEK Apr. 8, 1985
pp.20-21.

EC 19.   Alexander, C. P.   "'Buy More Foreign Goods'." TIME v.125 Apr. 22, 1985 pp.42-43.

EC 20.   Alm, Richard.   "Trade War with Japan?" U.S. NEWS AND WORLD REPORT v.98 Apr. 15, 1985 pp.22-23.

EC 21.   "America and Japan: a Ceremonial Handshake." ECONOMIST v.286 Jan. 22, 1983 pp.23-24.

EC 22.   "America and Japan: of Baseball Bats and Burden-sharing." ECONOMIST v.285: Dec. 11, 1982 p.23.

EC 23.   "America Hunts for a Japanese Plot to Put It Out of Business." ECONOMIST v.287 May 21/27, 1983 pp.79-80.

EC 24.   "America's Deficit; the Import Boom." ECONOMIST v.292 Sep. 29, 1984 pp.70+.

EC 25.   "America's Hidden Problem: the Huge Trade Deficit is Sapping Growth and Exporting Jobs." BUSINESS WEEK Aug. 29, 1983 pp.66-69+.

EC 26.   Armstrong, L., et al.   "Why Carmakers will Mourn if Export Quotas Die." BUSINESS WEEK Feb. 18, 1985 pp.46-47.

EC 27.   Baker, G. Robert.   "Japan-U.S. Economic Friction: an American View." JAPAN QUARTERLY v.31 Jan./Mar. 1984 pp.28-32.

EC 28.   Barry, John M.   "U.S. Retreats from Free Trade." DUN,S BUSINESS MONTHLY v.125 Apr. 1985 pp.30-32+.

EC 29.   Bartholomew, J.   "Dollar-Yen Dilemma of America's Own Making." FAR EASTERN ECONOMIC REVIEW v.114 Nov. 12-19, 1981 p.56.

EC 30.   Berger, M., and Wilson, J. W. "Now Japan is Where It's At for U.S. Chipmakers." BUSINESS WEEK Nov. 24, 1986 p.108.

EC 31.   Blackburn, M. "Onward and Upward--And Further Into the Red." FAR EASTERN ECONOMIC REVIEW v.114 Oct.23-29, 1981 p.72.

EC 32.   Blair, R. D., and Cheng, L. "On Dumping." SOUTHERN ECONOMIC JOURNAL v.50 Jan. 1984 pp.857-863.

EC 33.   Boland, J. C. "Trade Wars: Protectionism Rears Its Ugly Head." BARRON'S v.62 Sep. 27, 1982 pp.22+.

EC 34.   Bowring, P. "Beware of the Trade Tidal Wave." FAR EASTERN ECONOMIC REVIEW v.114 Nov. 13-19, 1981 pp.54.

EC 35.   "Breaking the Logjam in U.S.--Japan Trade Relations." DUN'S BUSINESS MONTHLY v.125 Apr. 1985 p.36. (An Interview with David Packard).

EC 36.   Brown, D. C. "Barriers, Progress Noted in Trade with Japan." BUSINESS MARKETING v.69 Nov. 1984 pp.12+.

EC 37.   Businger, D. "Exports to Japan May Recover, but Record U.S. Deficit is Likely." BUSINESS AMERICA v.6 Feb. 21, 1983 pp.37-38.

EC 38.   Canto, V. A., and Laffer, A. B. "The Effectivness of Orderly Marketing Agreements: the Color TV Case." BUSINESS ECONOMICS v.18 Jan. 1983 pp.38-45.

EC 39.   Cavanaugh, H. A. "On a New Kind of War." ELECTRONICS WORLD v.198 Sep. 1984 pp.31-33.

EC 40.   Chiesl, N. E., and Knight, L. L. "Japanese Buyers Attitudes toward the US Supply Sources." INDUSTRIAL MARKETING MANAGEMENT v.10 Oct. 1981 pp.243-251.

EC 41.   Cifelli, A. "It's a Cold Spring in
Washington for Japan." FORTUNE v.111 Apr. 15, 1985
p.120.

EC 42.   "Dangerous Standoff over US--Japanese
Trade." BUSINESS WEEK Mar. 15, 1982 pp.46+.

EC 43.   Dentzer, S. "Getting a Foot in Japan's
Door." NEWSWEEK v.105 Mar. 25, 1985 p.74.

EC 44.   Doe, P. "Hakuto's Goal: Re-engineer U.S.
Products in Japan." ELECTRONIC BUSINESS v.11 Mar. 1,
1985 pp.83+.

EC 45.   Doe, P. "Say it with Corn Oil." ELECTRONIC
BUSINESS v.10 July 10, 1984 pp.79-80.

EC 46.   Dole, R. "Freeing up Free Trade with
Japan." USA TODAY (monthly) v.111 July 1982 pp.54-56.

EC 47.   "The Domestic Discontent Bill." ECONOMIST
v.285 p.21 Dec. 18, 1982.

EC 48.   Donlan, T. G. "Shades of Smoot-Hawley? Rep.
John Dingell Wants to Get Tough with Japan." BARRON'S
v.65 Apr. 15, 1985 pp.8-9+.

EC 49.   Dooley, B. J. "Free Trade: Are U.S. Auto
Companies True Believers?" AMERICAN IMPORT/EXPORT
BULLETIN v.94 May 1981 pp.22+.

EC 50.   Eason, H. "American--Japanese Trade
Practices." NATION'S BUSINESS v.72 Dec. 1984 p.44.

EC 51.   Eason, H. "An Electronic Bridge Over
Troubled Waters: American and Japanese Leaders Talk
Trade in a Televised Washington-Tokyo Dialogue."
NATION'S BUSINESS v.72 Apr. 1984 pp.78-79.

EC 52.   Eason, H. "Exports to Japan: An Open or
Shut Case." NATION'S BUSINESS v.73 Apr. 1985

EC 53.   Eason, H. "Japan Rolls Out a Trade Carpet."
NATION'S BUSINESS v.72 Sep. 1984 pp.53-54.

EC 54.   "East and West Trade Insults." ECONOMIST
v.282 Feb. 6-12, 1982 p.73.

EC 55.   "Enact New Laws to Ban Imports? Yes:
Interview with Senator John C. Danforth, Republican of
Missouri; No: Interview with C. Fred Bergsten, Director
of the Institute for International Economics." U.S.
NEWS AND WORLD REPORT v.93 Jul. 19, 1982 pp.53-54.

EC 56.   "Exchange Rule Clarification Required for
Advanced Technology." BUSINESS JAPAN v.28 Sep. 1983
pp.14-15.   (re: U.S. National Security Act)

EC 57.   "Exports Ignite a Capital Spending Surge."
BUSINESS WEEK Oct. 15, 1984 p.57.

EC 58.   "Facing off with Japan." FORTUNE v.111 Apr.
29, 1985 p.8.

EC 59.   Finn, E. A., Jr. "Of Apples, Oranges and
Toyotas." FORBES v.139 Jan. 26, 1987 pp.34-35.

EC 60.   France, Boyd, et al.   "Collision Course:
Can the U.S. Avert a Trade War with Japan?" BUSINESS
WEEK Apr. 8, 1985 pp.50-55.

EC 61.   France, B., et al.   "Talks with Japan near
the Flash Point." BUSINESS WEEK Mar. 11, 1985
pp.34-35.

EC 62.   Frank, A. D. "Enough of Your Promises."
FORBES v.130 p.98 Dec. 20, 1982.

EC 63.   Frank, A. D. "The U.S. Side of the Street."
FORBES v.130 Jul. 19, 1982 pp.31-32.

EC 64.   Gall, N. "Black Ships are Coming?" FORBES
v.131 Jan. 31, 1983 pp.67-71+.

EC 65.   Gelman, E. "Trade War Ahead." NEWSWEEK
v.105 Apr. 15, 1985 pp.22-23.

EC 66.   Graham, John L. "A Hidden Cause of
America's Trade Deficit with Japan." COLUMBIA JOURNAL
OF WORLD BUSINESS v.16 Fall 1981 pp.5-15

EC 67.   Greenfield, D. "Japan's Trade Policies are
Frustrating to Many; Success Depends on Putting the
Pieces Together with a Japanese Design." AMERICAN
SHIPPING v.24 Aug. 1982 pp.44-45.

EC 68.   Greenwald, J. "Pressure from Abroad." TIME
v.125 Apr. 8, 1985 pp.52-53.

EC 69.   Gregory, G. "All's Fair in War." FAR EASTERN
ECONOMIC REVIEW v.117 July 2-8, 1982 pp.76-77.

EC 70.   Gregory, G. "Love-Hate Relationship." FAR
EASTERN ECONOMIC REVIEW v.120 June 30, 1983 pp.54-55.

EC 71.   "Guess Who's Pleading for U.S. Export
Cuts?" BUSINESS WEEK Apr. 13, 1981 pp.63-65.

EC 72.   Hampton, W. J., and Mervosh, E. "More
Japanese Cars: How Much Will They Hurt?" BUSINESS WEEK
Mar. 18, 1985 pp.117+.

EC 73.   Hanke, Steve H. "U.S.--Japanese Trade:
Myths and Realities." CATO JOURNAL v.3 Winter 1983-1984
pp.757-775.

EC 74.   Higashi, Kiyoshi. "U.S. Trade and
Industrial Structure." EXIM REVIEW v.3 no.1 1983
pp.3-23.

EC 75.   Hoadley, W. E. "U.S. vs. Japan: the
Economic Balance is now Shifting in Our Favor." DUN'S
BUSINESS MONTH v.123 June 1984 p.57.

EC 76. Hoadley, W. E. "Why U.S.--Japan Relations are Deteriorating--and How to Improve Them." DUN'S BUSINESS MONTH v.119 June 1982 p.39.

EC 77. Hollerman, L. "Trade Barriers Against Japan May Worsen U.S. Position." CENTER MAGAZINE v.15 May/June 1982 pp.20-28.

EC 78. Holstein, W. J., et al. "Another Japanese-style Trade Gap." BUSINESS WEEK May 13, 1985 pp.45-46.

EC 79. Iacocca, Lee A. "Why We Need Auto Quotas." FORTUNE v.110 Nov. 12, 1984 pp.227+.

EC 80. "'I'm Worried About a Full-Blown Trade War'; No One's Hands are Clean on Import Restrictions; Interview with J. Paul Lyet, Chairman, President's Export Council." U.S. NEWS AND WORLD REPORT v.93 Nov. 29, 1982 pp.59-60.

EC 81. "Involuntary Restraints; Japanese Car Exports." ECONOMIST v.288 July 9-15, 1983 pp.65-66.

EC 82. "Japan: An Upsurge in Sales of Chips to the U.S." BUSINESS WEEK Feb. 18, 1980 p.79.

EC 83. "Japan Remains Top Market for U.S. Farm Products." NATIONAL FOOD REVIEW no.35 Oct. 27, 1986 p.62.

EC 84. "Japan--U.S.: Wrangle Over Sakhalin Project." BEIJING REVIEW v.25 Aug. 16, 1982 pp.15-16.

EC 85. "Japan Worries that It Ain't Seen Nothing Yet." ECONOMIST v.293 Nov. 10, 1984 pp.75-76.

EC 86. "Japanese-American Trade: Barnyard Noises." ECONOMIST v.291 Apr. 7, 1984 p.73.

EC 87. "A Japanese Boost for U.S. Exports." BUSINESS WEEK June 14, 1982 pp.31-32.

EC 88. "Japanese Trade: Blaming the United States." SOCIETY v.23 Nov./Dec. 1985 p.2.

EC 89. "Japan's Car Exports: Restraint is Dead, Long live Restraint." ECONOMIST v.294 Feb. 2, 1985 pp.58+.

EC 90. "Japan's Perspective on Trade." CHALLENGE v.28 July/Aug. 1985 pp.18-26. (Interview with Hidetoshi Ukawa on the Trade Deficit)

EC 91. "Japan's Trade Promises." DUN'S BUSINESS MONTHLY v.119 Feb. 1982 pp.17-18.

EC 92. "Japan's Weak Answer to U.S. Trade Demands." BUSINESS WEEK Feb. 15, 1982 pp.43-44.

EC 93. Joseph, Raymond A. "Automation Helps RCA and Zenith Keep Color TV Leadership in Face of Imports." WALL STREET JOURNAL v.197 May 5. 1981 p.56.

EC 94. Kahn, H. "44 Economists Want VRA (Voluntary Restraint Agreements) to Die." AUTOMOTIVE NEWS Feb. 25, 1985 p.55.

EC 95. Kahn, H. "Japanese Makers Main Target as a New Trade Battle Begins." AUTOMOTIVE NEWS Mar. 8, 1982 pp.2+.

EC 96. Kelderman, J. "Japanese Balk at Threats of New U.S. Import Curbs." AUTOMOTIVE NEWS Dec. 7, 1981 pp.1+.

EC 97. Krause, Walter, and Monroe, Wilbur F. "Prospects for United States--Japan Trade Relations." COLUMBIA JOURNAL OF WORLD BUSINESS v.16 Summer 1981 pp.18-22.

EC 98. Lester, R. K. "U.S.--Japanese Nuclear Relations: Structural Change and Political Strain." ASIAN SURVEY v.22 May 1982 pp.417-433.

EC 99. Lewis, J. "End of the Road." FAR EASTERN ECONOMIC REVIEW v.112 May 8-14, 1981 pp.51+.

EC 100. Lincoln, Edward J. "U.S.-Japan Relations: Good? Terrible? SAIS (SCHOOL OF ADVANCED INTERNATIONAL STUDIES) REVIEW v.4 Winter/Spring 1984 pp.31-44.

EC 101. McClenahen, J. S. "Trade Action Now, Says US to Japan." INDUSTRY WEEK v.211 Dec. 14, 1981 pp.101-102.

EC 102. McClenahen, J. S., and McAbee, M. "Trade: Congress Declares War on Japan." INDUSTRY WEEK v.225 Apr. 15, 1985 pp.17-18.

EC 103. McCulloch, Rachel. "Trade Deficits, Industrial Competitiveness, and the Japanese." CALIFORNIA MANAGEMENT REVIEW v.27 Winter 1985 pp.140-156.

EC 104. MacEachron, E. "United States and Japan: the Bilateral Potential." FOREIGN AFFAIRS v.61 Winter 1982/1983 pp.400-415.

EC 105. Madison, Christopher. "The Protectionist Congress: Is this the Year that the Trade Barriers Go Up?" NATIONAL JOURNAL v.15 Jan. 1, 1983 pp.18-21.

EC 106. Madison, Christopher. "White House Accentuates the Positive on Japanese Economic, Defense Ties." NATIONAL JOURNAL v.15 Oct. 22, 1983 pp.162-167.

EC 107. Manning, R. "Reciprocity's Risks." FAR EASTERN ECONOMIC REVIEW v.116 Apr. 9/15, 1982 pp.48+.

EC 108. Mansfield, M. "U.S.--Japan Relations Present and Future." BUSINESS AMERICA v.7 Nov. 12, 1984 pp.10-14.

EC 109. Mansfield, Michael J. "The U.S.-Japan Relationship: An Overview." AMERICAN CHAMBER OF

COMMERCE JOURNAL v.2 June 1985 pp.73+.

EC 110.   Marcuss, Stanley J., and Kantor, Mark
Alan. "U.S. Antidumping & Countervailing Duty Laws."
AMERICAN CHAMBER OF COMMERCE IN JAPAN JOURNAL v.21 Apr.
1983 pp.19-20+.

EC 111.   Meissner, Frank. "Cracking the Japanese
Walnut." BUSINESS HORIZONS v.23 no.1 Feb. 1980
pp.64-69.

EC 112.   Nevin, John J. "Can U.S. Business Survive
Our Japanese Trade Policy?" HARVARD BUSINESS REVIEW
v.56 Sep./Oct. 1978 pp.165-177.

EC 113.   "The New Politics of U.S. Protectionism."
BUSINESS WEEK Dec. 27, 1982 pp.44-45.

EC 114.   "The New Squeeze on Japan." MACLEAN'S v.98
Apr. 22, 1985 pp.30-36.

EC 115.   Nicholson, Tom. "GM Takes on the Japanese."
NEWSWEEK v.47 May 11, 1981 p.56.

EC 116.   Okamura, Minoru. "Estimating Taste
Changes; Impacts of the U.S. Soybean Embargo on the
Japanese Demand for Meat." SOUTHERN ECONOMIC JOURNAL
v.49 Apr. 1983 pp.953-1065.

EC 117.   Olmer, L. H. "Perspectives on U.S.-Japan
Trade." BUSINESS AMERICA v.7 Nov. 12, 1984 pp.3-9.

EC 118.   Peters, T. J. "Closed Minds Can't Open
Markets." U.S. NEWS AND WORLD REPORT v.100 Mar. 3, 1986
p.59.

EC 119.   Pringle, R. "Japan: the Glint of Steel
Behind Tokyo's International Role." BANKER v.131 Aug.
1981 pp.77+.

EC 120.   "Removal of Non-Tariff Barriers." JAPAN
QUARTERLY v.29 Apr./June 1982 pp.162-165.

EC 121. "A Report on U.S.--Japan Agricultural Trade Problems." AMERICAN CHAMBER OF COMMERCE IN JAPAN v.21 Nov. 1984 pp.9+.

EC 122. Robertson, J. "Government Closeup: Proof of the Sushi is the Eating." ELECTRONICS NEWS v.32 Aug. 11, 1986 p.10. (re: U.S.-Japan Semiconductor Agreement)

EC 123. Robertson, J. "Japan Execs Chide U.S. Protectionist Leanings, Reciprocity Bills." ELECTRONIC NEWS v.28 Mar. 8, 1982 pp.1+.

EC 124. Rodrik, D. "Managing Resource Dependency: The United States and Japan in the Markets for Copper, Iron Ore and Bauxite." WORLD DEVELOPMENT v.10 July 1982 pp.541-560.

EC 125. Scheibla, S. H. "Washington's Joshua Bill Brock Leads the Fight Against Protectionism." BARRON'S v.64 Aug. 20, 1984 pp.13+.

EC 126. Schoenbaum, Thomas J. "Trade Friction with Japan and the American Policy Response." MICHIGAN LAW REVIEW v.82 Apr./May 1984 pp.1647-1661.

EC 127. Schwartz, L. "House Bill Proposes Restructuring of Japan--U.S. Trade Relations." ELECTRONIC NEWS v.27 Aug. 17, 1981 pp.Supplement D.

EC 128. Schwartz, L. "Report High-Tech Rivalry Causing Japan-U.S. Friction." ELECTRONIC NEWS v.30 July 9, 1984 p.Supplement X.

EC 129. Scouton, W. "Commerce Department Leaders Visit Asia, Urge Japan to Eliminate Trade Barriers." BUSINESS AMERICA v.4 Nov. 16, 1981 p.10.

EC 130. Sedjo, R. A. "United States--Japanese Solidwood Products Trade." COLUMBIA JOURNAL OF WORLD BUSINESS v.19 Spring 1984 pp.83-88.

EC 131. Sekiguchi, Sueo. "The Distribution System: a Nontariff Barrier? Japan's Notorious Distribution System Has Been Blamed for the Huge U.S. Trade Deficit with Japan." ECONOMIC EYE v.3 June 1982 pp.23-26.

EC 132. Shaw, S. J. "U.S. Trade Representatives Blast Japanese Export Policy." MINI-MICRO SYSTEMS v.17 May 1984 pp.66+.

EC 133. "A Shortcut through the Red Tape." BUSINESS WEEK June 11, 1984 pp.57+.

EC 134. Smith, J. V. "Japan Wants U.S. Exports." AMERICAN IMPORT/EXPORT MANAGEMENT v.101 Dec. 1984 pp.18-19.

EC 135. Smith, L. "What the U.S. Can Sell Japan." FORTUNE v.111 May 13, 1985 pp.92-96.

EC 136. Smith, Roy C. "Japan as a Vulnerable No. 1." BUSINESS WEEK Aug. 11, 1980 pp.13-14.

EC 137. Spencer, Edson W. "Japan: Stimulus or Scapegoat?" FOREIGN AFFAIRS v.62 Fall 1983 pp.123-137.

EC 138. Sundstrom, G., and Gawronski, F. J. "U.S. Auto Sales Rise in Japan, but Total is Still Tiny." AUTOMOTIVE NEWS Aug. 4, 1986 p.42.

EC 139. Tabner, J. "Japanese Recovery is Under Way; Export Surge Boosts Trade Surplus." BUSINESS AMERICA v.7 Aug. 20, 1984 pp.38-39.

EC 140. Taylor, W. A. "Why Japan Won't Cave in to U.S. Trade Demands." U.S. NEWS AND WORLD REPORT v.98 Apr. 22, 1985 pp.32-34.

EC 141. Tell, L. J. "U.S.--Japan Tension builds: Tokyo Decision on Phone Imports May be Key." BARRON'S v.65 Apr. 1, 1985 pp.40-41.

EC 142. Tharp, M. "Gap Still Yawns." FAR EASTERN ECONOMIC REVIEW v.117 Aug. 13/19, 1982 pp.89-90.

EC 143. Tharp, M. "Japan's New Boom." FAR EASTERN ECONOMIC REVIEW v.113 Sep. 18/24, 1981 p.117.

EC 144. Tharp, M. "Rumblings of War." FAR EASTERN ECONOMIC REVIEW v.114 Oct. 16/22, 1981 pp.86-88.

EC 145. Tharp, M. "Stalemate Lingers." FAR EASTERN ECONOMIC REVIEW v.121 Sep. 22, 1983 pp.85-86.

EC 146. Tharp, M. "Tokyo's Peace Offerings." FAR EASTERN ECONOMIC REVIEW v.119 Feb. 24, 1983 pp.65-66.

EC 147. Tharp, M. "Uncle Sam Wants Japan." FAR EASTERN ECONOMIC REVIEW v.117 July 9/15, 1982 pp.30-31.

EC 148. Thomas, R. "Japan Must Join the World." NEWSWEEK v.106 Nov. 4, 1985 pp.50-51.

EC 149. Timmer, C. Peter, and Reich, Michael R. "Japan and the U.S.: Trading Shots over Beef and Oranges." CHALLENGE Sep./Oct. 1983 pp.18-24. (Includes a Chronology of U.S.-Japan Agricultural Talks 1978-1983).

EC 150. Tomabechi, T. "U.S.--Japan Connection in the Changing World Marketplace: A Trader's Perspective." JOURNAL OF INTERNATIONAL AFFAIRS v.37 Summer 1983 pp.43-48.

EC 151. "Trade Puts a Double Whammy on the Economy." BUSINESS WEEK Nov. 1, 1982 pp.96-98+.

EC 152. "Trade Talks that Could Snap the Frayed U.S.-Japanese Ties." BUSINESS WEEK Oct. 4, 1982 p.64.

EC 153. "Trade War Looms with Japan." ENGINEERING NEWS-RECORD v.217 July 3, 1986 pp.84-85.

EC 154. "Trade With Japan: Likely to Stay Lopsided." BUSINESS WEEK June 22, 1981 pp.47-48.

EC 155. Trezise, Philip H. "The Realities of Japan--U.S. Economic Relations." PACIFIC COMMUNITY v.1 Apr. 1970 pp.353-368.

EC 156. Tsongas, Paul E. "Meeting the Challenge of the Japanese Competition." ELECTRONIC BUSINESS v.8 Oct. 1982 pp.33-35.

EC 157. Tsongas, Paul E. "Meeting the Japanese Challenge." MINI-MICRO SYSTEMS v.15 Jul. 1982 pp.106-107.

EC 158. Tsurumi, Yoshi. "Critical Choice for Japan: Cooperation or Conflict with the United States." COLUMBIA JOURNAL OF WORLD BUSINESS v.12 1977 pp.14-20.

EC 159. Turner, Charlie G. "Voluntary Export Restraints on Trade Going to the United States." SOUTHERN ECONOMIC JOURNAL v.49 Jan. 1983 pp.793-803.

EC 160. "Under Secretary Ulmer Warns of U.S.-Japan Trade Imbalance." BUSINESS AMERICA v.4 Dec. 14, 1981.

EC 161. "U.S.-Japan Trade Rhubarb continues." IRON AGE v.225 Feb. 1, 1982 pp.13+.

EC 162. Van Zandt, H. F. "East Opens Its Doors to the West." TELEPHONY v.200 June 1, 1981 pp.26-27.

EC 163. Victor, A. Paul. "Antidumping and Antitrust: Can the Inconsistencies be Resolved?" NEW YORK UNIVERSITY JOURNAL OF INTERNATIONAL LAW AND POLITICS v.15 Winter 1983 pp.339-350.

EC 164. Volpe, John. "U.S.-Japan Trade and the Yen/Dollar Relationship." AMERICAN CHAMBER OF COMMERCE OF JAPAN JOURNAL v.21 Feb. 1984 pp.59+.

EC 165.   Wallace, J. "The Festering Irritation with Japan." U.S. NEWS AND WORLD REPORT v.93 Aug. 23, 1983 pp.39-40.

EC 166.   Wente, M. "Does Detroit have the Japanese Licked at Last?" CANADIAN BUSINESS v.57 May 1984 p.11.

EC 167.   Werner, T. "Japan: Land of High Tariffs and Old Customs Challenges U.S. Business." AMERICAN IMPORT/EXPORT MANAGEMENT v.95 Dec. 1981 pp43+.

EC 168.   Whalley, John. "General Equilibrium Analysis of U.S.--EEC--Japanese Trade and Trade Distorting Policies: A Model and Some Initial Findings." ECONOMIE APPLIQUEE v.33 no.1 1980 pp.191-230.

EC 169.   Wilson, J. W., and Helm, L. "The Trade Pact on Chips is a Godsend--for the Japanese." BUSINESS WEEK Oct. 13, 1986 p.142.

EC 170.   Wilson, P. "U.S.--Japan Trade Relations." VITAL SPEECHES OF THE DAY v. 51 Oct. 1, 1985 pp.741-743.

EC 171.   Wilson, W., et al.   "Selling Chips to the Japanese: LSI Logic Has an Ace Up Its Sleeve." BUSINESS WEEK Jan. 28, 1985 pp.133-134.

ED.   International Trade

Monographic Works

ED 1.   Akrasanee, Narongchai, ed.   ASAEN--JAPAN RELATIONS: TRADE AND DEVELOPMENT. Singapore: Institute of Southeast Asian Studies, 1983. 191pp.

ED. International Trade

ED 2.   Japan External Trade Organization. ÄJETROÄ
WHITE PAPER ON INTERNATIONAL TRADE: JAPAN 1982. 34th
ed.   Tokyo: JETRO, 1982. 465pp.

ED 3.   Japan External Trade Organization. ÄJETROÄ
WHITE PAPER ON INTERNATIONAL TRADE: JAPAN 1984.

ED 4.   Perry, Charles M. THE WEST, JAPAN, AND CAPE
ROUTE IMPORTS: THE OIL AND NON-FUEL MINERAL TRADES.
Cambridge, Mass.: Institute for Foreign Policy
Analysis, 1982. 88pp.

ED 5.   Pringsheim, Klaus H. NEIGHBORS ACROSS THE
PACIFIC: THE DEVELOPMENT OF ECONOMIC AND POLITICAL
RELATIONS BETWEEN CANADA AND JAPAN. Westport, Conn.:
Greenwood Press, 1983. 241pp.

ED 6.   Roemer, John E. U.S.-JAPANESE COMPETITION IN
INTERNATIONAL MARKETS: A STUDY OF THE TRADE-INVESTMENT
CYCLE IN MODERN CAPITALISM. Berkeley, Calif.: Institute
of International Studies, University of California,
1975. 242pp.

ED 7.   Schlossstein, Steven. TRADE WAR: GREED,
POWER, AND INDUSTRIAL POLICY ON OPPOSITE SIDES OF THE
PACIFIC. New York: Congdon & Weed; dist.   by St.
Martin's Press, 1984. 296pp.

ED 8.   Shoemack, Harvey R. and DeRoin, Gene, eds.
JAPAN'S INTERNATIONAL TRADE POLICY: MYTHS AND
REALITIES. Chicago: Japan Trade Center, 1978. 104pp.

ED 9.   Tsurumi, Yoshi. TECHNOLOGY TRANSFER AND
FOREIGN TRADE: A CASE OF JAPAN, 1950-1966. New York:
Arno Press, 1980. 337pp.

ED 10.   United States. Congress. House. Committee
on Energy and Commerce. UNITED STATES TRADE RELATIONS
WITH CHINA AND JAPAN: 1983: STAFF REPORT. 98th
Congress, 1st Session, Committee Print 98-H.
Washington, D.C. : U.S. Government Printing Office,
1983. 219pp.

ED 11.   United States. Congress. House. Committee
on Ways and Means. Subcommittee on Trade. TASK FORCE
REPORT ON UNITED STATES-JAPANESE TRADE, WITH ADDITIONAL
VIEWS. Washington, D.C. : U.S. Government Printing
Office, 1979. 83pp.

ED 12.   United States. Congress. House. Committee
on Ways and Means. Subcommittee on Trade. TRADE WITH
JAPAN: HEARINGS, AUGUST 26 AND SEPTEMBER 18, 1980. 96th
Congress, 2nd Session. Serial 96-1211. Washington,
D.C. : U. S. Government Printing Office, 1980.

ED 13.   United States. Congress. House. Committee
on Ways and Means. Subcommittee on Trade. UNITED
STATES--JAPAN TRADE RELATIONS: HEARINGS BEFORE THE
SUBCOMMITTEE ON TRADE OF THE COMMITTEE ON WAYS AND
MEANS. 98th Congress, 1st Session, March 10 and April
26, 27, 1983. Serial 98-13. Washington, D.C. : U.S.
Government Printing Office, 1983. 548pp.

ED 14.   United States. Congress. House. Committee
on Ways and Means. Subcommittee on Trade. United
States--Japan Trade Task Force. UNITED STATES-JAPAN
TRADE REPORT. 96th Congress, 2nd Session. Committee
Print WMCP: 96-68. Washington, D.C. : U.S. Government
Printing Office, 1980. 92pp.

ED 15.   United States. Congress. Joint Economic
Committee. Subcommittee on International Trade, Finance
and Security Economics. U.S.--JAPANESE ECONOMIC
RELATIONS: HEARINGS, JUNE 19--JULY 13, 1981. 97th
Congress, 1st session.   Washington, D.C. : U.S.
Government Printing Office, 1981. 226p.

ED. International Trade

ED 16. United States. Congress. Senate. Committee
on Banking, Housing, and Urban Affairs. Subcommittee on
International Finance and Monetary Policy.
SEMICONDUCTOR TRADE AND JAPANESE TARGETING: HEARING
BEFORE THE SUBCOMMITTEE ... ON THE PROBLEMS OF UNFAAIR
TRADE PRACTICES AND JAPANESE BARRIERS TO TRADE IN THE
SEMICONDUCTOR INDUSTRY, JULY 30, 1985. Washington,
D.C.: U.S. Government Printing Office, 1985. 220pp.

ED 17. United States. Congress. Senate. Committee
on Foreign Relations. U.S. ECONOMIC RELATIONS WITH
JAPAN: HEARING, APRIL 7, 1983, ON THE IMPACT OF THE
YEN-DOLLAR EXCHANGE RATE. 98th Congress, 1st session,
Senate Hearing 98-67. Washington, D.C.: U.S. Government
Printing Office, 1983. 63pp.

ED 18. United States. General Accounting Office.
UNITED STATES-JAPAN TRADE: ISSUES AND PROBLEMS: REPORT.
By the Comptroller General of the United States.
Washington, D.C.: U.S. General Acounting Office, 1979.
205pp.

ED 19. Wonnacott, R. J. AGGRESSIVE U.S.
RECIPROCITY EVALUATED WITH A NEW ANALYTICAL APPROACH TO
TRADE CONFLICTS. Montreal: Institute of Research for
Public Policy, 1984. 68pp.

Articles

ED 20. "Africa--Japan Trade Focus." AFRICA; AN
INTERNATIONAL BUSINESS, ECONOMIC AND POLITICAL MAGAZINE
v.123 Nov. 1981 pp.115-126.

ED 21. Denman, R. "Trade Relations Between
Industrialized Countries in Times of Crisis." ATLANTIC
COMMERCE QUARTERLY v.20 Fall 1982 pp.258-265.

ED 22. Graham, John L. "Brazilian, Japanese and American Business Negotiations." JOURNAL OF INTERNATIONAL BUSINESS STUDIES v.14 no.1 1983 pp.47-61.

ED 23. Hay, K. A. J. "Haze on the Rising Sun." CANADIAN BANKER ICB REVIEW v.90 Feb. 1983 pp.12-17.

ED 24. "In Bed with Different Dreams." ECONOMIST v.294 Jan. 5, 1985 pp.15-16.

ED 25. Ingersoll, Robert S. "Toward a Bilateral Partnership: Improving Economic Relations." JOURNAL OF INTERNATIONAL AFFAIRS v.37 Summer 1983 pp.21-28.

ED 26. "Japan: Dedicated to Stable World Trade." JOURNAL OF COMMERCE v.348 June 8, 1981 pp.1C-10C.

ED 27. "Japanese Business Ties Close the Door to Foreign Interests." ASIAN BUSINESS v.18 Sep. 1982 pp.82-86.

ED 28. "Japanese Export Industries Targeting East European Markets." BUSINESS JAPAN v.31 July 1986 pp.16-17.

ED 29. "Japan's Trade War with the West Goes From Cold to Hot." ECONOMIST v.283 Apr. 24, 1982 pp.87-88.

ED 30. Keller, Dietmar. "The International Competitiveness of Europe, the USA and Japan." INTERECONOMICS v.20 Mar./Apr. 1985 pp.59-64.

ED 31. Kerns, H. "Target Japan Frowns as Counter-Trade Grows." FAR EASTERN ECONOMIC REVIEW v.119 Jan. 27, 1983 p.54.

ED 32. Koo, A. Y. C. "Japan in Intra-Regional Trade, Alternative Models." REVIEW OF ECONOMICS AND STATISTICS v.37 1955 pp.201-204.

ED. International Trade

ED 33.   Koo, A. Y. C. "The Role of Japan in Intra-regional trade of the Far East." REVIEW OF ECONOMICS AND STATISTICS v.39 1957 pp.31-40.

ED 34.   Kurihara, K. K. "Japan's Trade Position in a Changing World Market." REVIEW OF ECONOMICS AND STATISTICS v.37 1955 pp.412-417.

ED 35.   Langdon, Frank C. "Japan--United States Trade Friction; the Reciprocity Issue." ASIAN SURVEY v.23 May 1983 pp.653-666.

ED 36.   Lehmann, Jean-Pierre. "Agenda for Action on Issues in Euro-Japanese Relations." WORLD ECONOMY v.7 Sep. 1984 pp.257-276.

ED 37.   Matsuo, T. "Structural Analysis of Japan's Trade with Southeast Asia." ASIAN AFFAIRS v.3 1958 pp.25-44.

ED 38.   Mehta, F. A. "Price Competition Between India, Japan, and the United Kingdom in Indian Cotton Textile Market." REVIEW OF ECONOMICS AND STATISTICS v.39 1957 pp.75-78.

ED 39.   Mendl, Wolf. "Western Europe and Japan." THE YEAR BOOK OF WORLD AFFAIRS 1983 pp.97-112.

ED 40.   Narayana, Chem. "Aggregate Images of American and Japanese Products: Implications of International Marketing." COLUMBIA JOURNAL OF WORLD BUSINESS v.16 Summer 1981 pp.31-35.

ED 41.   Nations, R. "Rocky Road to Tokyo." FAR EAST ECONOMIC REVIEW v.121 Aug. 4, 1983 pp.53-55.

ED 42.   Panglaykim, J. "Business Relations Between Indonesia and Japan." THE DEVELOPING ECONOMIES v.12 no.3 1974 pp.281-303.

ED 43.   Ray, E. J., and Marvel, H. P. "The Pattern
of Protection in the Industrial World." REVIEW OF
ECONOMIC STATISTICS v. 66 Aug. 1984 pp. 452-458.

ED 44.   Sundstrom, G. "Japanese Move to Ease
Importation of Autos." AUTOMOTIVE NEWS Sep. 1, 1986
p. 1.

ED 45.   Ushiba, N. "Possibility of Expanding Trade
of Japan with Communist Bloc." ASIAN AFFAIRS v. 4 1959
pp. 61-72.

ED 46.   Watanabe, Toshio, and Kajiwara, Hirokazu.
"Pacific Manufactured Trade and Japan's Options." THE
DEVELOPING ECONOMIES v. 21 no. 4 1983 pp. 313-339.

ED 47.   Wilson, Dick. "Japan: the Other Side of the
Trade War." BANKER v. 132 Nov. 1982 pp. 31-32+.

EE. Tariff Policy; Protectionism

Monographic Works

EE 1.   Greenway, David. TRADE POLICY AND THE NEW
PROTECTIONISM. New York: St. Martin's Press, 1983.
240pp.

EE 2.   Japan Economic Institute of America.
AGRICULTURAL PROTECTIONISM. Washington, D. C.: The
Institute, 1983. 20pp.

EE 3.   Krauss, Melwyn B. NEW PROTECTIONISM. New
York: New York University Press, 1978. 119pp.

BE. Tariff Policy; Protectionism

Articles

EE 4.   Agress, P. "U.S. Calls on Japan to Eliminate Import Barriers." BUSINESS AMERICA v.5 Mar 22, 1982 pp.3-6.

EE 5.   Berger, M. "The Japanese Trade Barrier Bugaboo." NEW LEADER v.65 May 3, 1982 pp.6-7.

EE 6.   Bergsten, C. F. "What to Do About the U.S.--Japan Economic Conflict." FOREIGN AFFAIRS v.60 Summer 1982 pp.1059-1075.

EE 7.   Brady, J. "Was Iacocca a Racist?" ADVERTISING AGE v.56 Mar. 21, 1985 p.44.

EE 8.   Carter, C. C. "Japanese Car Quotas." FORTUNE v.110 Dec. 24, 1984 pp.103-104.

EE 9.   Chang, Stephanie. "The Benefits and Liabilities of Tariff Restrictions on U.S.-Japan Trade Relations." AMERICAN CHAMBER OF COMMERCE JAPAN JOURNAL v.21 July/Aug. 1984 pp.10-11+.

EE 10.   DeMott, J. S. "Pounding on Tokyo's Door." TIME v.125 Mar. 25, 1985 pp.54-55.

EE 11.   Doan, Michael. "Will the U.S. Strike Back on Trade Barriers? Keep Out Foreign Cars, Dump Dairy Surpluses Abroad--These Ideas and More are being Pushed in the Wake of a Global Conference that Fizzled." U.S. NEWS AND WORLD REPORT v.93 Dec. 13, 1982 pp.90.

EE 12.   "The Doors that Farmers Want Japan to Open." BUSINESS WEEK Oct. 25, 1982 pp.28-29.

EE 13.   Eason, H. "The Pull of Protectionism." NATION'S BUSINESS v.72 May 1984 pp.53+.

EE 14. Galvin, R. W. "Japanese Protectionism."
(Address given June 2, 1982.) VITAL SPEECHES OF THE DAY
v. 48 Aug. 1, 1982.

EE 15. Givens, William L. "The U.S. Can No Longer
Afford Free Trade: A Laudable Idea Has Become an
Inadequate Policy as Japan Wins Dominance Of a Series
Of Industries by Selective Use Of Protectionism."
BUSINESS WEEK Nov. 22, 1982 p. 15.

EE 16. Grover, R. "Protectionism's Unlikely Point
Man." BUSINESS WEEK Apr. 29, 1985 pp27-28.

EE 17. Hein, John. "A New Protectionism Rises."
ACROSS THE BOARD v. 20 Apr. 1983 pp. 22-30.

EE 18. "Imports vs. Jobs: the Push for
Protectionism; a Protectionist Trade War Could be a
Disaster; Unrestricted Free Trade, however, Causes as
Many Problems as Protectionism." DOLLARS AND SENSE
May/Jun. 1982 pp. 3-5.

EE 19. McAbee, Michael. "Clever Japanese: Trade
Barriers Come in Creative Packages." INDUSTRY WEEK
v. 213 Apr. 5, 1982 pp. 26-27.

EE 20. McAbee, Michael. "Trade: New Wave of
Barriers?" INDUSTRY WEEK v. 223 Oct. 1, 1984 pp. 36-37.

EE 21. McClenahen, J. S. "Japan: a Bulwark of
Barriers." INDUSTRY WEEK v. 225 Apr. 29, 1985 pp. 18-19.

EE 22. Manning, R. "No Give, No Take." FAR EASTERN
ECONOMIC REVIEW v. 118 Nov. 19-25, 1982 p. 80.

EE 23. Manning, R. "Uneasy Truce." FAR EASTERN
ECONOMIC REVIEW v. 115 Feb. 5/11, 1982 pp. 73-74.

EE 24. "Must Trade Barriers Go Up with
Unemployment?" ECONOMIST v. 283 May 15/21, 1982
pp. 33-34.

BE. Tariff Policy; Protectionism

EE 25. Nakamae, Tadashi. "Why Fear Protectionism?" JAPAN QUARTERLY v.30 Apr./Jun. 1983 pp.122-125.

EE 26. Nevin, John J. "Doorstop for Free Trade." HARVARD BUSINESS REVIEW v.61 p.88-95 Mar.-Apr. 1983.

EE 27. Pine, Art. "Protectionist Push: Threat of a Trade War Rises as Recession Spurs Competition, Nations Impose Curbs." WALL STREET JOURNAL v.200 Nov. 17, 1982 p.56.

EE 28. Pine, Art, and Lehner, Urban C. "Trade Winds: Protectionist Feelings Against Japan Increase in the U.S. and Europe." WALL STREET JOURNAL v.201 Jan. 14, 1983 pp.1+.

EE 29. Poe, B. "Still Facing Hurdles." DATAMATION v.32 Dec. 15, 1986 pp.33-34.

EE 30. Schreffler, R. "Quotas, Continued: Of Cars, Cattle, Citrus and Cigs." DISTRIBUTION v.83 Aug. 1984 pp.62+.

EE 31. Tharp, M. "Time and Protectionism Wait for No Man." FAR EASTERN ECONOMIC REVIEW v.114 Nov. 13/19, 1981 pp.55-56.

EE 32. "Trade Barriers, Japanese Style." U.S. NEWS AND WORLD REPORT v.92 Feb 1, 1982 p.52.

EE 33. Wallace, Laura. "Trade Trouble: Protectionist Pressures Are Rising in Europe as Economies Stagnate." WALL STREET JOURNAL v.197 Jan. 30, 1981 pp.1+.

EE 34. Wolfowitz, Paul D. "Protectionism and U.S.--Japan Trade." DEPARTMENT OF STATE BULLETIN v.85 July 1985 pp.50-54.

EF. Japanese Investments and Companies in the U.S.

Monographic Works

EF 1.   AFFILIATES AND OFFICES OF JAPANESE FIRMS IN THE USA AND CANADA. Tokyo: Japan External Trade Organization, 1986. 562pp.

EF 2.   Alexander, Lamar. FRIENDS: JAPANESE AND TENNESSEANS. Tokyo: Kodansha International, 1986. 192pp.

EF 3.   Freedman, Audrey, and Bauer, David. JAPANESE INVESTMENT IN THE UNITED STATES: AN OPINION SURVEY OF ELECTED OFFICIALS. New York: Conference Board, 1983. 9pp.

EF 4.   Heller, H. Robert, and Heller, Emily E. JAPANESE INVESTMENT IN THE UNITED STATES, WITH A CASE STUDY OF THE HAWAIIAN EXPERIENCE. New York: Praeger, 1974. 161pp.

EF 5.   Kujawa, Duane. JAPANESE MULTINATIONALS IN THE UNITED STATES: CASE STUDIES. New York: Praeger, 1986. 304pp.

EF 6.   MacKnight, Susan. JAPAN'S EXPANDING MANUFACTURING PRESENCE IN THE UNITED STATES: A PROFILE. Washington, D. C.: Japan Economic Institute of America, 1981. 25pp.

EF 7.   Negandi, Anant R., and Baliga, B. R. TABLES ARE TURNING: GERMAN AND JAPANESE MULTINATIONAL COMPANIES IN THE UNITED STATES. Cambridge, Mass.: Oeleschlager, Gunn and Hain, 1981. 166pp.

EF. Japanese Investments in U.S.

Articles

EF 8.   Agress, P. "Japan's MIPRO Opens Washington Office, Offers Services to American Exporters." BUSINESS AMERICA v. 4 June 1, 1981 p. 14.

EF 9.   Armstrong, L. et al.   "The New Wheeler-Dealers in U.S. Real Estate are Japanese." BUSINESS WEEK Oct. 27, 1986 p. 55.

EF 10.   Brecher, C., and Pucik, V. "Foreign Banks in the U.S. Economy: The Japanese Example." COLUMBIA JOURNAL OF WORLD BUSINESS v. 15 no. 1 1980 pp. 5-13.

EF 11.   Bronte, Stephen. "The Japanese Attack on Corporate America." EUROMONEY Sep. 1982 pp. 195-196+.

EF 12.   Bylinski, G. "Japanese Score on a U.S. Fumble." FORTUNE v. 103 June 1, 1981 pp. 68-72.

EF 13.   Chang, S. "The Gods and the U.A.W. are Smiling: Mazda's New Boss Plans to Make Cars, and Jobs, for Yanks." PEOPLE WEEKLY v. 23 Feb. 18, 1985 pp. 90-91.

EF 14.   Cook, D. "Why the UAW Can't Afford to Lose at Honda." BUSINESS WEEK Dec. 2, 1985 pp. 32-33.

EF 15.   Cook, J. "East Goes West, Antes Up." FORBES v. 137 Apr. 7, 1986 p. 125.

EF 16.   Cook, J. "Tiger by the Tail." FORBES v. 127 Apr. 13, 1981 pp. 119-25+.

EF 17.   Dervin, R. "Foreign Investors Consider U.S. Property Stable: Japanese Investment is Expected to be a Megatrend." NATIONAL REAL ESTATE INVESTOR v. 28 Sep. 1986 pp. 80+.

EF 18.   Edid, M., et al.   "Why Mazda is Settling in at the Heart of Union Territory." BUSINESS WEEK Sep. 9, 1985 pp. 94-95.

EF 19.   "Foreign Investors in the United States: a Symposium." REAL ESTATE REVIEW v.14 Fall 1984 pp.34-42.

EF 20.   Goodman, G. "American Samurai." SALES AND MARKETING MANAGEMENT v.127 Oct. 12, 1981 pp.45-46+.

EF 21.   Guzda, H. P. "Industrial Democracy: Made in the U.S.A." MONTHLY LABOR REVIEW v.107 May 1984 pp.23-40.

EF 22.   Harari, Ehud, and Ziera, Yoram. "Morale Problems in Non-American Multinational Corporations in the United States." MANAGEMENT INTERNATIONAL REVIEW v.14 no.6 1974 pp.43-57.

EF 23.   Helm, L., and Levine, J. B. "Japan's Giants Go Shopping for U.S. Startups." BUSINESS WEEK Nov. 3, 1986 pp.46+.

EF 24.   Hoerr, J. "Pleading Labor's Case at Japan's U.S. Plants." BUSINESS WEEK May 13, 1985 pp.30-31.

EF 25.   Hollerman, Leon. "Japanese Direct Investment in California." ASIAN SURVEY v.21 Oct. 1981 pp.1080-1095.

EF 26.   Holstein, W. J., et al.   "Japan's Bigger and Bolder Forays into the U.S." BUSINESS WEEK Nov. 17, 1986 pp.80-81.

EF 27.   Inaba, M. "Japan Companies Spurn California for East, North." ELECTRONIC NEWS v.32 Aug 18, 1986 pp.11+.

EF 28.   "Innovative Japanese Drugs Move into the U.S." BUSINESS WEEK May 10, 1982 pp.150-151+.

EF 29.   Ioannou, L. "Money and the Japanese Market Too." VENTURE v.8 Aug. 1986 pp.92+.

EF 30.   "Japan: Business Feels the Heat of U.S.

EF. Japanese Investments in U.S.

Antibias Laws." BUSINESS WEEK Nov. 23, 1981 pp.57-58.

EF 31.   "Japan: Robots Get a Warm Welcome in
Kentucky." BUSINESS WEEK Apr. 19, 1982. pp.48-49.

EF 32.   "Japanese Automakers Site Plants in US."
INDUSTRIAL DEVELOPMENT v.149 Nov./Dec. 1980 pp.23-38.

EF 33.   "Japanese Car Makers Raise U.S. Stakes."
DUN'S BUSINESS MONTHLY v.125 Jan. 1985 p.23.

EF 34.   "Japanese Learn to Get Along with
Suspicious U.S. Unions." INTERNATIONAL MANAGEMENT V.38
Aug. 1983 p.3-4.

EF 35.   "Japanese U.S. Plants Go Union." BUSINESS
WEEK Oct 5, 1981 pp.10-11.

EF 36.   "Japan's U.S. Plants Go Union." BUSINESS
WEEK Oct. 5, 1981 pp.70+.

EF 37.   Johnson, R. T., and Ouchi, William G. "Made
In America (Under Japanese Management)." HARVARD
BUSINESS REVIEW v.52 no.5 1974 pp.61-69.

EF 38.   Johnson, R. T. "Success and Failure of
Japanese Subsidiaries in America." COLUMBIA JOURNAL OF
WORLD BUSINESS v.12 no.1 1977 pp.30-37.

EF 39.   Kawata, Makoto. "Making It Work: Japanese
Direct Investment in the United States." JOURNAL OF
JAPANESE TRADE AND INDUSTRY v.3 Jan./Feb. 1984
pp.25-27.

EF 40.   Krisher, Bernard. "Different Kind of
Tiremaker Rolls into Nashville." FORTUNE v.105 Mar. 22,
1982 pp.136-141+.

EF 41.   Krisher, Bernard. "How the Japanese Manage
in the U.S." FORTUNE v.103 June 15, 1981 pp.97-103.

EF 42. Larsen, R. J. "Yamazaki--Another Japanese Heavyweight Enters the U.S. Market." IRON AGE v.224 June 10, 1981 pp.43+.

EF 43. Lincoln, J. R.; Olson, J.; and Hanada, M. "Cultural Orientations and Individual Reactions to Organizations: a Study of Employees of Japanese-Owned Firms." ADMINISTRATIVE SCIENCE QUARTERLY v.26 Mar. 1981 pp.93-115.

EF 44. Lindamood, J. "Left Coast Design." CAR AND DRIVER v.31 Sep. 1985 pp.59-64.

EF 45. Lowell, J. "Raising the Stakes in America." WARD'S AUTO WORLD v.22 July 1986 pp.73-75.

EF 46. Marcial, G. G. "Nomura's 'Must-Heed' List." BUSINESS WEEK June 24, 1985 p.98.

EF 47. "Marshall Urges Japan to Build Autos in U.S." IRON AGE v.223 Sep. 15, 1980 pp.15+.

EF 48. Meadows, E. "Japan Runs into America Inc." FORTUNE v.105 Mar. 22, 1982 pp.56-61.

EF 49. Meagher, "A Japanese Challenge to Fifth Avenue." BARRONS v.63 Oct. 10, 1983 p.63.

EF 50. Minard, L. "Saab, Mercedes, Volvo, BMW, Jaguar, Watch Out!" FORBES Sep. 10, 1984 pp.62+.

EF 51. Miner, S. "Study Finds Japan Ready to Take Over U.S. Supplier Field." AUTOMOTIVE NEWS July 21, 1986 p.3.

EF 52. "Mitsubishi a Japanese Giant's Plans for Growth in the U.S." BUSINESS WEEK July 20, 1981 pp.128-132.

EF 53. "Mitsubishi Revs Up to Go Solo." BUSINESS WEEK May 3, 1982 pp.129+.

EF. Japanese Investments in U.S.

EF 54. "Nippon Electric: Chipping through Silicon Valley." ECONOMIST v. 280 July 4, 1981 pp. 68-69.

EF 55. Novotny, R. "Working for the Japanese." PERSONNEL ADMINISTRATOR v. 29 Feb. 1984 pp. 14+.

EF 56. Parker, S. T. "Look Who's Being Cut Out of Top Jobs in the U. S." IRON AGE v. 224 Aug. 3, 1981 pp. 35+.

EF 57. Pendleton, J. "Will Americans Buy an Ohio Honda? Japan Tests Perceptions of Made in U. S. A. Quality." ADVERTISING AGE v. 54 sec. 2 Aug. 29, 1983 pp. M4-M5+.

EF 58. "The Powerful Lobby that Works for Japan in Washington: Big-name Lawyers, PR Men, and Former Officials Discreetly Argue Tokyo's Case." BUSINESS WEEK pp. 148+ Oct. 17, 1983.

EF 59. Reich, R. B. "Japan, Inc., U. S. A." CURRENT v. 270 Feb. 1985 pp. 36-40.

EF 60. Rice, F. "America's New No. 4 Automaker--Honda." FORTUNE v. 112 Oct. 28, 1985 pp. 30-33.

EF 61. Rice, F. "Moving the Battle to Detroit's Back Yard." FORTUNE v. 109 June 25, 1984 p. 22.

EF 62. Seamonds, J. A. "Is U. S. Honeymoon Over for Japan's Car Makers?" U. S. NEWS AND WORLD REPORT v. 99 Dec. 9, 1985 pp. 82.

EF 63. Sears, Cecil E. "Japanese Real Estate Investments in the United States." URBAN LAND v. 46 Feb. 1987 pp. 6-11.

EF 64. Sease, Douglas R. "New Inroads: Japanese Firms Set up More Factories in U. S., Alarm Some

Americans; They Widen Role in Autos, Even Enter Steelmaking." WALL STREET JOURNAL v.205 Mar. 29, 1985 pp.1+.

EF 65.   Sender, H. "Turmoil in the T-Bond Market." INSTITUTIONAL INVESTOR v.20 Aug. 1986 p.276.

EF 66.   Sethi, S. P., and Swanson, C. "How Japanese Multinationals Skirt Our Civil Rights Laws." BUSINESS AND SOCIETY REVIEW no.44, Winter 1983, pp.46-51.

EF 67.   Sheets, K. R. "Landlords from the Far East." U.S. NEWS AND WORLD REPORT v.100 Apr. 7, 1986 pp.53-54.

EF 68.   Sheler, J. L. "A Tale of Two Worlds in Tennessee." U.S. NEWS AND WORLD REPORT Dec. 20, 1982 pp.84-85.

EF 69.   Smolowe, J. "From Tennessee to Tokyo" NEWSWEEK v.100 Aug. 9, 1982 p.59.

EF 70.   Sorge, M. "Japanese Plants in U.S. Seen Cementing Good Relationship." AUTOMOTIVE NEWS June 16, 1980 pp.44+.

EF 71.   Sorge, M. "Nissan's Southern Strategy." AUTOMOTIVE NEWS Oct. 19, 1981 pp.E-1+.

EF 72.   Stavro, B. "Made in the U.S.A." FORBES v.135 Apr. 22, 1985 pp.50-51.

EF 73.   "Stepping into the Circle." ECONOMIST v.290 Mar. 17, 1984 pp.70+.

EF 74.   "Sumitomo in America: Women Scorned." ECONOMIST v.283 Apr. 24, 1982 pp.95-96.

EF 75.   "Supreme Court to Hear Japanese Job Bias Suit." IRON AGE v.224 Dec. 16, 1981 v.17-18.

EF. Japanese Investments in U.S.

EF 76. Tanzer, A. "The Silicon Valley Greater Co-prosperity Sphere." FORBES v.134 Dec. 17, 1984 pp.31-32.

EF 77. Tanzer, A. "Dollar Shokku." FORBES v.137 Mar. 10, 1986 pp.30-31.

EF 78. Tanzer, A. "Unfriendly Raider." FORBES v.138 Nov. 3, 1986 pp.229-230.

EF 79. "Tokyo on the Hudson." CHEMICAL BUSINESS Jan. 11, 1982 p.5.

EF 80. "Toyota Takes a Foreign Trip with General Motors." ECONOMIST v.286 Feb. 5-11, 1983 pp.65-66.

EF 81. "Toyota's Choice." TIME v.126 Dec. 16, 1985 p.47.

EF 82. Tracy, E. J. "Mazda's Bet on Import Quotas." FORTUNE v.111 Jan. 7, 1985 p.42.

EF 83. Treece, J. B., and Hampton, W. J. "Japan vs. Detroit, Round 2: the Midsize Market." BUSINESS WEEK July 22, 1985 p.65.

EF 84. "U.S. Amada Opens Plant in California." IRON AGE v.224 Nov. 23, 1981 pp.26+.

EF 85. "A U.S. Beachhead for Japanese Fast Food." BUSINESS WEEK July 2, 1979 pp.23-24.

EF 86. "Yankees Out of North America: Foreign Employer Job Discrimination Against American Citizens." MICHIGAN LAW REVIEW v.83 Oct. 1984 pp.237-256.

EG. Japanese Capital Investment;
Investments Overseas

Monographic Works

EG 1.   Hasegawa, Sukehiro. JAPANESE FOREIGN AID,
POLICY AND PRACTICE. New York: Praeger, 1975. 172pp.

EG 2.   Kojima, Kiyoshi. JAPANESE DIRECT FOREIGN
INVESTMENT, A MODEL OF MULTINATIONAL BUSINESS
OPERATIONS. Tokyo: Tuttle, 1978.

EG 3.   Oriental Economist. JAPANESE OVERSEAS
INVESTMENT, 1984-1985: A COMPLETE LISTING BY FIRMS AND
COUNTRIES. Tokyo: Nihonbashi-Hongokuchu, 1984 335pp.

EG 4.   Rix, Alan. JAPAN'S ECONOMIC AID:
POLICY-MAKING AND POLITICS. New York: St. Martin's
Press, 1980. 286pp.

EG 5.   Sekiguchi, Sueo. JAPANESE DIRECT FOREIGN
INVESTMENT. Montclair, N.J.: Allenheld, Osmun, 1979.
133pp.

EG 6.   Tsurumi, Yoshi. THE JAPANESE ARE COMING: A
MULTINATIONAL INTERACTION OF FIRMS AND POLITICS.
Cambridge, Mass.: Ballinger, 1976. 333pp.

EG 7.   Yoshihara, Kunio. JAPANESE INVESTMENT IN
SOUTHEAST ASIA. Honolulu: University of Hawaii Press,
1978. 230pp.

EG 8.   Yoshitomi, Masaru. JAPAN AS CAPITAL EXPORTER
AND THE WORLD ECONOMY. New York: Group of Thirty, 1985.
32pp.

EG. Japanese Capital Export

Articles

EG 9.   Alexander, C. P. "A Global Money Machine."
TIME v.   125 Jan. 14, 1985 pp.48-50.

EG 10.   Araki, Motoaki. "Trends in Japan's Direct
Investment Abroad for Fiscal Year 1983." EXIM REVIEW
v.5 no.2 1985 pp.37-68.

EG 11.   Beauchamp, M. "Close the Door, They're
Coming in the Windows." FORBES v.137 Jan. 27, 1986
p.81+.

EG 12.   Bellanger, S. "Understanding Japanese
Capital Flows." BANKERS MAGAZINE v.169 Sep./Oct. 1986.

EG 13.   Burke, William Maran. "Japan's Entrance
into the International Financial Community." AMERICAN
JOURNAL OF ECONOMICS AND SOCIETY v.23 July 1964
pp.325-335.

EG 14.   Debes, C. et al.   "Japan's Investment Binge
in Southeast Asia." BUSINESS WEEK Nov. 3, 1986
pp.42-43.

EG 15.   Helm, L. "A Strong Yen: the Key that will
open a Closed Market?" BUSINESS WEEK Mar. 10, 1986
pp.45-46.

EG 16.   "Japan Is Buying Its Way into U.S.
University Labs." BUSINESS WEEK Sep. 24, 1984
pp.72-73+.

EG 17.   "Japanese Capital Changes Pace." ECONOMIST
v.300 July 5, 1986 p.66.

EG 18.   "Japan's Direct Investment Overseas
Expands." FUJI BANK BULLETIN v.36 Jan./Feb. 1985
pp.4-11.

EG 19.   "Japan's Ubiquitous Traders have a Finger in Every Pie." ASIAN BUSINESS v.18 July 1982 pp.19-24.

EG 20.   Kawahara, Isao. "Trends in Japan's Direct Investment Abroad for FY 1979." EXIM REVIEW v.2 May 1981 pp.2-19.

EG 21.   Koshiro, Kazutoshi. "How Overseas Investment Affects Employment at Home." ECONOMIC EYE v.3 June 1982 pp.34-36.

EG 22.   Nishikawa, Jun. "Japanese Overseas Investment and Developing Countries." WASEDA ECONOMIC PAPERS v.20 1981 pp.57-80.

EG 23.   O'Donnell, T. "Unhealthy Yen for Loans." FORBES v.128 July 6, 1981 pp.50+.

EG 24.   Osborn, Neil. "Now, the Japanese Attack the World's Financial Markets." EUROMONEY Oct. 1985 pp.76-91.

EG 25.   Ozawa, Terutomo. "Japan's New Resource Diplomacy; Government-backed Group Investment." JOURNAL OF WORLD TRADE LAW v.14 Jan./Feb. 1980 pp.3-13.

EG 26.   Rafferty, Kevin. "Japanese Corporate Finance Goes Global." INSTITUTIONAL INVESTOR v.20 Nov. 1986 pp.289-290+.

EG 27.   Taira, Koji. "Colonialism in Foreign Subsidiaries: Lessons from Japanese Investment in Thailand." ASIAN SURVEY v.20 no.4 1980 pp.373-396.

EG 28.   Thomee, F. "Japanese Yen for Exporting." EUROMONEY June 1981 pp.141-142.

EG 29.   Wise, D. W. "Corporate Debentures and the Internationalization of the Japanese Bond Market." COLUMBIA JOURNAL OF WORLD BUSINESS v.17 Fall 1982 pp.40-46.

EG. Japanese Capital Export

EG 30.   Yamada, Mitsuhiko. "Japan's Direct Overseas Investment and its Impact on Domestic Industry." JOURNAL OF JAPANESE TRADE AND INDUSTRY v.1 Sep. 1982 pp.18-23.

EG 31.   "A Yen for Foreign Investment" ECONOMIST v.300 July 19, 1986 pp.14+.

EH. Japanese Corporations Abroad

Monographic Works

EH 1.   Katano, Hikoji. JAPANESE ENTERPRISES IN ASEAN COUNTRIES: STATISTICAL OUTLOOK. Kobe: Kobe University Press, 1981. 371pp.

EH 2.   Ozawa, Terutomo. MULTINATIONALISM, JAPANESE STYLE THE POLITICAL ECONOMY OF OUTWARD DEPENDENCY. Princeton, N.J.: Princeton University Press, 1979. 289p.

Articles

EH 2a.   Amano, Matt M. "Organizational Changes of a Japanese Firm in America." CALIFORNIA MANAGEMENT REVIEW v.21 Spring 1979 pp.51-59.

EH 3.   Gregory, Gene A. "Japanese Joint Ventures Abroad: Source of Tension." RIVISTA INTERNAZIONALE DI SCIENZE ECONOMICHE E COMMERCIALI v.25 Aug.-Sep. 1978 pp.753-774.

EH 4.   "The Hidden Japanese Weakness: Manufacturing Abroad." INTERNATIONAL MANAGEMENT v.38 July 1983 p.2.

EH 5.   Ichimura, Shinichi. "Japanese Firms in
Asia." JAPANESE ECONOMIC STUDIES v.10 no.1 1981
pp.31-52.

EH 6.   "Japanese Multinationals--Covering the World
with Investment." BUSINESS WEEK June 16, 1980
pp.92-102.

EH 7.   Mino, Hokaji. "Conduct of Japanese
Enterprises Entering Foreign Markets and Their
Communiations with Communities." BUSINESS JAPAN v.27
Sep. 1982 pp.26-29; Oct. 1982 pp.22-27.

EH 8.   Otten, Alan L. "Japanese Firms Press
European Ventures to Help Profits and Deter
Protectionism." WALL STREET JOURNAL v.203 Apr. 16, 1982
p.44.

EH 9.   "Why Japanese Institutions are Going
International." EUROMONEY Mar. 1985 pp.33-75.

EH 10.   Yoshihara, Hideki. "Japanese Multinational
Enterprises; A View from Outside." KOBE ECONOMIC AND
BUSINESS REVIEW v.25 1979 pp.15-35.

EI. Multinational Corporations

Monographic Works

EI 1.   Negandi, Anant R., ed.   FUNCTIONING OF THE
MULTINATIONAL CORPORATION: A GLOBAL COMPARATIVE STUDY.
New York: Pergamon Press, 1980. 294pp.

EI 2.   Tsurumi, Yoshi. MULTINATIONAL MANAGEMENT.
2nd ed. Cambridge, Mass.: Ballinger, 1984. 490pp.

EI. Multinational Corporations

EI 3.   Tsurumi, Yoshi. THE JAPANESE ARE COMING: A
MULTINATIONAL INTERACTION OF FIRMS AND POLITICS.
Cambridge, Mass.: Ballinger, 1976. 333pp.

EI 4.   Yoshino, Michael Y. JAPAN'S MULTINATIONAL
ENTERPRISES. Cambridge, Mass.: Harvard University
Press, 1976. 191pp.

Articles

EI 5.   Flanigan, J. "'Multinational' as We Know It,
Is Obsolete." FORBES v.136 Aug. 26, 1985 pp.30-32.

EI 6.   Gregory, G. "Japan's New Multinationalism:
The Canon Giessen Experience." COLUMBIA JOURNAL OF
WORLD BUSINESS v.11 no.1 1976 pp.122-129.

EI 7.   Negandi, A. R. "Adaptability of American,
European and Japanese Multinational Corporations in
Developing Countries." in Negandi, A. R., ed.
FUNTIONING OF THE MULTINATIONAL CORPORATION: A GLOBAL
COMPARATIVE STUDY. New York: Pergamon Press, 1980.
pp.136-164.   Also, with Baliga, B. R., "Multinationals
in Industrially Developed Countries: A Comparative
Study of American, German and Japanese Multinationals."
pp.117-135.

EI 8.   Ozawa, Terutomo. "Japan's Multinational
Enterprise: The Political Economy of Outward
Dependency." WORLD POLITICS V.30 1977/1978 pp.517-537.

EI 9.   Takamiya, Makoto. "Japanese Multinationals
in Europe: Internal Operations and Their Public Policy
Implications." COLUMBIA JOURNAL OF WORLD BUSINESS v.16
Summer 1981 pp.5-17.

EI 10.   Tsurumi, Yoshi. "Japanese Multinational
Firms." JOURNAL OF WORLD TRADE LAW v.7 no.1 1973
pp.74-90.

EI 11.   Tsurumi, Yoshi. "The Multinational Spread of Japanese Firms and Asian Neighbors' Reactions." in Apter, D., and Goodman, L., eds.   THE MULTINATIONAL CORPORATIONS AND SOCIAL CHANGE. New York: Praeger, 1976. pp. 118-147.

EI 12.   Yamazaki, K.; Kobayashi N.; and Doi, T. "Toward Japanese-Type Multinational Corporations." JAPANESE ECONOMIC STUDIES v. 5 no. 4 1977 pp. 41-70.

EI 13.   Yoshihara, Hideki. "The Japanese Multinational." LONG RANGE PLANNING v. 10 no. 2 1977 pp. 41-45.

IX.

CHAPTER 6

F. LABOR, EMPLOYMENT, SOCIAL POLICY, WOMEN

FA. General Works; Background

Monographic Works

FA 1.   Abegglen, James C. THE JAPANESE FACTORY:
ASPECTS OF ITS SOCIAL ORGANIZATION. Rev. ed.   Tokyo: C.
E. Tuttle, 1986. 200pp.

FA 2.   Abegglen James C. MANAGEMENT AND WORKER: THE
JAPANESE SOLUTION. Tokyo: Kodansha International, 1973.
200pp.

FA 3.   Ballon, Robert J., ed.   THE JAPANESE
EMPLOYEE. Tokyo: Sophia University Press, 1969. 317pp.

FA 4.   Ballon, Robert J., and Inohara, Hideo.
JAPANESE LABOR TERMS. Bulletin--Sophia University
Socio-Economic Institute, no.21.   Tokyo: Sophia
University Press, 1970. 49pp.

FA. General Works; Background

FA 5.   Farley, Miriam Southwell. ASPECTS OF JAPAN'S
LABOUR PROBLEMS. New York: John & Day, 1950. 263pp.

FA 6.   Harada, Shuichi. LABOUR CONDITIONS IN JAPAN.
New York: Columbia University Press, 1928. 293pp.

FA 7.   Nakayama, Ichiro. INDUSTRIALIZATION AND
LABOR-MANAGEMENT RELATIONS IN JAPAN. Mouer, Ross E.,
trans.   Tokyo: Japan Institute of Labor, 1975. 415pp.

FA 8.   Ueda, Teijiro. THE GROWTH OF POPULATION AND
OCCUPATIONAL CHANGES IN JAPAN: 1920-1935. Tokyo:
Institute of Pacific Relations, 1936. 16pp.

Articles

FA 9.   Abegglen, James C. "Subordination and
Autonomy: Attitudes of Japanese Workers." AMERICAN
JOURNAL OF SOCIOLOGY v.63 1957 pp.181-189.

FA 10.   Gleason, Alan Harold. "Chronic
Underemployment: A Comparison Between Japan and the
United States." ANNALS OF THE HITOTSUBASHI ACADEMY v.10
Aug. 1959 pp.64-80.

FA 11.   Ibe, Kyonosuke. "It Took the Japanese to
Build Japan." BUSINESS WEEK Oct. 6, 1980 pp.17-18.

FA 12.   Ishida, Hideto. "Japanese-Style Human
Resource Management: Can It Be Exported?" SUMITOMO
QUARTERLY v.5 1981 pp.15-18.

FA 13.   Komiya, Ryutaro, and Uchida, Tadao. "The
Labour Coefficient and the Size of Establishment in Two
Japanese Industries." in Barna, T., ed.   STRUCTURAL
INTERDEPENDENCE AND ECONOMIC DEVELOPMENT London:
Macmillan, 1963. pp.265-276.

FA 14.   Levine, Solomon B. "The Labor Movement and
Economic Development in Japan." INDUSTRIAL RELATIONS
RESEARCH ASSOCIATION PROCEEDINGS v.7 Dec. 1954
pp.48-59.

FA 15.   Maguire, Mary Ann, and Kloliczak, Alice.
"Attitudes of Japanese and American Workers;
Convergence on Diversity." THE SOCIOLOGICAL QUARTERLY
v.24 Winter 1983 pp.107-122.

FA 16.   Okita, Saburo. "Manpower Policy in Japan."
INTERNATIONAL LABOR REVIEW v.88 July 1964 pp.45-58.

FA 17.   "Role of Labor in Japan's Economic Growth."
SUMITOMO QUARTERLY Mar. 1982 pp.1-6. (Interview with
Takao Sasaki director of the Socio-Economic Policy
Research Institute)

FA 18.   Takezawa, S. "The Quality of Working Life:
Trends in Japan." LABOUR AND SOCIETY v.1 1976
pp.29-48.

FA 19.   Tsuda, Masumi. "The Formation and
Characteristics of the Work Group in Japan." in
International Conference on Business History (4th;
1977; Fuji Education Center). LABOR AND MANAGEMENT:
PROCEEDINGS OF THE FOURTH FUJI CONFERENCE. Tokyo:
University of Tokyo Press. 1979. pp.29-42.

FA 20.   Watanabe, Tsunehiko. "Price Changes and the
Rate of Change of Money Wage Earnings in Japan:
1955-1962." QUARTERLY JOURNAL OF ECONOMICS v.80 Feb.
1966 pp.31-47.

FA 21.   Whitehill, Arthur M. "Cultural Values and
Employee Attitudes: United States and Japan." JOURNAL
OF APPLIED PSYCHOLOGY v.48 no.1 1964 pp.69-72.

FB. Social Policy

Monographic Works

FB 1.   Emi, Koichi.   ESSAYS, ON THE SERVICE
INDUSTRY AND SOCIAL SECURITY IN JAPAN. Tokyo:
Kinokuniya Book-Store Co., 1978. 186pp.

FB 2.   Takezawa, Shinichi, et al.   IMPROVEMENTS IN
THE QUALITY OF WORKING LIFE IN THREE JAPANESE
INDUSTRIES. Geneva: International Labour Office, 1982.
175pp.

Articles

FB 3.   "Aging Work Force Strains Japan's
Traditions." BUSINESS WEEK Apr. 20, 1981 pp.72+.

FB 4.   Fisher, Paul. "Major Social Security Issues:
Japan 1972. SOCIAL SECURITY BULLETIN v.36 Mar. 1973
pp.26-38.

FB 5.   Ishida, Hideto. "Japanese Workers and the
Quality of Working Life." SUMITOMO QUARTERLY v.4 1980
pp.15-18.

FB 6.   Kotaka, Yasuo. "Opinions of the Japanese
Top Company Executives on the social Conditions Closely
Relating to the Long-Range Development of Business and
Industry." KEIO BUSINESS REVIEW v.1 1962 pp.23-47.

FB 7.   Martin, Linda G. "Japanese Response to an
Aging Labor Force." POPULATION RESEARCH AND POLICY
REVIEW v.1 Jan. 1982 pp.19-41.

FB 8. Noguchi, Yukio. "Problems of Public Pensions in Japan." HITOTSUBASHI JOURNAL OF ECONOMICS v. 24 June 1983 pp. 43-68.

FB 9. Norbeck, Edward, and Befu, Harami. "Religion and Society in Modern Japan: Continuity and Change." RICE UNIVERSITY STUDIES v. 56 no. 1 1970.

FB 10. Ozawa, Martha N. "Social Security Reform in Japan." SOCIAL SERVICE REVIEW v. 59 Sep. 1985 pp. 476-495.

FB 11. Seki, H. "Employment Problems and Policies in an Ageing Society: the Japanese Experience." INTERNATIONAL LABOUR REVIEW v. 119 May/June 1980 pp. 351-65.

FB 12. "Social Problems." BUSINESS WEEK Dec. 14, 1981 pp. 116-120.

FC. Employment; Labor Market

Monographic Works

FC 1. EMPLOYMENT AND EMPLOYMENT POLICY. Japanese Industrial Relations Series; 1. Tokyo: Japan Institute of Labour, 1979. 28pp.

FC 2. Organization for Economic Cooperation and Development. MANPOWER POLICY IN JAPAN. Paris: OECD, 1973. 183pp.

FC 3. Shimada, Haruo. THE JAPANESE EMPLOYMENT SYSTEM. Tokyo: Japan Institute of Labour, 1980. 36pp.

FC. Employment; Labor Market

FC 4.   Taira, Koji. ECONOMIC DEVELOPMENT & THE
LABOR MARKET IN JAPAN. Studies of the East Asian
Institute Series. New York: Columbia University Press,
1970. 282pp.

FC 5.   Woronoff, Jon. JAPAN'S WASTED WORKERS.
Totowa, N.J.: Allanheld, Osmun, 1983. 296pp.

Articles

FC 6.   Alm, Richard. "America vs.   Japan: Can U.S.
Workers Compete?" U.S. NEWS AND WORLD REPORT v.99 Sep.
2, 1985 pp.40-45.

FC 7.   Antom, A. F. "Corporate Careers with
Japanese Companies in the U.S." CREATIVE COMPUTING v.10
Aug. 1984 pp.152-160.

FC 8.   Bednarzik, R. W. "The Impact of
Microelectronics on Employment: Japan's Experience."
MONTHLY LABOR REVIEW v.108 Sep. 1985 pp.45-48.

FC 9.   Cole, Robert E. "Functional Alternatives and
Economic Development: An Empirical Example of Permanent
Employment in Japan." AMERICAN SOCIOLOGICAL REVIEW v.38
1973 pp.424-438.

FC 10.   Cole, Robert E. "Late-Developer
Hypothesis: An Evaluation of Its Relevance for Japanese
Employment Practices." JOURNAL OF JAPANESE STUDIES v.4
no.2 1978 pp.247-265.

FC 11.   Cole, Robert E. "Permanent Employment in
Japan: Facts and Fantasies." INTERNATIONAL LABOR
RELATIONS REVIEW v.26 1972 pp.615-630.

FC 12. Cole, Robert E. "The Theory of Institutionalization: Permanent Employment and Tradition in Japan." ECONOMIC DEVELOPMENT AND CULTURAL CHANGE v. 20 no. 1 1971 pp. 47-70.

FC 13. Crawcour, S. "The Japanese Employment System" JOURNAL OF JAPANESE STUDIES v. 4 no. 2 1978 pp. 225-245.

FC 14. "The Greying of Japan." INTERNATIONAL MANAGEMENT v. 37 June 1982 pp. 26-28.

FC 15. Haitani, Kanji. "Changing Characteristics of the Japanese Employment System." ASIAN SURVEY v. 8 1978 pp. 1029-1045.

FC 16. Hamada, Koichi, and Kurosaka, Yoshiro. "The Relationship Between Production and Unemployment in Japan: Okun's Law in Comparative Perspective." EUROPEAN ECONOMIC REVIEW v. 25 June 1984 pp. 71-94.

FC 17. Hanami, T. "The Lifetime Employment System in Japan: Its Reality and Future." ATLANTA ECONOMIC REVIEW v. 26 no. 3 1976 pp. 35-39.

FC 18. Hashimoto, Masanori. "Bonus Payments, On-the-Job Training, and Lifetime Employment in Japan." JOURNAL OF POLITICAL ECONOMY v. 87 no. 5 1979 pp. 1086-1104.

FC 19. Jacoby, Sanford. "The Origins of Internal Labor Markets in Japan." INDUSTRIAL RELATIONS v. 18 Spring 1979 pp. 184-196

FC 20. Koike, Kazuo. "Japanese Workers in Large Firms." KEIZAI KAGAKU v. 26 1978 pp. 1-37.

FC 21. McClenahen, J. S. "Japan Readjusts Its Employment Emphasis." INDUSTRY WEEK v. 207 Dec. 8, 1980 p. 33-34.

FC. Employment; Labor Market

FC 22. Marsh, Robert M., and Mannari, Hiroshi. "A New Look at 'Lifetime Commitment' in Japanese Industry." ECONOMIC DEVELOPMENT AND CULTURAL CHANGE v. 20 1972 pp. 611-630.

FC 23. Masamura, Kimihiro, and Amakasu, Keisuke. "Jobs and High Technology: (1) Minimizing High Tech's Adverse Effects" (2) Maximizing High Tech's Favorable Effects." ECONOMIC EYE v. 5 June 1984 pp. 27-32.

FC 24. Metz, Edmund J. "Job Security: the Quality of Worklife Issue." MANAGERIAL PLANNING v. 31 Sep./Oct. 1982 pp. 4-9.

FC 25. Mosk, Carl, and Nakata, Yoshi-Iumi. "The Age-Wage Profile and Structural Change in the Japanese Labor Market for Males, 1964-1982." JOURNAL OF HUMAN RESOURCES v. 20 Winter 1985 pp. 100-116.

FC 26. Ogawa, N. "Economic Implications of Japan's Aging Population: a Macro-Economic Demographic Modelling Approach." INTERNATIONAL LABOUR REVIEW v. 121 Jan./Feb. 1982 pp. 17-33.

FC 27. Ozawa, Terutomo. "Japanese World of Work: An Interpretive Survey." MSU BUSINESS TOPICS v. 28 Spring 1980 pp. 45-55.

FC 28. Pucik, V. "Lifetime Employment in Japan--An Alternative to the 'Culture-Structure' Causal Model." JOURNAL OF INTERNATIONAL AFFAIRS v. 33 no. 1 1979 pp. 158-161.

FC 29. Rohlen, Thomas P. "Permanent Employment Faces Recession, Slow Growth and an Ageing Workforce." JOURNAL OF JAPANESE STUDIES v. 5 no. 2 1979 pp. 235-272.

FC 30. Shimada, Haruo. "International Trade and Labour Market Adjustment; the Case of Japan." ECONOMIA & LAVORO v. 19 Sep. 1985 pp. 3-30.

FC 31.   Shimada, Haruo. "The Japanese Labor Market after the Oil Crisis: A Factual Report (I)." KEIO ECONOMIC STUDIES v.14 1977 pp.49-65.

FC 32.   Shunzo, Nitta. "Japanese Industry Enters a New Stage; Increasingly Knowledge Intensive Industrial Structure and Changes in Employment Structure." ECONOMIC AND INDUSTRIAL DEMOCRACY v.6 May 1985 pp.139-160.

FC 33.   Smith, C. "The 'Job-for-life' Illusion." WORLD PRESS REVIEW v.33 Feb. 1986 p.50.

FC 34.   Sorge, M. "Paradise Lost? Japan Labor Outlook is Rocky." AUTOMOTIVE NEWS Sep. 1, 1980 pp.E8+.

FC 35.   Taira, Koji. "The Characteristics of Japanese Labor Markets." ECONOMIC DEVELOPMENT AND CULTURAL CHANGE v.10 no.2 1962 pp.150-168.

FC 36.   Taira, Koji. "Industrial Policy and Employment in Japan." CURRENT HISTORY v.82 Nov. 1983 pp.362-65+.

FC 37.   Taira, Koji. "Japan's Low Unemployment: Economic Miracle or Statistical Artifact?" MONTHLY LABOR REVIEW vol.106 July 1983 pp.3-10.

FC 38.   Taira, Koji. "The Labor Market in Japanese Employment." BRITISH JOURNAL OF INDUSTRIAL RELATIONS v.2 July 1964 pp.212+.

FC 39.   Tanaka, F. J. "Lifetime Employment in Japan." CHALLENGE v.24 July/Aug. 1981 pp.23-29.

FC 40.   Tominaga, Kenichi. "Occupational Mobility in Japanese Society: Analysis of Labor Market in Japan." THE JOURNAL OF ECONOMIC BEHAVIOR AND ORGANIZATION v.2 no.2 1962 pp.1-37.

FC. Employment; Labor Market

FC 41.   Valery, N. "Hire and Fire." ECONOMIST v.288
Jul. 9-15, 1983 pp.14+.

FC 42.   Yashiro, Naohiro. "The Economic Rationality
of Japanese-style Employment Practices." ECONOMIC EYE
v.2 Mar. 1981 pp.21-24.

FC 43.   Zager, Robert. "Managing Guaranteed
Employment." HARVARD BUSINESS REVIEW v.56 May/June 1978
pp.105-115.

FD. Salaries, Wages

Monographic Works

FD 1.   Ballon, Robert J. JAPAN'S BASIC SALARY.
Bulletin--Sophia University Socio-Economic Institute,
no.40. Tokyo: Sophia University Press, 1972. 18pp.

FD 2.   Ballon, Robert J. JAPAN'S LIFELONG
REMUNERATION SYSTEM. Bulletin--Sophia University
Socio-Economic Institute, no.16. Tokyo, Sophia
University Press, 1968. 49pp.

FD 3.   Ballon, Robert J. JAPAN'S LIFE-TIME SALARY
SYSTEM. Bulletin--Sophia University Socio-Economic
Institute, no 11. Tokyo: Sophia University Press,
1966. 41pp.

FD 4.   Ballon, Robert J. JAPAN'S SALARY SYSTEM, THE
BASIC SALARY. Bulletin--Sophia University
Socio-Economic Institute, no.55. Tokyo: Sophia
University Press, 1975. 22p.

FD 5.   Ballon, Robert J. JAPAN'S SALARY SYSTEM, THE BONUS. Bulletin--Sophia University Socio-Economic Institute, no.57. Tokyo: Sophia University Press, 1975. 24pp.

FD 6.   Ballon, Robert J. JAPAN'S SALARY SYSTEM, MONTHLY ALLOWANCES. Bulletin--Sophia University Socio-Economic Institute, no.58. Tokyo: Sophia University Press, 1975. 25pp.

Articles

FD 7.   Alston, Jon P. "Awarding Bonuses the Japanese Way." BUSINESS HORIZONS v.25 Sep./Oct. 1982 pp.46-50.

FD 8.   Doi, Noriyuki. "Industrial Concentration And Employee Compensation; Some Evidence from Japan." RIVISTA INTERNAZIONALE DI SCIENZE ECONOMICHE E COMMERIALE v.31 Sep. 1984 pp.844-857.

FD 9.   Hashimoto, Masanori, and Raisian, John. "Employment Tenure and Earning Profiles in Japan and the United States." AMERICAN ECONOMIC REVIEW v.74 Sep. 1985 pp.721-735.

FD 10.   Hotani, Rokuro, and Hayashi, Takashi. "The Evolution of Wage Structure in Japan." INDUSTRIAL AND LABOR RELATIONS REVIEW v.25 Oct. 1961 pp.52-66.

FD 11.   "Japanese Wages: the Militancy of the Orient." ECONOMIST v.279 Apr. 25, 1981 pp.78+.

FD 12.   Kaido, Susumu. "Wages in Japan." INTERNATIONAL CONGRESS OF ORIENTALISTS v.5 1963 pp.466-471.

FD. Salaries, Wages

FD 13. Kamata, S. "Employee Welfare Takes a Back Seat at Toyota: Reflections from a Japanese Assembly Line." BUSINESS AND SOCIETY REVIEW no. 46 Summer 1983 pp. 26-31.

FD 14. Magota, R. "The End of the Seniority-Related (Nenko) Wage System." JAPANESE ECONOMIC STUDIES v. 7 no. 3 1979 pp. 71-125.

FD 15. Montgomery, Edward. "Income Security and Economic Growth." JOURNAL OF CONTEMPORARY STUDIES v. 7 Fall 1984 pp. 79-102, (Compares U.S., Japan, Sweden)

FD 16. "Salary Workers: Survey of Average Worker." BUSINESS JAPAN v. 28 Feb. 1983 pp. 14-15.

FD 17. Taira, Koji. "Japanese 'Enterprise Union' and Interfirm Wage Structure." INDUSTRIAL AND LABOR RELATIONS REVIEW v. 15 Oct. 1961 pp. 33-51.

FD 18. Taira, Koji. "Market Forces and Public Power in Wage Determination: Early Japanese Experience." SOCIAL RESEARCH v. 30 Winter 1963 pp. 434-457.

FD 19. Wood, R. C. "Japan's Multitier Wage System." FORBES v. 126 Aug. 18, 1980 pp. 53+.

FD 20. Yamamura, Kozo. "An Observation on the Post-War Japanese Anti-Monopoly Policy." INDIAN JOURNAL OF ECONOMICS v. 45 no. 176 July 1964 pp. 31-68.

FE. Prices

Articles

FE 1. Agmon, T. "Country Risk: the Significance of the Country Factor for Share-Price Movements in the

United Kingdom, Germany and Japan." JOURNAL OF BUSINESS v. 46 Jan. 1973 pp. 24-32.

FE 2. "Analysis of Price Comparisons in Japan and the United States." ECONOMIC BULLETIN (Tokyo) v. 13 Sep. 1963 pp. 1-18.

FE 3. Greenhut, M. L. "Spatial Pricing in the United States, West Germany and Japan." ECONOMICA v. 4 no. 189 Feb. 1981 pp. 79-86.

FE 4. Kogiku, Kiichiro. "Inflation and Price Stability." in KODANSHA ENCYCLOPEDIA OF JAPAN (see item A 28) v. 3 pp. 303.

FE 5. Kurebashi, S. "The Problem of Prices." POLITICO (Pavia) v. 32 June 1967 pp. 389-395.

FE 6. Miyazawa, Kenichi. "Input-Output Analysis." in KODANSHA ENCYCLOPEDIA (See Item A 28) v. 3 pp. 312-313.

FE 7. Moore, Geoffrey H., and Cullity, John P. "Trends and Cycles in Productivitiy, Unit Costs, and Prices; An International Perspective." in Moore, Geoffrey H., ed. BUSINESS CYCLES, INFLATION, AND FORECASTING. 2nd ed. Cambridge, Mass.: Ballinger, 1983. pp. 245-280.

FE 8. Nakao, Takeo. "Application of Duesenberry's Model to the Growth in Stocks of Consumer Durable Goods in Japan." REVIEW OF ECONOMICS AND STATISTICS v. 60 Feb. 1978 pp. 33-38.

FE 9. Otani, I. "Some Empirical Evidence on the Determinants of Wage and Price Movements in Japan, 1950-1973." INTERNATIONAL MONETARY FUND STAFF PAPERS v. 22 July 1975 pp. 469-493.

FE 10. Shimomura, O. "Consumer Price Problems." ORIENTAL ECONOMIST v. 31 Nov. 1963 pp. 617-625; and Dec. 1963 pp. 674-680.

FE 11.   Shinjo, Koji. "Business Pricing Policies
and Inflation: The Japanese Case." REVIEW OF ECONOMICS
AND STATISTICS v.59 Nov. 1977 pp.447-455.

FE 12.   Shirai, T. "Prices and Wages in Japan:
Towards an Anti-Inflationary Policy?" INTERNATIONAL
LABOR REVIEW v.103 Mar. 1971 pp.227-246.

FE 13.   Suruga, Terukazu.   "Consumption Patterns
and Price Indices of Yearly Income Quintile Groups: The
Case of Japan 1963-1976." ECONOMIC STUDIES QUARTERLY
v.31 Apr. 1980 pp.23-32.

FE 14.   Toyoda, T. "Price Expectations and the
Short-Run and Long-Run Phillips Curves in Japan,
1956-1968." REVIEW OF ECONOMICS AND STATISTICS v.54
Aug. 1972 pp.267-274.

FE 15.   Tsuchiya, Keizo. "Agricultural Prices and
Diversification in Japan." PHILIPPINE ECONOMIC JOURNAL
v.14 no.1-2 1975 pp.295-299.

FE 16.   Tsurumi, Yoshi. "The Case of Japan: Price
Bargaining and Controls on Oil Products." JOURNAL OF
COMPARATIVE ECONOMICS June 1978 pp.126-143.

FE 17.   Watanabe, T. "Price Changes and the Rate of
Change of Money Wage Earnings in Japan 1955-1962."
QUARTERLY JOURNAL OF ECONOMICS v.80 Feb. 1966
pp.31-47.

FE 18.   Yoshihara, Kunio; Furuya, Kenichi; and
Suzuki, Takao. "The Problem of Accounting for
Productivity Change in the Construction Price Index."
JOURNAL OF THE AMERICAN STATISTICAL ASSOCIATION v.66
Mar. 1971 pp.33-41.

FF. Labor Unions, Laboring Classes

Monographic Works

FF 1.   Ayukawa, Iwao F. A HISTORY OF LABOR IN
MODERN JAPAN. Honolulu: East-West Center Press, 1966.
406pp.

FF 2.   Ballon, Robert J. THE JAPANESE LABOR
MOVEMENT (1957-1960). Bulletin--Sophia University
Socio-Economic Institute, no.2. Tokyo: Sophia
University Press, 1960. 37pp.

FF 3.   Cole, Robert E. JAPANESE BLUE COLLAR: THE
CHANGING TRADITION. Berkeley: University of California,
1971. 300pp.

FF 4.   Cook, Alice H. AN INTRODUCTION TO JAPANESE
TRADE UNIONISM. Ithaca, N.Y.: Cornell University Press,
1966. 216pp.

FF 5.   Cook, Alice H. JAPANESE TRADE UNIONISM. New
York: New York State School of Industrial Relations,
Cornell University, 1965. 216pp.

FF 6.   Gordon, Andrew. THE EVOLUTION OF LABOR
RELATIONS IN JAPAN: HEAVY INDUSTRY, 1853-1955.
Cambridge, Mass.: Harvard University Press, 1985.
524pp.

FF 7.   LABOR AND THE ECONOMY ILLUSTRATED. Japanese
Industrial Relations Series; 4. Tokyo: Japan Institute
of Labour, 1980. 28pp.

FF 8.   Large, Stephen S. THE RISE OF LABOR IN
JAPAN: THE YUAIKAI 1912-19. Tokyo: Sophia University
Press, 1972.

FF. Labor Unions, Laboring Classes

FF 9. Okochi, Kazuo. LABOR IN MODERN JAPAN. Tokyo: Science Council of Japan., 1958. 117pp.

Articles

FF 10. Ishikawa, Akihiro. "Japanese Trade-Unionism in a Changing Environment." INTERNATIONAL SOCIAL SCIENCE JOURNAL v.36 no.2 1984 pp.271-281.

FF 11. "A New Force in Japanese Organized Labor: Interview with Toshifumi Tateyama, Chairman of JPTUC äJapanese Private Sector Trade Union Councilä." JOURNAL OF JAPANESE TRADE AND INDUSTRY v.3 Nov./Dec. 1984 pp.36-38.

FF 12. "A Spark of Militancy in the Land of Loyalty." BUSINESS WEEK Sept. 5, 1983 pp.96+.

FF 13. Takezawa, S. "The Blue Collar Worker in Japanese Industry." INTERNATIONAL JOURNAL OF COMPARATIVE SOCIOLOGY v.10 1969 pp.178-193.

FF 14. Treece, J. B. "How a Powerless Work Force Sharpens Industry's Edge." BUSINESS WEEK Apr. 15, 1985 p.35.

FF 15. Tsuda, Masumi. "Class Consciousness of Japanese Workers." RIVISTA INTERNAZIONALE DI SCIENZE ECONOMICHE E COMMERICIALI v.29 Dec. 1982 pp.1169-81. Also in HITOTSUBASHI JOURNAL OF SOCIAL STUDIES v.16 Apr. 1984 pp.5-18.

FF 16. Tung, Rosalie L. "Human Resource Planning in Japanese Multinationals: A Model for U.S. Firms?" JOURNAL OF INTERNATIONAL BUSINESS STUDIES v.15 Fall 1984 pp.139-149.

FG. Human Resources Development, Training

Monographic Works

FG 1.   Amaya, Tadashi. HUMAN RESOURCE DEVELOPMENT
IN INDUSTRY. Japanese Industrial Relations Series; 10.
Tokyo: Japan Institute of Labour, 1983. 34pp.

FG 2.   Azumi, Koya. HIGHER EDUCATION AND BUSINESS
RECRUITMENT IN JAPAN. New York: Teachers College Press,
Columbia University, 1969. 126pp.

FG 3.   Ishikawa, Toshio. VOCATIONAL TRAINING.
Japanese Industrial Relations Series; 7. Tokyo: Japan
Institute of Labour; 7. 32pp.

FG 4.   Levine, Solomon B., and Kawada, Hisashi.
HUMAN RESOURCES IN JAPANESE INDUSTRIAL DEVELOPMENT.
Princeton, N.J.: Princeton University Press, 1980.
332pp.

FG 5.   Wakabayashi, Mitsuru. MANAGEMENT CAREER
PROGRESS IN A JAPANESE ORGANIZATION. Ann Arbor: UMI
Research Press, 1980. 377pp.

Articles

FG 6.   Clegg, C. "Trip to Japan: a Synergistic
Approach to Managing Human Resources." PERSONNEL
MANAGEMENT v.18 Aug. 1986 pp.35-39.

FG 7.   Gregory, G. "Why Japan's Engineers Lead."
MANAGEMENT TODAY May 1984 pp.50-54.

FG. Human Resources Development

FG 8. Kempner, Thomas. "Education for Management in Five Countries: Myth and Reality." JOURNAL OF GENERAL MANAGEMENT v.9 Winter 1983-1984 pp.5-23.

FG 9. Koike, Kazua. "The Formation of Worker Skill in Small Japanese Firms." JAPANESE ECONOMIC STUDIES v.11 Summer 1983 v.3-57.

FG 10. Rehder, R. R. "Education and Training: Have the Japanese Beaten Us Again?" PERSONNEL JOURNAL v.62 Jan. 1983 pp.42-7.

FG 11. Rohlen, Thomas P. "Sponsorship of Cultural Continuity in Japan: a Company Training Program." JOURNAL OF ASIAN AND AFRICAN STUDIES v.5 1970 pp.184-192.

FG 12. Sekiguchi, Shiro. "How Japanese Business Treats Its Older Workers." MANAGEMENT REVIEW v.69 Oct. 1980 pp.15-18.

FG 13. Tanaka, Hiroshi. "The Japanese Method of Preparing Today's Graduate to Become Tomorrow's Manager." PERSONNEL JOURNAL v.59 Feb. 1980 pp.109-112.

FG 14. Tanaka, H. "New Employee Education in Japan." PERSONNEL JOURNAL v.60 Jan. 1981 pp.51-52.

FH. Industrial Relations

Monographic Works

FH 1. Ballon, Robert J. JAPANESE-LIKE INDUSTRIAL RELATIONS. Bulletin--Sophia University Socio-Economic Institute, no. 48. Tokyo: Sophia University Press, 1973. 25pp.

FH 2.   Cole, Robert E. WORK, MOBILITY, AND
PARTICIPATION: A COMPARATIVE STUDY OF AMERICAN AND
JAPANESE INDUSTRY. Berkeley: University of California,
1979. 293pp.

FH 3.   Dore, Ronald Phillips. BRITISH FACTORY,
JAPANESE FACTORY; THE ORIGINS OF NATIONAL DIVERSITY IN
INDUSTRIAL RELATIONS. Berkeley: University of
California Press, 1973. 432pp.

FH 4.   Fujita, Yoshitaka. EMPLOYEE BENEFITS AND
INDUSTRIAL RELATIONS. Japanese Industrial Relations
Series; 12. Tokyo: Japan Institute of Labour, 1984.
48pp.

FH 5.   Hanami, Tadashi. LABOR RELATIONS IN JAPAN
TODAY. Tokyo: Kodansha International; dist.   by Harper
and Row, 1979. 253pp.

FH 6.   INDUSTRIAL SAFETY AND HEALTH. Japan
Industrial Relations Series; 9. Tokyo: Japan Institute
of Labour, 1982. 32pp.

FH 7.   Japan. Institute of Labour. LABOR UNIONS AND
LABOR-MANAGEMENT RELATIONS. Tokyo, 1979. 40pp.

FH 8.   Japanese National Commission for Unesco,
ed.   HISTORY OF INDUSTRIAL EDUCATION IN JAPAN
1868-1900. Tokyo: The Commission, 1959. 197pp. 429pp.

FH 9.   Levine, Solomon B. INDUSTRIAL RELATIONS IN
POSTWAR JAPAN. Urbana, Ill.: University of Illinois
Press, 1958. 200pp.

FH 100.   Odaka, Kunio. TOWARD INDUSTRIAL DEMOCRACY:
MANAGEMENT AND THE WORKERS IN MODERN JAPAN. East Asian
Monographs: No. 80. Cambridge, Mass.: Harvard
University Press, 1975. 270pp.

FH. Industrial Relations

FH 11.   Okochi, Kazuo; Karsh, Bernard; Levine,
Solomon B., eds.   WORKERS AND EMPLOYERS IN JAPAN: THE
JAPANESE EMPLOYMENT RELATIONS SYSTEM. Princeton, N.J.:
Princeton University Press, 1974, c1973.   538pp.

FH 12.   Organization for Economic Cooperation and
Development. THE DEVELOPMENT OF INDUSTRIAL RELATIONS
SYSTEMS: SOME IMPLICATIONS OF THE JAPANESE EXPERIENCE.
Paris: OECD, 1977. 53pp.

FH 13.   Shirai, Taishiro. CONTEMPORARY INDUSTRIAL
RELATIONS IN JAPAN. Madison: University of Wisconsin
Press, 1983. 421pp.

FH 14.   Sugimoto, Yoshio.; Shimada, Haruo; and
Levine, S. B. INDUSTRIAL RELATIONS IN JAPAN. Melbourne:
Japanese Studies Center, 1982. 57pp.

FH 15.   Whitehill, Arthur M., and Takezawa,
Shinichi. CULTURAL VALUES IN MANAGEMENT--WORKER
RELATIONS. Chapel Hill, N.C.: University of North
Carolina, 1961. 113pp.

FH 16.   Whitehill, Arthur M., and Takezawa,
Shinichi. THE OTHER WORKER: A COMPARATIVE STUDY OF
INDUSTRIAL RELATIONS IN THE UNITED STATES AND JAPAN.
Honolulu: East-West Center Press, 1968.

FH 17.   Whitehill, Arthur M., and Takezawa,
Shinichi. WORK WAYS: JAPAN AND AMERICA. Tokyo: Japan
Institute of Labor, 1982. 230pp.

Articles

FH 18.   Aonuma, Yoshimatsu. "Japanese Explains
Japan's Business Style." ACROSS THE BOARD v.18 Feb.
1981 pp.41-50.

FH 19.   Bernstein, J. "Japanese Successes are
Analyzed." AUTOMOTIVE NEWS Apr. 6, 1981 p. 23.

FH 20.   Bowman, J. S. "The Rising Sun in America."
PERSONNEL ADMINISTRATOR v. 31 Sep. 1986 pp. 63-67+; and
Oct. 1986 pp. 81-84+.

FH 21.   Chokki, T. "Labor Management in the Cotton
Spinning Industry." in International Conference On
Business History (4th: 1977: Fuji Education Center.
LABOUR AND MANAGEMENT: PROCEEDINGS OF THE FOURTH FUJI
CONFERENCE. Tokyo: University of Tokyo Press, 1979.
pp. 145-167.

FH 22.   Chung, K. H. and Gray, M. A. "Can We Adopt
the Japanese Methods of Human Resource Management?"
PERSONNEL ADMINISTRATOR v. 27 May 1982 pp. 41-46+.

FH 23.   Crawcour, S., and Hata, H. "Japanese Labour
Relations." in Drysdale, P., and Kitaoji, H., eds.,
JAPAN & AUSTRALIA: TWO SOCIETIES AND THEIR INTERACTION.
Canberra: Australian National University Press, 1981.
pp. 236-253.

FH 24.   Daito, E. "Management and Labor: The
Evolution of Employer--Employee Relations in the Course
of Industrial Development." in International Conference
On Business History (4th: 1977: Fuji Education Center.
LABOUR AND MANAGEMENT: PROCEEDINGS OF THE FOURTH FUJI
CONFERENCE. Tokyo: University of Tokyo Press, 1979.
pp. 1-25.

FH 25.   Dore, Ronald Phillips. "Commitment--For
What, by Whom and Why." in Asian Regional Conference on
Industrial Relations (Tokyo, Japan, 1971). THE SOCIAL
AND CULTURAL BACKGROUND OF LABOR--MANAGMENT RELATIONS
IN ASIAN COUNTRIES. Tokyo: Japan Institute of Labor,
1972. pp. 106-126.

FH. Industrial Relations

FH 26.   Evans, R. "Evolution of the Japanese System of Employer--Employee Relations, 1868-1945." BUSINESS HISTORY REVIEW v.44 no.1 1970 pp.110-125.

FH 27.   Hall, B. "Team Play is Key for Mazda Leader." AUTOMOTIVE NEWS Sep. 1, 1980 p.E7-E8.

FH 28.   Hall, J. L., et al.   "Will Your Workers Sing the Company Song?" TRAINING AND DEVELOPMENT JOURNAL v.38 Jul. 1984 pp.68-70.

FH 29.   Hamada, Tomoko. "Wings of Change: Economic Realism and Japanese Labor Management." ASIAN SURVEY v.20 no.4 Apr. 1980 pp.397-406.

FH 30.   Kassalow, E. M. "Japan as an Industrial Relations Model." JOURNAL OF INDUSTRIAL RELATIONS v.25 no.2 1983 pp.201-219.

FH 31.   Khlynov, Vladimir. "How the 'Diamond' is 'Polished' or, the Secret of the Vaunted Japanese Industriousness." NEW TIMES (Moscow) Jan. 1985 pp.20-21.

FH 32.   Kishimoto, Eitaro. "Labour--Management Relations and the Trade Unions in Post-war Japan." THE KYOTO UNIVERSITY ECONOMIC REVIEW v.38 1968 pp.1-35.

FH 33.   Koike, Kazuo. "Japan's Industrial Relations: Characteristics and Problems." JAPANESE ECONOMIC STUDIES v.7 1978 pp.42-90.

FH 34.   "Labor-Management Agreement" BUSINESS JAPAN v.28 May 1983 pp.12-13.   Äre: Nissan Motor Co. Å

FH 35.   Levine, Soloman B. "Changing Strategies of Unions and Management: Evaluation of Four Industrialized Countries." BRITISH JOURNAL OF INDUSTRIAL RELATIONS v.18 no.1 1980 pp.70-81.

FH 36.   Levine, Solomon B. "Industrial Relations in the New Japan." PACIFIC AFFAIRS v. 30 Fall 1957 pp. 209-220.

FH 37.   Levine, Solomon B., and Taira, Koji. "Japanese Industrial Relations--Is One Economic 'Miracle' Enough?" MONTHLY LABOR REVIEW v. 101 Mar. 1978 pp. 31-33.

FH 38.   Nakayama, N. "The Modernization of Industrial Relations in Japan." BRITISH JOURNAL OF INDUSTRIAL RELATIONS v. 3 no. 2 1965 pp. 225-236.

FH 39.   Peredo, S. "Labor Relations--Japanese Style." MACLEAN'S v. 95 Mar. 8, 1982 p. 41.

FH 40.   Raskin, A. H. "Can Management and Labor Really Become Partners?" ACROSS THE BOARD v. 19 July/Aug. 1982 pp. 12-16.

FH 41.   Sakurabayashi, Makoto, and Ballon, Robert J. "Labor-Management Relations in Modern Japan: A Historical Survey of Personnel Administration." in Roggendorf, Joseph, ed. STUDIES IN JAPANESE CULTURE. Tokyo: Sophia University Press, 1963. pp. 245-266.

FH 42.   Schwartz, L. "Laud Japan Worker--Management Rapport." ELECTRONICS NEWS v. 29 July 25, 1983 pp. : supp. N.

FH 43.   Shimada, Haruo. "Japan's Success Story: Looking Behind the Great Legend." CURRENT v. 255 Sep. 1983 pp. 35-42.   Also in TECHNOLOGY REVIEW v. 86 May/June 1983 pp. 46-52.

FH 44.   Sumiyo, M. "The Development of Japanese Labour-Relations." THE DEVELOPING ECONOMIES v. 4 no. 4 1966 pp. 499-515.

FH 45.   Takagi, Ikuro. "Corporate Labor Policies in Flux." ECONOMIC EYE v. 3 Dec. 1982 pp. 16-19.

FH. Industrial Relations

FH 46. Whitehill, Arthur M., and Takezawa, Shinichi. "Workplace Harmony: Another Japanese Miracle?" COLUMBIA JOURNAL OF WORLD BUSINESS v.13 Fall 1978 pp.25-39.

FH 47. Yamamoto, Yoshito. "Employment Adjustments from the Perspective of Labor Law and Labor-Management Relations." JAPANESE ECONOMIC STUDIES v.8 Spring 1980 pp.28-66.

FI. Women

Monographic Works

FI 1. Cook, Alice H., and Hayashi, Hiriko. WORKING WOMEN IN JAPAN: DISCRIMINATION, RESISTANCE AND REFORM. Ithaca, N.Y.: Cornell University Press, 1980. 124pp.

FI 2. Lebra, Takie Sugiyama. JAPANESE WOMEN: CONSTRAINT AND FULFILLMENT. Honolulu: University of Hawaii Press, 1984. 345pp.

FI 3. Robins-Mowry, Dorothy. THE HIDDEN SUN: WOMEN OF MODERN JAPAN. Boulder, Colo.: Westview Press, 1983. 394pp.

FI 4. Trager, James. LETTERS FROM SACHIKO: A JAPANESE WOMAN'S VIEW OF LIFE IN THE LAND OF THE ECONOMIC MIRACLE. New York: Atheneum, 1982. 218pp.

Articles

FI 5. Ahl, David H. "Women's Rights?: Not in Japan." CREATIVE COMPUTING v.10 Aug. 1984 pp.62-64.

FI 6. Anderson, Kathryn H., and Hill, Anne M. "Marriage and Labor Market Discrimination in Japan." SOUTHERN ECONOMIC JOURNAL v.49 Apr. 1983 pp.941-953.

FI 7. Ayakawa, Masako, and Sato, Keiko. "The Growing Female Labor Force: Its Impact on the Japanese Economy." JAPANESE FINANCE AND INDUSTRY Jan./Mar. 1983 pp.36-39.

FI 8. "In Search of Women's Independence." JAPAN QUARTERLY v.29 Sep. 1982 pp.301-323.

FI 9. Koprowski, E. J. "Cultural Myths: Clues to Effective Management." ORGANIZATIONAL DYNAMICS v.12 pp.39-51 Autumn 1983.

FI 10. Lebra, T. S. "Japanese Women in Male Dominant Careers: Cultural Barriers and Accommodations for Sex-Role Transcendence." ETHNOLOGY v.20 Oct. 1981 pp.291-306.

FI 11. Miyamoto, M. "The Underground Warrior." WORKING WOMAN v.7 May 1982 pp.106-108. (Excerpt from A BOOK OF FIVE RINGS).

FI 12. Shimada, Haruo, and Higuchi, Yoshio. "An Analysis of Trends in Female Labor Force Participation in Japan." ECONOMIA & LAVORO v.19 June 1985 pp.3-18.

FI 13. Takeuchi, Hiroshi. "Corporate Management in Japan; Industrial Relations." STUDIA DIPLOMATICA v.36 no.3 1983 pp.223-234.

FI 14. Takeuchi, Hiroshi. "Working Women in Business Corporations: the Management Viewpoint." JAPAN QUARTERLY v.29 July/Sep. 1982 pp.319-23.

CHAPTER 7

G. THE JAPANESE CORPORATE WORLD

GA. General Works

Monographic Works

GA 1.   Hunsburger, Warren S. JAPAN: NEW INDUSTRIAL
GIANT. New York: American-Asian Educational Exchange,
1972. 80pp.

GA 2.   Japan Society. COMPARATIVE INDUSTRIES: JAPAN
AND THE UNITED STATES IN THE 1980s. New York: The
Society, 1980.

GA 3.   Mannari, Hiroshi. THE JAPANESE BUSINESS
LEADERS. Tokyo: University of Tokyo Press, 1974. 291pp.

GA 4.   Sato, Kazuo, and Hoshino, Yasuo, eds.   THE
ANATOMY OF JAPANESE BUSINESS. Armonk, N.Y.: M. E.
Sharpe, 1984. 352pp.

GA. Corporate World

GA 5. Sato, Kazuo, ed. INDUSTRY AND BUSINESS IN JAPAN. White Plains, N.Y.: M.E. Sharpe, 1980. 465pp.

GA 6. Shimizu, Ryuei. THE GROWTH OF FIRMS IN JAPAN. Tokyo: Keio Tsushin, 1980. 233pp.

GA 7. Stokes, Henry Scott. THE JAPANESE COMPETITOR. London: Financial Times, 1976. 251pp.

Articles

GA 8. Abegglen, James C., and Nishimura, Toshiro. "Can Japanese Companies Be Acquired?: (1) Why Japan Mistrusts Mergers; (2) M & A Law in Japan: Rules of the Unplayed Game." MERGERS AND ACQUISITIONS v.17 Winter 1983 pp.16+.

GA 9. Casement R. "Best of Both Worlds." ECONOMIST v.283 June 19/25, 1982 pp.Survey,29-30.

GA 10. "Corporate Mergers are Progressing: Trend Moving Toward Oligopoly." JAPAN ECONOMIC JOURNAL Jan. 3, 1967 p.11.

GA 11. Fruin, W. M. "The Japanese Company Controversy." JOURNAL OF JAPANESE STUDIES v.4 no.2 1978 pp.267-300.

GA 12. "Inc. Special Report: Small Business in Japan." INC. v.4 p.75-88 Nov. 1982.

GA 13. "Japan Corporate Finance." EUROMONEY Sep. 1984 pp.135-176

GA 14. "Japanese Corporate Finance." EUROMONEY Sep. 1983 pp.105-132.

GA 15. "Japanese Industry Survey." ECONOMIST v.280 July 18. 1981 pp.survey 1-29.

GA 16. Kerns, H. "Retailing: Frustrating Foreign Businessmen." FAR EASTERN ECONOMIC REVIEW v.118 Dec. 3-9, 1982 pp.83-85.

GA 17. Kobayashi, S. "The Creative Organization: A Japanese Experiment." PERSONNEL v.47 no.6 1970 pp.8-17.

GA 18. Kuniya, N., and Kobayashi, K. "Current Trends in Organizational Development in Japan." INTERPERSONAL DEVELOPMENT v.5 no.3 1974/1975 pp.136-155.

GA 19. Lee, M. "Business Under Siege." FAR EASTERN ECONOMIC REVIEW v.113 July 24/30, 1981 pp.43-44.

GA 20. Nadler, L. "Beware the Solution on the White Horse." TRAINING AND DEVELOPMENT JOURNAL v.35 May 1981 pp.76-80.

GA 21. Nakamura, Takatoshi. "Japan's Giant Enterprises: Their Power and Influence." JAPANESE ECONOMIC STUDIES v.12 Summer 1984 pp.50-90.

GA 22. Osako, M. "Technology and Social Structure in a Japanese Automobile Factory." SOCIOLOGY OF WORK AND OCCUPATIONS v.4 no.4 1977 pp.397-426.

GA 23. Rapp, William V. "Japan: Its Industrial Policies and Corporate Behavior." COLUMBIA JOURNAL OF WORLD BUSINESS v.12 Spring 1977 pp.17-24.

GA 24. Robbins, S. P. "The Theory Z Organization from a Power-Control Perspective." CALIFORNIA MANAGEMENT REVIEW v.25 no.2 1983 pp.67-75.

GA 25. Takahashi, K., and Kurokawa, Y. "Corporate Bankruptcy Prediction in Japan." JOURNAL OF BANKING AND FINANCE v.8 June 1984 pp.229-247.

GA. Corporate World

GA 26. Thompson, Robert T., Jr. "Labor
Productivity and Employee Relations." BUSINESS AND
ECONOMIC REVIEW v.29 Mar. 1983 pp.33-42.

GA 27. "Top 100 Japanese Companies." ASIAN
BUSINESS v.18 Oct. 1982 pp.42-43.

GA 28. Tsuchiya, M. "Management Organization of
Vertically Integrated Non-Zaibatsu Business." in
International Conference on Business History (1st;
1974; Fuji Ecuation Center). STRATEGY OF BIG BUSINESS:
PROCEEDINGS OF THE FIRST FUJI CONFERENCE. Tokyo:
University of Tokyo Press, 1975. pp.65-78.

GA 29. Tsurumi, Yoshi. "Two Models of Corporation
and International Transfer of Technology." COLUMBIA
JOURNAL OF WORLD BUSINESS v.14 no.2 1979 pp.43-50.

GA 30. Urabe, Kuniyoshi. "The Separation of
Ownership and Management in the Large Corporations in
Japan." ANNALS OF THE SCHOOL OF BUSINESS ADMINISTRATION
KOBE UNIVERSITY no.1 1957 pp.5-19.

GA 31. Weinshall, T. D., and Tawara, J. "The
Managerial Structure of a Nationally Mixed Organization
in Japan: A Sociometric Case Study." ORGANIZATION AND
ADMINISTRATIVE SCIENCES v.8 1977/1978 pp.209-217.

GA 32. Wright, Richard W., and Suzuki, Sadahiko.
"Financial Structure and Bankruptcy Risk in Japanese
Companies." JOURNAL OF INTERNATIONAL BUSINESS STUDIES
v.16 no.1 1985 pp.97-110.

GA 33. Yoshihara, Hideki. "Research on Japan's
General Trading Firms: An Overview." JAPANESE ECONOMIC
STUDIES v.9 no.3 1981 pp.61-86.

B. Industrial and Business Organizations;
   Structure; Operations

Monographic Works

GB 1. Aoki, Masahiko. ECONOMIC ANALYSIS OF THE
JAPANESE FIRM. Contributions to Economic Analysis
Series: Vol. 151. New York: Elsevier, 1984. 425pp.

GB 2. Arai, Shunzo. AN INTERSECTION OF EAST AND
WEST: JAPANESE BUSINESS MANAGEMENT. Tokyo: Rikugei
Publishing House, 1971. 212pp.

GB 3. Ballon, Robert J., and Inohara, Hideo. THE
JAPANESE ENTERPRISE. Bulletin--Sophia University
Socio-Economic Institute, no.45. Tokyo: Sophia
University Press, 1973. 16pp.

GB 4. Clark, Rodney. THE JAPANESE COMPANY. New
Haven: Yale University Press, 1979. 282pp.

GB 5. Dimock, Marshall E. THE JAPANESE
TECHNOCRACY: MANAGEMENT AND GOVERNANCE IN JAPAN. New
York: Walker/Weatherhill, 1968. 197pp.

GB 6. Kono, Toyohiro. STRATEGY AND STRUCTURE OF
JAPANESE ENTERPRISES. Armonk, N.Y.: M. E. Sharpe, 1984.
352pp.

GB 7. Vogel, Ezra F., ed. MODERN JAPANESE
ORGANIZATION AND DECISIONMAKING. Berkeley and Los
Angeles: University of California Press, 1975. 340pp.

GB 8. (not used)

GB. Organizational Structure

Articles

GB 9.   Balloun, J. S. "Japan and the Excellent
Organization." MANAGERIAL PLANNING v. 30 May/June 1982
pp. 10-15.

GB 10.   Buchan, P. B. "Boards of Directors:
Adversaries or Advisors." CALIFORNIA MANAGEMENT REVIEW
v. 24 Winter 1981 pp. 31-39.

GB 11.   Chakravarty, S. N. "Economic Darwinism."
FORBES v. 138 Oct. 6, 1986 pp. 52+. (Interview with
James C. Abegglen)

GB 12.   Cheng-Kuang, Hsu, et al.   "An Examination
of the Determinants of Organizational Structure."
AMERICAN JOURNAL OF SOCIOLOGY v. 88 Mar. 1983
pp. 975-996.

GB 13.   "Consensus Rules--Okay?" ECONOMIST v. 286
Mar. 26/Apr. 1, 1983 pp. survey 70+.

GB 14.   Fruin, W. M. "The Family as a Firm and the
Firm as a Family in Japan: The Case of Kikkoman Shoyu
Company Limited." JOURNAL OF FAMILY HISTORY v. 5 1980
pp. 432-449.

GB 15.   Fruin, W. M. "From Philanthropy to
Paternalism in the Noda Soy Sauce Industry:
Pre-Corporate and Corporate Charity in Japan." BUSINESS
HISTORY REVIEW v. 56 no. 2 1982 pp. 168-191.

GB 16.   "Guide to Japanese Trading Companies." MASS
TRANSIT v. 11 Oct. 1984 pp. 38-39.

GB 17.   Hattori, I. "A Proposition of Efficient
Decision-Making in the Japanese Corporation." COLUMBIA
JOURNAL OF WORLD BUSINESS v. 13 Summer 1978 pp. 7-15.

GB 18. Hayashi, Kichiro. "Corporate Planning Practices in Japanese Multinationals." ACADEMY OF MANAGEMENT JOURNAL v.21 no.2 1978 pp.211-226.

GB 19. "Inside a Japanese Corporation." SCHOLASTIC UPDATE v. 116 Nov. 11, 1983 pp.25-26.

GB 20. "Japanese Companies Throw a Good Party." WALL STREET JOURNAL v.198 Dec. 9, 1981 pp.34.

GB 21. Kobayashi, M. K., and Burke, W. Warner. "Organizational Development in Japan." COLUMBIA JOURNAL OF WORLD BUSINESS v.11 Summer 1976 p.113-123.

GB 22. Koshiro, K. "Humane Organization of Work in the Plants: Production Techniques and The Organization of Work in Japanese Large Factories." EKONOMIA v.63 1979 pp.35-69.

GB 23. Kure, Bunji. "The Financial Structure of Japanese Companies." SUMITOMO QUARTERLY Winter 1982 pp.11-14.

GB 24. Kuroda, Iwao, and Oritani, Yoshiharu. "A Reexamination of the Unique Features of Japan's Corporate Financial Structure: A Comparison of Corporate Balance Sheets in Japan and the United States." Spackman, Dennis M., translator. JAPANESE ECONOMIC STUDIES v.8 Summer 1980 pp.82-117.

GB 25. Lehner, Urban C. "The Nuts and Bolts of Japan's Factories." WALL STREET JOURNAL v.197 Mar. 31, 1981 p.32.

GB 26. Marsh, Robert M., and Mannari, Hiroshi. "Technology and Size as Determinants of the Organizational Structure of Japanese Factories." ADMINISTRATIVE SCIENCE QUARTERLY v.26 1981 pp.35-57.

GB 27. Mead, Christopher A. "A Very Japanese Company." INC. v.3 Nov. 1981 pp.67-68.

GB. Organizational Structure

GB 28. Nishiyama, Tadanori. "The Structure of Managerial Control: Who Owns and Controls Japanese Businesses?" JAPANESE ECONOMIC STUDIES v. 11 Fall 1982 pp. 37-77.

GB 29. Ohmae, Kenichi. "Yokkakari: The Cycle of Dependence in the Japanese Corporation." MANAGEMENT REVIEW v. 64 no. 6 1975 pp. 42-45.

GB 30. "Outsiders Inside Japanese Companies." FORTUNE v. 106 p. 114-115+ July 12, 1982.

GB 31. Schonberger, Richard J. "A Revolutionary Way to Streamline the Factory." WALL STREET JOURNAL v. 204 Nov. 15, 1982 p. 26.

GB 32. Schreffler, R. "Renovations for Japan's Trading Houses." DISTRIBUTION v. 83 Oct. 1984 pp. 17+.

GB 33. Shimizu, Ryuei. "A Positive Study in Organization and Other Related Matters--Referring Mainly to a Survey of Organizational Effectiveness on 260 Firms of Japan." KEIO BUSINESS REVIEW v. 5 1978 pp. 17-105.

GB 34. Skinner, K. A. "Conflict and Command in a Public Corporation in Japan." JOURNAL OF JAPANESE STUDIES v. 6 no. 2 1980 pp. 301-329.

GB 35. Skinner, Wickham. "The Focused Factory." HARVARD BUSINESS REVIEW v. 52 May/June 1974 pp. 113-121.

GB 36. Sogawa, H. "Comparative Analysis of Business Behavior Among Manufacturing Firms in Japan by a Field Survey on 607 Manufacturing Firms." KEIO BUSINESS REVIEW v. 15 1978 pp. 125-145.

GB 37. Suzuki, Y. "The Strategy and Structure of Top 100 Japanese Industrial Enterprises 1950-1970." STRATEGIC MANAGEMENT JOURNAL v. 1 1980 pp. 265-291.

GB 38.   Wheelwright, Steven C. "Japan--Where
Operations Really Are Strategic." HARVARD BUSINESS
REVIEW v.59 July/Aug. 1981 pp.67-74.

GB 39.   Wheelwright, Steven C. "Operations as
Strategy--Lessons From Japan." STANFORD GSB Fall
1981/1982 pp.2-7.

GB 40.   Yanagihara, N. "The Strategy and Structure
of Japanese Industrial Corporations." KSU ECONOMIC AND
BUSINESS REVIEW 1974 pp.24-45.

GC. Corporate Strategies in General

Monographic Works

GC 1.   Boisot, Max. INTANGIBLE FACTORS IN JAPANESE
CORPORATE STRATEGY. The Atlantic Papers, no. 50.
Paris: Atlantic Institute of International Affairs;
Totowa, N.J.: Allenheld, Osmun, 1983. 55pp.

Articles

GC 2.   Abegglen, James C., and Rapp, William.
"Japanese Managerial Behavior and 'Excessive
Competition'." THE DEVELOPING ECONOMIES v.8 Dec. 1970
pp.427-444.

GC 3.   Capon, N.; Farley, J.; and Hulbert, J.
"International Discussion of Corporate Strategic
Planning Practices." COLUMBIA JOURNAL OF WORLD BUSINESS
v.15 Fall 1980 pp.5-13.

GC. Corporate Strategies (General)

GC 4. Chernotsky, H. I. "Selecting U.S. Sites: A Case Study of German and Japanese Firms." MANAGEMENT INTERNATIONAL REVIEW v.23 no.2 1983 pp.45-55.

GC 5. "Corporations Launch Corporate Reforms to Survive Hard Times." BUSINESS JAPAN v.28 May 1983 pp.14-15.

GC 6. "Corporations Trim for Hard Fight Ahead." BUSINESS JAPAN v.28 Jun. 1983 pp.13-14.

GC 7. Crampe, Michiko Ito, and Benes, Nicholas Edward. "Majority Ownership Strategies for Japan." UCLA PACIFIC BASIN LAW JOURNAL v.1 Winter 1982 pp.41-82.

GC 8. Goto, A. "Statistical Evidence on the Diversification of Japanese Large Firms." JOURNAL OF INDUSTRIAL ECONOMICS v.29 Mar. 1981 pp.271-277.

GC 9. "Japan's Corporations Get Smart." EUROMONEY Sep. 1985 pp.85-117.

GC 10. Kraar, Louis. "Japan's Canon Focuses on America." FORTUNE v.103 Jan. 12, 1981 pp.81-84.

GC 11. Murakami, T. "Recent Changes in Long Range Corporate Planning in Japan." LONG RANGE PLANNING v.11 Apr. 1978 pp.2-5.

GC 12. Nagashima, Yukiniri. "Response of Japanese Companies to Environment Changes." LONG RANGE PLANNING v.8 Feb. 1976 p.21.

GC 13. Ohmae, Kenichi. "Japan vs Japan: Only the Strong survive." WALL STREET JOURNAL v.197 Jan. 26, 1981 p.20.

GC 14. Shibata, Y. "Japanese Give the Chop to Former Allies." EUROMONEY Aug. 1986 pp.89-90+.

GC 15. "Theme: Japanese Finance; Companies and Banks Go through Pains of Adjustment." ASIAN FINANCE v.6 Aug. 15, 1980 pp.31-33+.

GC 16. Young, A. K. "Internationalization of the Japanese General Trading Companies." COLUMBIA JOURNAL OF WORLD BUSINESS v.9 no.1 1974 pp.78-86.

GD. Corporate Strategies of Individual Industries and Companies

Monographic Works

GD 1. Abe, Masatoshi. "Dynamic Microeconomic Models of Production, Investment and Technological Change of the U.S. and Japanese Iron and Steel Industries." Doctoral Dissertation, University of Wisconsin, Madison, 1970. 277pp.

GD 2. Chang, Chan Sup. THE JAPANESE AUTO INDUSTRY AND THE U.S. MARKET. New York: Praeger, 1981. 214pp.

GD 3. Cole, Robert E. THE JAPANESE AUTOMOBILE INDUSTRY = MODEL AND CHALLENGE FOR THE FUTURE? Ann Arbor: Center for Japanese Studies, University of Michigan, 1961. 147pp.

GD 4. Dodwell Marketing Consultants. KEY PLAYERS IN THE JAPANESE ELECTRONIC INDUSTRY. Tokyo, 1985. 555pp.

GD 5. Dodwell Marketing Consultants. STRUCTURE OF THE JAPANESE AUTO PARTS INDUSTRY. 3rd ed. Tokyo, 1986. 456pp.

GD. Industry/Company Strategies

GD 6.   Dodwell Marketing Consultants. STRUCTURE OF
THE JAPANESE MOTOR COMPONENTS INDUSTRY. Tokyo, 1983.
246pp.

GD 7.   Dodwell Marketing Consultants. STRUCTURE OF
THE JAPANESE RETAIL AND DISTRIBUTION INDUSTRY. Tokyo,
1981. 372pp.

GD 8.   Gould, Rowland. THE MATSUSHITA PHENOMENON.
Tokyo: Diamond Sha, 1970. 224pp.

GD 9.   Kamata, Satoshi. JAPAN IN THE PASSING LANE;
AN INSIDER'S SHOCKING ACCOUNT OF LIFE IN A JAPANESE
AUTO FACTORY. New York: Pantheon, 1983. 211pp.

GD 10.   Kawahito, Kiyoshi. THE JAPANESE STEEL
INDUSTRY: WITH AN ANALYSIS OF THE U.S. STEEL IMPORT
PROBLEM. New York: Praeger, 1972. 203pp.

GD 11.   Longworth, John W. BEEF IN JAPAN: POLICIES,
PRODUCTION, MARKETING, AND TRADE. New York: University
of Queensland Press, 1984. 327pp.

GD 12.   Lyons, N. THE SONY VISION. New York: Crown
Publishers, 1976. 235pp.

GD 13.   McLean, Mick, ed.   JAPANESE ELECTRONICS
CHALLENGE,   by TECHNOVA. New York: St. Martin's, 1982.
163pp.

GD 14.   ORIGIN AND DEVELOPMENT OF IRON AND STEEL
TECHNOLOGY IN JAPAN. New York: Unipub, 1980. 81pp.

GD 15.   Osako, Masako. "Auto Assembly Technology
and Social Integration in a Japanese Factory: A Case
Study." Doctoral Dissertation, Northwestern University,
Evanston, Ill., 1973. 333pp.

GD 16.   Shingo, Shigeo. STUDY OF TOYOTA PRODUCTION
SYSTEM FROM INDUSTRIAL ENGINEERING VIEWPOINT. Tokyo:
Japan Management Association, 1981. 363pp.

GD 17. Sobel, Robert. IBM vs. JAPAN: THE STRUGGLE FOR THE FUTURE. New York: Stein and Day, 1985. 304pp.

Articles

GD 18. Armstrong, L., et al. "Toyota's Fast Lane." BUSINESS WEEK Nov. 4, 1985 pp. 42-44.

GD 19. "Auto Makers Mount a U.S. Invasion." BUSINESS WEEK Apr. 23, 1979 p. 58.

GD 20. Brooks, Rosanne. "East and West Blend at Yamaha Tank Plant." AMERICAN METAL MARKET Mar. 9, 1981 p. 18.

GD 21. Bylinski, G. "Japanese Chip Challenge." FORTUNE v. 103 Mar. 23, 1981 p. 16.

GD 22. Clutterbuck, David. "Kawasaki Stresses Its Environmental Responsibilities." INTERNATIONAL MANAGEMENT v. 31 Apr. 1976 p. 14.

GD 23. Crain, Kenneth E. "Life with the World's Top Importer." AUTOMOTIVE NEWS Feb. 22, 1982 p. 30.

GD 24. Davidson, William H. "Small Group Activity At Musashi Semiconductor Works." SLOAN MANAGEMENT REVIEW v. 23 pp. 3-14 Spring 1982.

GD 25. Donaldson, L. "Regaining Control at Nipont." JOURNAL OF GENERAL MANAGEMENT v. 4 no. 4 1979 pp. 14-30.

GD 26. Edwards, M. "Fifth Generation Systems: East Meets West in Battle of Info Supremacy." COMMUNICATIONS NEWS v. 21 Jul. 1984 pp. 54-60.

GD. Industry/Company Strategies

GD 27. Feigenbaum, Edward, and McCorduck, Pamela. "The Fifth Generation: Japan's Computer Challenge to the World." CREATIVE COMPUTING v.10 Aug. 1984 pp.103-111.

GD 28. "First Independent Japanese Auto Plant in EC Starts Production." BUSINESS JAPAN v.31 Oct. 1986 pp.42-43. (re: European Community)

GD 29. Gross, L. "Bargained Birthright?" FORBES v.131 Jun. 6, 1983 p.46.

GD 30. Hill, R. "Japanese Fibers Firm Restructures to Restore Profits." INTERNATIONAL MANAGEMENT v.32 no.5 1977 pp.41-43.

GD 31. "Hitachi in the '80s: A Focus on Computers." BUSINESS WEEK Mar. 2, 1981 pp.38-39.

GD 32. "Honda: Building Overseas to Meet Demand Diplomatically." BUSINESS WEEK Jan. 28, 1980. pp.112+

GD 33. "How Mazda Was Rotated." MANAGEMENT TODAY Feb. 1980 pp.62-65.

GD 34. Ike, Brian. "The Japanese Textile Industry; Structural Adjustment and Government Policy." ASIAN SURVEY May 1980 pp.532-551.

GD 35. Inaba, M. "In Wake of Trade Pact: Japan Semicon Firms Eye Expansion in U.S." ELECTRONICS NEWS v.32 Aug. 11, 1986 pp.36+.

GD 36. "Japan Chemicals To Be Restructured Under MITI Plan." CHEMICAL MARKETING REPORTER v.223 Feb. 14, 1983 pp.5+.

GD 37. "Japanese Retailers Get Ready to Move into U.S." BUSINESS WEEK Aug. 4, 1980 p.32.

GD 38. "Japanese Skills Called Key to a Brighter Future." AUTOMOTIVE NEWS May 25, 1981 p.24.

GD 39. "Japanese Steel: Milling Around America."
ECONOMIST v.300 Aug 16, 1986 p.46.

GD 40. "Japanese Steel Industry, Secrets for Its
Spectacular Productivity Improvement." ORIENTAL
ECONOMIST v.49 Mar. 1981 pp.18-23.

GD 41. "Japan's Service Industries Still Hide
Behind Barriers." ASIAN BUSINESS v.18 Aug. 1982
pp.68-70.

GD 42. "Kawasaki Steel: Using Technology as a Tool
to Bolster Exports." BUSINESS WEEK Jan. 29, 1979
pp.119-120.

GD 43. Kraar, Louis. "Japan's Automakers Shift
Strategies." FORTUNE v.102 Aug. 11, 1980 pp.106-111.

GD 44. "Made-in-America Japanese Car." TIME v.115
Jan. 28, 1980 p.64.

GD 45. Mashahiro, Matsuzaki. "Textiles; Probing
the Way to Revitalization." JAPAN QUARTERLY v.29 no.2
June 1982 pp.205-211.

GD 46. Meltzer, R. I. "Color TV Sets and
U.S.--Japanese Relations: Problems of Trade Adjustment
Policymaking." ORBIS v.23 Summer 1979 pp.421-446.

GD 47. Menzies, H. D. "Can the Twain Meet at
Mitsubishi?" FORTUNE v.103 Jan. 26, 1981 pp.41-44+.

GD 48. "Nissan Plant Outlays Total $500 Million."
IRON AGE v.225 Feb. 1, 1982 pp.15+.

GD 49. Otake, Hideo. "Corporate Power in Social
Conflict; Vehicle Safety and Japanese Motor
Manufacturers." INTERNATIONAL JOURNAL OF THE SOCIOLOGY
OF LAW v.10 Feb. 1982 pp.75-103.

GD. Industry/Company Strategies

GD 50.   Ouchi, William G. "Teamwork and
Competition: How the Japanese Computer Industry has
Developed." CREATIVE COMPUTING v.10 Aug. 1984
pp.145-151.

GD 51.   Porter, D. "Japanese Makers Push for End to
U.S. Quotas as Expiration Nears." AUTOMOTIVE NEWS Oct.
6, 1986 p.2.

GD 52.   Rappa, Michael A. "Capital Financing
Strategies of the Japanese Semiconductor Industry."
CALIFORNIA MANAGEMENT REVIEW v.27 Winter 1985 pp.85-99.

GD 53.   "Reorganization Trend Given Fresh Impetus
by Isuzu-Fuji Move." JAPAN ECONOMIC JOURNAL Dec. 27,
1966 p.12+.

GD 54.   Robertson, J. "U.S. Charges Japan with
EpROM Dumping." ELECTRONICS NEWS v.32 Nov. 3, 1986
p.36.

GD 55.   Rutledge, P. "Bringing Mitsui Together
Again." INTERNATIONAL MANAGEMENT v.29 no.2 1974
pp.28-31.

GD 56.   Salmans, S. "How Mazda Was Rotated."
MANAGEMENT TODAY Feb. 1980 pp.62-65.

GD 57.   Sheard, P. "Auto-Production Systems in
Japan: Organizational and Locational Features."
AUSTRALIAN GEOGRAPHICAL STUDIES v.21 1983 pp.49-68.

GD 58.   Shimoda, H. "Fifth Generation Computer:
From Dream to Reality." Interview with K. Fuchi.
ELECTRONIC BUSINESS v.10 Nov. 1, 1984 pp.68+.

GD 59.   Shimokawa, Koichi. "Entrepreneurship and
Social Environment Change in the Japanese Automobile
Industry; On the Key Elements of High Productivity and
Innovation." SOCIAL SCIENCE INFORMATION v.2 1982
pp.273-300.

GD 60. "Sogo Shosha: Japan's Transit Connection."
MASS TRANSIT v.11 Oct. 1984 pp.14-16+.

GD 61. "Sony: a Diversification Plan Tuned to the
People Factor." BUSINESS WEEK Feb. 9, 1981 pp.88-89.

GD 62. Symonds, W. C. "National Steel's New Game
Plan Is Made in Japan." BUSINESS WEEK June 3, 1985
p.78.

GD 63. Takai, Toshio. "Setting the Record Straight
on Semiconductors." JOURNAL OF JAPANESE TRADE AND
INDUSTRY Jul./Aug. 1983 pp.24-30. (Response to the
American report entitled, "The Effect of Government
Targeting on World Semiconductor Competition: A Case
History of Japanese Industrial Strategy and Its Costs
for America," issued by the Semiconductor Industry
Association, Feb. 3, 1983."

GD 64. Tindall, R. E. "Mitsubishi Group: World's
Largest Mutinational Enterprise?" MSU BUSINESS TOPICS
v.22 no.2 1974 pp.27-34.

GD 65. Tsurumi, Yoshi. "How to Handle the Next
Chrysler." FORTUNE v.101 June 16, 1980 pp.87-88.

GD 66. Uenohara, Michiyuki. "The Japanese
Electronic Industry; Its History, Present Situation,
and Future Prospects." MANAGEMENT JAPAN v.15 Aug. 1982
pp.7-17.

GD 67. Uttal, Bro. "Exports won't come easy for
Japan's Computer Industry." FORTUNE v.98 Oct. 9, 1978
pp.138-146.

GD 68. Uttal, Bro. "Japan's Big Push in
Computers." FORTUNE v.98 Sep. 25, 1978 pp.64-72.

GD 69. Yamamura, Kozo. "The Founding of
Mitsubishi: A Case Study in Japanese Business History."
BUSINESS HISTORY REVIEW v.41 Summer 1967 pp.156+.

GD. Industry/Company Strategies

GD 70. Yasuoka, S. "The Tradition of Family
Business in the Strategic decision Process and
Management Structure of Zaibatsu Business: Mitsui,
Sumitomo, and Mitsubishi." in International Conference
on Business History (1st; 1974; Fuji Education Center)
STRATEGY AND STRUCTURE OF BIG BUSINESS: PROCEEDINGS OF
THE FIRST FUJI CONFERENCE . Tokyo: University of Tokyo
Press, 1975. pp.81-101.

XI.

CHAPTER 8

H. JAPANESE MANAGEMENT

HA. Theories; Principles; Cultural Background

Monographic Works

HA 1. British Institute of Management, ed. MODERN
JAPANESE MANAGEMENT. London: Management Publications,
1970. 141pp.

HA 2. Dreyfack, Raymond. MAKING IT IN MANAGEMENT,
THE JAPANESE WAY. Rockville Centre, N.Y. : Farnsworth,
1982. 344pp.

HA 3. Hayashi, Shuji. CULTURE AND MANAGEMENT IN
JAPAN. Tokyo: University of Tokyo Press, Press, 1986.
250pp.

HA 4. Lee, Sang M. , and Schwendiman, Gary.
JAPANESE MANAGEMENT: CULTURAL AND ENVIRONMENTAL
CONSIDERATIONS. New York: Praeger, 1982. 299pp.

HA. Theories; Principles

HA 5.   Long, William A., and Seo, K. K. MANAGEMENT
IN JAPAN AND INDIA: WITH REFERENCE TO THE UNITED
STATES. New York: Praeger, 1977. 293pp.

HA 6.   Schaupp, Dietrich L. A CROSS-CULTURAL STUDY
OF A MULTINATIONAL COMPANY: ATTITUDINAL RESPONSES TO A
PARTICIPATIVE MANAGEMENT. New York: Praeger, 1978.
166pp.

Articles

HA 7.   Allen, R. L. "Theory Z: People, Productivity
& Profit" CHAIN STORE AGE GENERAL MERCHANDISE EDITION
v.59 July 1983 pp.128+

HA 8.   Baillie, A. S. "The Deming Approach: Being
Better than the Best." ADVANCED MANAGEMENT JOURNAL v.51
Autumn 1986 pp.15-23.

HA 9.   Brown, W. "Japanese Management: The Cultural
Background." MONUMENTA NIPPONICA v.21 no.1-2 1966
pp.47-60.

HA 10.   Buchanan, Daniel H. "Differential Economic
Progress: Japan versus 'Asia'." AMERICAN ECONOMIC
ASSOCIATION PAPERS AND PROCEEDINGS v.41 May 1951
pp.359-366.

HA 11.   Buckley, P. J., and Mirza, H. "The Wit and
Wisdom of Japanese Management; An Iconoclastic
Analysis." MANAGEMENT INTERNATIONAL REVIEW v.25 1985
pp.16-33.

HA 12.   Chandler, M. K. "Management Rights: Made in
Japan." COLUMBIA JOURNAL OF WORLD BUSINESS v.1 no.1
1966 pp.131-140.

HA 13.   Curtis, Gerald L. "Organizational
Leadership in Japan's Economic Community." JOURNAL OF
INTERNATIONAL AFFAIRS v. 26 1972 pp. 172-185.

HA 14.   De Mente, B. "The Japanese Executive and
His Management Philosophy." WORLDWIDE P & I PLANNING
v. 2 no. 1 1968 pp. 42-50.

HA 15.   Doktor, R. "Culture and The Management of
Time: A Comparison of Japanese and American Top
Managment Practice." ASIA PACIFIC JOURNAL OF MANAGMENT
v. 1 no. 1 1983 pp. 65-71.

HA 16.   Ellenberger, James N. "Japanese Management:
Myth or Magic." AMERICAN FEDERATIONIST v. 89 Apr. /June
1982 pp. 3-12.

HA 17.   England, G. W., and Koike, R. "Personal
Value Systems of Japanese Managers." JOURNAL OF
CROSS-CULTURAL PSYCHOLOGY v. 1 no. 1 1970 pp. 21-40.

HA 18.   Fox, W. M. "Japanese Management: Tradition
Under Strain." BUSINESS HORIZONS v. 20 Aug. 1977
pp. 76-85.

HA 19.   Fujimori, Mitsuo. "Japanese Management
Philosophies: Formation and Changes." KEIO BUSINESS
REVIEW v. 20 1983 pp. 105-116.

HA 20.   Harbison, F. "Management in Japan." in
Harbison, F., and Myers, C. A., MANAGEMENT IN THE
INDUSTRIAL WORLD: AN INTERNATIONAL ANALYSIS. New York:
McGraw-Hill, 1959. pp. 249-264.

HA 21.   Hesseling, P., and Konnen, E. "Culture and
Subculture in a Decision-Making Exercise." HUMAN
RELATIONS v. 22 no. 1 1969 pp. 31-51.

HA 22.   Iizuka, A. "The Spirit of Harmonious
Competition." TECHNOLOGY REVIEW v. 85 Aug. /Sep. 1982
pp. 53-54.

HA. Theories; Principles

HA 23.   Imai, M. "Shukko, Jomukai, Ringi--The
Ingredients of Executive Selection in Japan." PERSONNEL
v. 46 no. 4 1969 pp. 20-30.

HA 24.   Inaoka, Tadayuki. "Culture in Business:
People Management And Development in Japan." AMERICAN
CHAMBER OF COMMERCE JAPAN JOURNAL v. 20 July/Aug. 1983
pp. 13+.

HA 25.   Jain, H. C. "Casting a New Light on
Japanese Management." MANAGEMENT WORLD v. 13 June 1984
pp. 8-11.

HA 26.   "Japanese Perspective on Management." DUN'S
BUSINESS MONTHLY v. 119 p. 52.

HA 27.   Kanase, Takeshi, and Tadaaki, Nemoto.
"Empirical Study on Ideal Personal Characteristics of
Japanese OR/MS Leaders." INTERFACES v. 9 Feb. 1979
pp. 56-62.

HA 28.   Kelley, L., and Reeser, C. "The Persistence
of Culture as a Determinant of Differentiated Attitudes
on the Part of American Managers of Japanese Ancestry."
ACADEMY OF MANAGEMENT JOURNAL v. 16 no. 1 1973 pp. 67-76.

HA 29.   Kono, Toyohiro. "Japanese Management
Philosophy: Can It Be Exported?" LONG RANGE PLANNING
v. 15 June 1982 pp. 90-102.

HA 30.   Krause, W. P. "Will Success Spoil Japanese
Management." COLUMBIA JOURNAL OF WORLD BUSINESS v. 8
no. 4 1973 pp. 26-30.

HA 31.   Leflufy, B. "The Secret of Japanese
Management Isn't Rice Diets--It's Practising What We
Preached." CANADIAN BUSINESS v. 55 Dec. 1982 pp. 143+.

HA 32.   Lim, H. "Japanese Agenda for Management
Development." TRAINING AND DEVELOPMENT JOURNAL v. 36
Mar. 1982 pp. 62-67.

HA 33. Lim, H. "Japanese Management: A Skill Profile." TRAINING AND DEVELOPMENT JOURNAL v. 35 Oct. 1981 pp. 18-21.

HA 34. McMillan, Charles J. "Social Values and Management Innovation: The Case of Japan." in Dlugos, G., and Weiemair, K., eds. MANAGEMENT UNDER DIFFERING VALUE SYSTEMS: POLITICAL, SOCIAL AND ECONOMICAL PERSPECTIVES IN A CHANGING WORLD. Berlin: Walter de Gruyter, 1981. pp. 815-832.

HA 35. Marsland, S. and Beer, M. "The Evolution of Japanese Management: Lessons for U.S. Managers." ORGANIZATIONAL DYNAMICS v. 11 Winter 1982 pp. 49-67.

HA 36. Maruyama, M. "Japanese Management Theories and Japanese Criticisms." FUTURES v. 15 June 1983 pp. 170-180.

HA 37. Misumi, Jyuji, and Peterson, M. F. "The Performance-maintenance (PM) Theory of Leadership: Review of a Japanese Research Program." ADMINISTRATIVE SCIENCE QUARTERLY v. 30 1985 pp. 198-223.

HA 38. Misumi, Jyuji, and Tasaki, Toshiaki. "A Study of the Effectiveness of Supervisory Patterns in a Japanese Hierarchical Organization." JAPANESE PSYCHOLOGICAL RESEARCH v. 7 no. 4 1965 pp. 151-162.

HA 39. Mroczkowski, Tomasz. "Theory Z: Myths, Realities, and Alternatives." INDUSTRIAL RELATIONS (Quebec) v. 38 Jan. 1984 pp. 19-20+.

HA 40. Nakase, T. "The Introduction of Scientific Management in Japan and Its Characteristics--Case Studies of Companies in the Sumitomo Zaibatsu." in International Conference on Business History (4th: 1977: Fuji Education Center). LABOR AND MANAGEMENT: PROCEEDINGS OF THE FOURTH FUJI CONFERENCE. Tokyo: University of Tokyo Press, 1979. pp. 171-202.

HA 41. Noda, K., and Glazer, H. "Traditional Japanese Management Decision-Making." MANAGEMENT INTERNATIONAL REVIEW v. 8 no. 2-3 1968 pp. 124-131.

HA 42. Odiorne, G. S. "The Trouble with Japanese Management Systems." BUSINESS HORIZONS v. 27 July-Aug. 1984 pp. 17-23.

HA 43. Oh, T. K. "Japanese Management: A Critical Review." ACADEMY OF MANAGEMENT REVIEW v. 1 Jan. 1976 pp. 14-25.

HA 44. Ohmae, Kenichi. "Beyond the Myths." (Address given April 20, 1982.) VITAL SPEECHES OF THE DAY v. 48 July 1, 1982 pp. 555-57.

HA 45. Ono, T. "Modernization of Business Administration in Japan." INTERNATIONAL STUDIES OF MANAGEMENT AND ORGANIZATION v. 1 no. 3 1971 pp. 274-291.

HA 46. "The Other Side of the Japanese Miracle." INTERNATIONAL MANAGEMENT Oct. 1982 pp. 19-20.

HA 47. Ouchi, William G. "Going from A to Z . . . Thirteen Steps to a Theory Z Organization." MANAGEMENT REVIEW v. 70 May 1981 pp. 8-16.

HA 48. Ouchi, William G., and Price, R. "Hierarchies, Clans and Theory Z: A New Perspective on Organization Development." ORGANIZATIONAL DYNAMICS v. 6 Autumn 1978 pp. 25-44.

HA 49. Ouchi, William G. "Organizational Paradigms: a Commentary on Japanese Management and Theory Z Organizations." ORGANIZATIONAL DYNAMICS v. 9 Spring 1981 pp. 36-43.

HA 50. Ouchi, William G., and Jaeger, A. M. "Type Z Organization: Stability in the Midst of Mobility." ACADEMY OF MANAGEMENT REVIEW v. 3 no. 2 1978 p. 305.

HA 51. Phalon, R. "Hell Camp." FORBES v.133 June 18, 1984 pp.56-58. (Kanrisha Management Training Camp)

HA 52. "Refuting Theory Z: the Sun Sets." MANAGEMENT WORLD v.11 Dec. 1982 p.15.

HA 53. Robinson, Richard D. "Can the Japanese Keep It Up?" TECHNOLOGY REVIEW v.85 Aug./Sep. 1982 pp.46-52.

HA 54. Ross, S. "What Is Japan, and What Is Not Japan?" BUSINESS AND SOCIETY REVIEW no.37 Spring 1980-81 pp.31-36.

HA 55. Shortell, S. M. "Theory Z: Implications and Relevance for Health Care Management." HEALTH CARE MANAGEMENT REVIEW v.7 Fall 1982 pp.7-21.

HA 56. Soejima, M. "Japan: Management in a Personal Dimension." INDUSTRY WEEK v.182 July 15, 1974 pp.66+.

HA 57. Stening, B. W. "Japanese Management: Panacea, Prophylactic or Passing Fancy?" ECONOMIC ACTIVITY v.24 no.3 1981 pp.15-19.

HA 58. Sullivan, J. J. "A Critique of Theory Z." ACADEMY OF MANAGEMENT REVIEW v.8 Jan 1983 pp.132-42.

HA 59. Suzuki, H. "Innovation and Integration in Japanese Management: The Fusion of Oriental and Occidental Civilizations." in International Management Congress (15th; Tokyo; 1969). THE ROLE OF MANAGEMENT: INNOVATION, INTEGRATION AND INTERNATIONALIZATION: PROCEEDINGS. Tokyo: Kogakusha, 1969. pp.31-37.

HA 60. Taira, Koji. "Factory Legislation and Management Modernization During Japan's Industrialization 1896-1916." BUSINESS HISTORY REVIEW v.44 no.1 1970 pp.84-109.

HA. Theories; Principles

HA 61.   Takamiya, S. "Characteristics of Japanese
Management and Its Recent Tendencies: Effectiveness of
Japanese Management." in International Management
Congress (15th; Tokyo; 1969). THE ROLE OF MANAGEMENT:
INNOVATION, INTEGRATION AND INTERNATIONALIZATION:
PROCEEDINGS OF THE 15TH CIOS INTERNATIONAL MANAGEMENT
CONGRESS. Tokyo: Kogakusha, 1969. pp.394-405.

HA 62.   Takezawa, S. "Socio-Cultural Aspects of
Management in Japan: Historical Development and New
Challenges." INTERNATIONAL LABOUR REVIEW v.94 no.2 1966
pp.148-174.

HA 63.   Tanaka, S. "The Relationship between
Management Behaviour and Social Structure." in
International Management Congress (15th; Tokyo; 1969).
THE ROLE OF MANAGEMENT: INNOVATION, INTEGRATION AND
INTERNATIONALIZATION: PROCEEDINGS OF THE 15TH CIOS
INTERNATIONAL MANAGEMENT CONGRESS. Tokyo: Kogakusha,
1969. pp.147-159.

HA 64.   "Theory Z Author Says Middle Management
Must Change System: Lifetime Jobs Called Japan's Ace."
AUTOMOTIVE NEWS Aug. 23, 1982 pp.32.

HA 65.   "Theory Z: The Sun Rises." MANAGEMENT
REVIEW v.11 Dec. 1982 p.14.

HA 66.   Tsuda, Masumi. "For Understanding of
Japanese-Style Management." DENTSU JAPAN
MARKETING/ADVERTISING Jan. 1982 pp.32-35+.

HA 67.   Whitely, W., and England, G. W. "Managerial
Values as a Reflection of Culture and the Process of
Industrialization." ACADEMY OF MANAGEMENT JOURNAL v.20
no.3 1977 pp1439-453.

HA 68.   Whitely, W., and England, G. W.
"Variability in Common Dimensions of Managerial Values
Due to Value Orientation and Country Differences."
PERSONNEL PSYCHOLOGY v.33 1980 pp.77-89.

HB. Management Practices; Techniques and Styles

Monongraphs

HB 1. Bradley, Keith, and Gelb, Alan. CO-OPERATION AT WORK: THE MONDRAGON EXPERIENCE. London; Exeter, N.H.: Heinemann Educational, 1983 102pp.

HB 2. Hibi, Sohei. HOW TO MEASURE MAINTENANCE PERFORMANCE. Tokyo: Asian Productivity Organization, 1977. 192pp.

HB 3. Kobayashi, Shigeru. CREATIVE MANAGEMENT. New York: American Management Association, 1971. 259pp.

HB 4. Lee, Sang M., and Schwendiman, Gary, eds. MANAGEMENT BY JAPANESE SYSTEMS. New York: Praeger, 1982. 562pp.

HB 5. Monden, Yasuhiro; Shibakawa, Rinya; Takayanagi, Satoru; and Nagao, Teruya. INNOVATIONS IN MANAGEMENT: THE JAPANESE CORPORATION. Norcross, Ga.: Institute Engineering Management Press, Institute of Industrial Engineers, 1985. 251pp.

HB 6. Noetzli, Irene M. A VIEW OF JAPANESE MANAGEMENT, ESPECIALLY MANAGEMENT DEVELOPMENT IN LARGE BUSINESS ENTERPRISES. Zurich: Schulthess Polygraphischer Verlag, 1982. 281pp.

HB 7. Pascale, Richard Tanner, and Athos, Anthony G. THE ART OF JAPANESE MANAGEMENT: APPLICATIONS FOR AMERICAN EXECUTIVES. New York: Simon and Shuster, 1981. 221pp.

HB. Management Practices

HB 8.   White, Michael and Trevor, Malcolm. UNDER
JAPANESE MANAGEMENT: THE EXPERIENCES OF BRITISH
WORKERS. London: Heinemann, 1983.

HB 9.   Yoshino, Michael Y. JAPAN'S MANAGERIAL
SYSTEM: TRADITION AND INNOVATION. Boston: M. I. T. Press,
1968. 292pp.

Articles

HB 10.   Alston, Jon P. "Three Principles of
Japanese Management." PERSONNEL JOURNAL v. 62 pp. 758+
Sep. 1983.

HB 11.   "American Myths vs. the Real Reasons for
Japan's Success." MANAGEMENT REVIEW v. 70 June 1981
pp. 55-56.

HB 12.   Benson, G. L. "How Employee Assumptions
Influence Managerial Behavior." SUPERVISORY MANAGEMENT
v. 28 Mar. 1983 pp. 2-8.

HB 13.   Boisot, M. "Convergence Revisited: The
Codification and Diffusion of Knowledge in a British
and Japanese Firm." JOURNAL OF MANAGEMENT STUDIES v. 20
Apr. 1983 pp. 159-190.

HB 14.   Bowen, W. "Why the Japanese Seem to be
Eight Feet Tall." FORTUNE v. 100 July 16, 1979
pp. 179-182.

HB 15.   Cathey, P. "Japanese Managers Find Best Way
to Direct U. S. Workers." IRON AGE v. 225 May 21, 1982
pp. 69+.

HB 16.   Chadwin, M. L. and Cross., E. M. "Japanese
Management Style Right for DP?" JOURNAL OF SYSTEMS
MANAGEMENT v. 34 Mar. 1983 pp. 6-9.

HB 17. Collison, R. "Japanese Fix." CANADIAN BUSINESS v.54 Nov. 1981 pp.36-43+.

HB 18. Cooper, C. L. "Participative Management Practice and Work Humanisation in Japan." PERSONNEL REVIEW v.7 no.2 1978 pp.25-30.

HB 19. Deming, W. Edwards. "What Top Management Must Do." BUSINESS WEEK July 16, 1981 pp.19-21.

HB 20. Deutsch, C. M. "Trust: the New Ingredient in Management." BUSINESS WEEK July 6, 1981 p.104-5.

HB 21. Dillon, L.S. "Japanese Rules for Communication." PERSONNEL ADMINISTRATOR v.29 pp.92+ Jan. 1984.

HB 22. Doktor, R. "Some Tentative Comments on Japanese and American Decision Making." DECISION SCIENCES v.14 Fall 1983 pp.607-612.

HB 23. Endo, C. A. "Formal Management Relations Practices in Japanese Business and Industrial Organizations." INTERNATIONAL JOURNAL OF CONTEMPORARY SOCIOLOGY v.11 no.1 1974 pp.22-33.

HB 24. Feinberg, M. R. "The Value of Motivating Managers." RESTAURANT BUSINESS v.83 Apr. 10, 1984 p.88.

HB 25. Fusfeld, D. R. "Labor-Managed and Participatory Firms: a Review Article." ******* v.17 Sep. 1983 pp.769-89.

HB 26. Gold, B. "Strengthening Managerial Approaches to Improving Technological Capabilities." STATEGIC MANAGEMENT v.4 July/Sep. 1983 pp.209-20.

HB 27. Grosjean, Paul. "Japanese Management Methods: Explaining The Success Story." CREATIVE COMPUTING v.10 Aug. 1984 pp.163-167.

HB. Management Practices

HB 28.   Hahori, Ichiro. "A Proposition on
Efficient Decision-Making in the Japanese Corporation."
COLUMBIA JOURNAL OF WORLD BUSINESS v. 13 Summer 1978
pp. 7-15.

HB 29.   Hammond, B. "Inscrutable World-Beaters."
DIRECTOR v. 34 Nov. 1981 p. 28.

HB 30.   Harbron, J. D. "How Japan Executives Manage
the Zaibatsu." BUSINESS QUARTERLY Summer 1980
pp. 15-18.

HB 31.   Hatakeyama, Y. "The Unsung Hero of Japanese
Management: the Middle Manager." MANAGEMENT REVIEW v. 71
Jul. 1982 p. 33.

HB 32.   Hatvany, Nina, and Pucik, Vladimir.
"Integrated Management System: Lessons From the
Japanese Experience." ACADEMY OF MANAGEMENT REVIEW v. 6
July 1981 p. 469-80.

HB 33.   Hayashi, Kichiro. "Japanese Management of
Multinational Operations: Sources and Means of
Control." INTERNATIONAL MARKETING v. 4 1978 pp. 47-57.

HB 34.   Hayes, Robert H. "Why Japanese Factories
Work." HARVARD BUSINESS REVIEW v. 59 July/Aug. 1981
pp. 57-66.   Also in McKINSEY QUARTERLY Fall 1982
pp. 32-48.

HB 35.   Hazama, H. "Characteristics of
Japanese-Style Management." JAPANESE ECONOMIC STUDIES
v. 6 no. 3-4 1978 pp. 110-173.

HB 36.   Hill, R. "Japanese Company Boss Who Gives
No Orders." INTERNATIONAL MANAGEMENT v. 32 Apr. 1977
pp. 27-29.

HB 37.   Hunt, E. H. and Gray, G. R. "Participative
Approach--Time to Catch Up." MANAGEMENT WORLD v. 10 May
1981 pp. 30-31.

HB 38.   Ishida, Hideto. "The Japanese Style of Management." SUMITOMO QUARTERLY v.1 no.3 1980 pp.1-4.

HB 39.   Ishikawa, Akihiro. "A Survey of Studies in the Japanese Style of Management." ECONOMIC AND INDUSTRIAL DEMOCRACY v.3 Feb 1982 pp.1-15.

HB 40.   Itami, H. "Japanese Management." ATLANTA ECONOMIC REVIEW v.23 1973 pp.38-40.

HB 41.   "Japan Gives the B-Schools an "A" --for Contacts." BUSINESS WEEK Oct. 19, 1981 pp.   132+.

HB 42.   "Japanese Are Better Managers, AMSA Says." IRON AGE v.225 Feb. 19, 1982 pp.11+.

HB 43.   "Japanese Managers Tell How Their System Works." FORTUNE v.96 Nov. 1977 pp.126+.

HB 44.   Johnston, J. "Word of Memo: Less Paper, More Communication--Japanese Style." MANAGEMENT WORLD v.12 p.46-7 Feb./Mar. 1983.

HB 45.   Kawashima, Takeyoshi. "Dispute Resolution in Contemporary Japan." in von Mehren, Arthur Taylor, ed.   LAW IN JAPAN: THE LEGAL ORDER IN A CHANGING SOCIETY. Cambridge, Mass.: Harvard University Press, 1963.

HB 46.   Kerns, H. "Japan Wins--By a Mile." FAR EASTERN ECONOMIC REVIEW v.114 Dec. 4/10, 1981 pp.97-98.

HB 47.   Kraar, Louis. "The Japanese Are Coming--With Their Own Style of Management." FORTUNE v.91 Mar. 1975 pp.116-120.

HB 48.   Kuzela, L. "Putting Japanese Style Management to Work" INDUSTRY WEEK v.206 Sep. 1, 1980 pp.61-61+.

HB. Management Practices

HB 49. McMillan, Charles J. "Production Planning
in Japan." JOURNAL OF GENERAL MANAGEMENT v.8 Summer
1983 v.44-72.

HB 50. Main, J. "The Trouble with Managing
Japanese-style." FORTUNE v.109 Apr. 2, 1984 pp.50-52+.

HB 51. Marengo, F. D. "Learning from the Japanese:
What or How?" MANAGEMENT INTERNATIONAL REVIEW v.19 no.4
1979 pp.39-46.

HB 52. Matsuno, S. and Stoever, W. A. "Japanese
Boss, American Employees." WHARTON MAGAZINE v.7 p.44-8
Fall 1982.

HB 53. Moran, Robert T. "Japanese Participative
Management--or How Rinji Seido Can Work for You." SAM
ADVANCED MANAGEMENT JOURNAL v.44 Summer 1979 pp.14-21.

HB 54. Morimiya, Y. "Japanese Approach to Risk
Treatment." RISK MANAGEMENT v.28 Nov. 1981 pp.46-49.

HB 55. Ohmae, Kenichi. "Foresight in Strategic
Planning." McKINSEY QUARTERLY Autumn 1982 pp.14-31. (An
excerpt from THE MIND OF THE STRATEGIST)

HB 56. Ohmae, Kenichi. "Foresighted Management
Decision Making: See the Options Before Planning
Strategy." MANAGEMENT REVIEW v.71 May 1982 pp.46-55.

HB 57. Ouchi, William G., and Johnson, J. B.
"Types of Organizational Control and Their Relationship
to Emotional Well Being." ADMINISTRATIVE SCIENCE
QUARTERLY v.23 1978 pp.293-317.

HB 58. Ozawa, Terutomo. "Japanese Chic." ACROSS
THE BOARD v.19 Oct. 1982 pp.6-13.

HB 59. Pascale, Richard Tanner. "Our Curious
Addiction to Corporate Grand Strategy." FORTUNE v.105
Jan. 25, 1982 pp.115-16.

HB 60. Phillips, L. A. "All Aboard the Japan Transfer." TECHNOLOGY REVIEW v. 80 May/June 1982 p. 80.

HB 61. Prasad, S. B. "A New System of Authority in Japanese Management." JOURNAL OF ASIAN AND AFRICAN STUDIES v. 3 no. 3-4 1968 pp. 216-225.

HB 62. Pucik, V. "Promotions and Intraorgani- zational Status Differentiation Among Japanese Managers." ACADEMY OF MANAGEMENT PROCEEDINGS 1981 41st Annual Meeting, San Diego, 1981. pp. 59-63.

HB 63. Schaeffer, D. "So What Do the Japanese Offer?" SUPERVISION v. 44 Nov. 1982 pp. 7-8.

HB 64. Sethi, S. P. "Japanese Management Practices." COLUMBIA JOURNAL OF WORLD BUSINESS v. 9 no. 4 1974 pp. 94-104.

HB 65. Shimizu, Ryuei. "A Study of Top Management Abilities: Through a Field Research on 79 Companies in the Electronics and Chain Restaurant Industries." KEIO BUSINESS REVIEW v. 20 1983 pp. 53-81.

HB 66. Stanton, E. S. "A Critical Reevaluation of Motivation, Management, and Productivity." PERSONNEL JOURNAL v. 62 March 1983 pp. 208-14.

HB 67. Stening, B. W., and Everett, J. E. "Japanese Managerial Attitudes at Home and Abroad." JOURNAL OF SOCIAL PSYCHOLOGY v. 111 1980 pp. 19-25.

HB 68. Stewart, Lea P.; Gudykunst, William B.; Ting-Toomey, Stella, et al. "The Effects of Decision-making Style on Openness and Satisfaction within Japanese Organizations." COMMUNICATIONS MONOGRAPHS v. 53 Sep. 1986 pp. 222-236.

HB 69. Takamiya, S. "Group Decision-Making in Japanese Management." INTERNATIONAL STUDIES OF MANAGEMENT AND ORGANIZATION v. 2 no. 2 1972 pp. 183-196.

HB. Management Practices

HB 70.   Takezawa, S. "Changing Worker Values and
Management Innovations in Japanese Industry." LABOUR
AND SOCIETY v.4 no.2 1979 pp.125-141.

HB 71.   Takezawa, S. "Changing Workers' Values and
Implications of Policy in Japan." in Davis, L. E. and
Cherns, A. B., eds. THE QUALITY OF WORKING LIFE. New
York: Free Press, 1975. pp.1 and 327-346.

HB 72.   "Togetherness Approach." CHEMICAL BUSINESS
Mar. 8, 1982 p.6.

HB 73.   Townsend, R. "Why the Japanese are So
Successful." MANAGEMENT REVIEW v.69 Oct. 1980 pp.29+.

HB 74.   Tracy, P., and Azumi, K. "Determinants of
Administrative Control: A Test of a Theory with
Japanese Factories." AMERICAN SOCIOLOGICAL REVIEW v.41
1976 pp.80-93.

HB 75.   Tsuda, Masumi. "Japanese-Style Management:
Principle and System." JAPANESE ECONOMIC STUDIES v.7
no.4 1979 pp.3-32.

HB 76.   "U.K. Conference Explodes Myths About Key
to Japan's Success." PERSONNEL MANAGEMENT v.15 p.12
Feb. 1983.

HB 77.   Urabe, Kuniyoshi. "A Critique of Theories
of the Japanese-Style Management System." JAPANESE
ECONOMIC STUDIES v.7 no.4 1979 pp.33-50.

HB 78.   "Vendor Relations: Get Firsthand View of
the Japanese Approach." PURCHASING v.92 Apr. 15, 1982
pp.24-5.

HB 79.   Wada, S. "How Sony Management Won Over Its
U.S. Workforce." MANAGEMENT REVIEW v.72 Feb. 1983
pp.31-32.

HB 80. Wadaki, Matsutaro; Shimizu, Ryuei; Fujimori, Mitsuo; and Sogowa, Hirokuni. "Decision-Making by Top-Management and Business Performance in Firms of Japan." KEIO BUSINESS REVIEW v.11 1972 pp.1-27.

HB 81. Wakabayashi, M., et al. "Managerial Career Development: Japanese Style." INTERNATIONAL JOURNAL OF INTERCULTURAL RELATIONS v.4 no.3-4 1980 pp.391-420.

HB 82. Weyr, T. "Japanese Management: The Quick Fix?" WORKING WOMAN v.7 Apr. 1982 pp.28+.

HB 83. Wilson, M. and Adkins, L. "How the Japanese Run U.S. Subsidiaries." DUN'S BUSINESS MONTH v.122 Oct. 1983 pp.32-35+

HB 84. Wood, R. C. "All in the Household." INC. v.4 Nov. 1982 pp.75-76+.

HB 85. Wright, J., and Jenney, B. W. "Secrets of Japanese Success." MANAGEMENT TODAY Jan. 1981 pp.64-67+.

HB 86. Yamada, T. "Japanese Management Practices--Change is On the Way as Traditional Habits Are Challenged." CONFERENCE BOARD RECORD v.6 no.11 1969 pp.22-23.

HB 87. Yoshino, M. Y. "Administrative Attitudes and Relationships in a Foreign Culture." MSU BUSINESS TOPICS v.16 no.1 1968 pp.59-66.

HB 88. "Younger Blood Rising To the Top in Japanese Companies." INTERNATIONAL MANAGEMENT v.38 July 1983 p.3.

HC. Personnel Management

Monographic Works

HC 1.   Dickerman, Allen B. TRAINING JAPANESE
MANAGERS. New York: Praeger, 1974. 104pp.

HC 2.   Freedman, Audrey. JAPANESE MANAGEMENT OF
U.S. WORK FORCES. The Conference Board Research
Bulletin no.119. New York: The Conference Board,
1982. 15pp.

HC 3.   Thurley, K.; Reitsperger, W.; Trevor, M.;
and Worm, P. THE DEVELOPMENT OF PERSONNEL MANAGEMENT IN
JAPANESE ENTERPRISES IN GREAT BRITAIN. London: London
School of Economics, 1980. 65pp.

HC 4.   Van Helvoort, E. THE JAPANESE WORKING MAN:
WHAT CHOICE? WHAT REWARD? Vancouver: University of
British Columbia, 1979. 158pp.

Articles

HC 5.   Beresford, M. "Why the Japanese Excel at
Personnel Management." INTERNATIONAL MANAGEMENT v.37
Mar. 1982 pp.20E3+.

HC 6.   Bowman, J. S. "Japanese Management:
Personnel Policies in the Public Sector." PUBLIC
PERSONNEL MANAGEMENT v.13 Fall 1984 pp.197-247.

HC 7.   Dewar, Donald L. "Returning Dignity to the Employee: the Path to Quality." NORTHERN CALIFORNIA REVIEW OF BUSINESS AND ECONOMICS v. 9 Nov. 1982 pp. 2-3+.

HC 8.   Hazama, H. "Formation of the Management System in Meiji Japan: Personnel Management in Large Corporations." THE DEVELOPING ECONOMIES v. 14 no. 4 1977 pp. 402-419.

HC 9.   Johnson, Chalmers. "The Reemployment of Retired Government Bureaucrats in Japanese Big Business." ASIAN SURVEY v. 14 1974 pp. 953-965.

HC 10.   Mino, Hokaji. "Seeking a Survival Strategy for Personnel Problems." BUSINESS JAPAN v. 27 Aug. 1982 pp. 26-30.

HC 11.   Neff, R. "Foibles Help Bring Japanese Back Down to Earth." INTERNATIONAL MANAGMENT v. 39 Aug. 1984 pp. 38-39.

HC 12.   Pucik, V. "White Collar Human Resource Management: A Comparison of the U. S. and Japanese Automobile Industries." COLUMBIA JOURNAL OF WORLD BUSINESS v. 19 Fall 1984 pp. 87-94.

HC 13.   Pucik, V. "White-Collar Human Resource Management in Large Japanese Manufacturing Firms." HUMAN RESOURCE MANAGEMENT v. 23 Fall 1984 pp. 257-276.

HC 14.   Starling, G. "Performance Appraisal in the Z Organization." PUBLIC PERSONNEL MANAGEMENT v. 11 Winter 1982 pp. 343-51.

HC 15.   Werter, William B., Jr. "Productivity Improvement Through People." ARIZONA BUSINESS v. 28 Feb. 1981 pp. 14-19.

HC 16.   "Why the Japanese Excel at Personnel Management." INTERNATIONAL MANAGEMENT Mar. 1982 pp. 20E-3--20E-6.

HD. Comparative Management

Monographic Works

HD 1.   England, G. W. THE MANAGER AND HIS VALUES:
AN INTERNATIONAL PERSPECTIVE FROM THE UNITED STATES,
JAPAN, KOREA, INDIA AND AUSTRALIA. Cambridge, Mass.:
Ballinger, 1975. 177pp.

HD 2.   Haire, Mason; Ghiselli, Edwin E.; and
Porter, Lyman W. MANAGERIAL THINKING: AN INTERNATIONAL
STUDY. New York: Wiley, 1966. 298pp.

HD 2a.   Heirs, Ben J., and Pehrson, Gordon. THE MIND
OF THE ORGANIZATION. Rev. ed.   New York: Harper & Row,
1982.   140pp.

HD 3.   Lancaster, Clay. THE JAPANESE INFLUENCE IN
AMERICA. New York: Abbeville Press, 1983, c1963. 314pp.

HD 4.   Leibenstein, Harvey. INSIDE THE FIRM: THE
INEFFICIENCIES OF HIERARCHY. Boston: Harvard University
Press, 1987. 304pp.

HD 5.   Okimoto, Daniel I.; Sugano, Takuo; and
Weinstein, Franklin B., eds.   COMPETITIVE EDGE: THE
SEMICONDUCTOR INDUSTRY IN THE U.S. AND JAPAN. Stanford,
Calif.: Stanford University Press, 1984. 275pp.

HD 6.   Pegels, Carl. JAPAN vs. THE WEST:
IMPLICATIONS FOR MANAGEMENT. Boston: Kluwer Nijhoff,
1984. 219pp.

HD 7.   Robinson, Richard D. THE JAPAN SYNDROME--IS
THERE ONE? CASES TO THE POINT. Atlanta: Georgia State
University, 1983. 225pp.

HD 8.   Shapiro, Harris, J., and Cosenza, Teresa.
THE AMERICANIZATION OF JAPANESE MANAGEMENT. Cambridge,
Mass.: Ballinger, 1987. 260pp.

HD 9.   Takezawa, Shinichi, and Whitehill, Arthur
M. WORK WAYS: JAPAN AND AMERICA. Tokyo: Japan Institute
of Labour, 1983. 230pp.

HD 10.   Trevor, Malcolm; Schendel, Jochen; and
Wilpert, Bernhard. THE JAPANESE MANAGEMENT DEVELOPMENT
SYSTEM: GENERALISTS AND SPECIALISTS IN JAPANESE
COMPANIES ABROAD. London: Pinter, 1987. 278pp.

HD 11.   Trevor, Malcolm. JAPAN'S RELUCTANT
MULTINATIONALS: JAPANESE MANAGEMENT AT HOME AND ABROAD.
New York: St. Martin's Press, 1983. 223pp.

Articles

HD 12.   Adam, E. E. "Towards a Typology of
Production and Operations Management Systems." ACADEMY
OF MANAGEMENT REVIEW v.8 July 1983 pp.365-75.

HD 13.   Bickerstaffe, G. "The Mixed Scorecard of
Japanese Management Abroad." INTERNATIONAL MANAGEMENT
v.38 July 1983 pp.12-16.

HD 14.   Bishop, D. "True Lessons of Japan."
MANAGEMENT TODAY Dec. 14, 1981 pp.42-45+.

HD 15.   Blotnick, S. "Supermen?" FORBES v.128 Aug.
17, 1981 pp.132-133.

HD 16.   Bowman, J. S., and Caison, F. K. "Japanese
Management in America: Experts Evaluate Japanese
Subsidiaries." ADVANCED MANAGEMENT JOURNAL v.51 Summer
1986 pp.22-28.

HD. Comparative Management

HD 17. Brockway, G. P. "America's Setting Sun."
NEW LEADER v.65 June 14, 1982 pp.8-9.

HD 18. Bryan, L. A. "Japanese and the American
First-Line Supervisor." TRAINING AND DEVELOPMENT
JOURNAL v.36 Jan. 1982 pp.62-68.

HD 19. Cathey, P. "Just How Different are American
and Japanese Managing Styles?" IRON AGE v.225 June 25,
1982 pp.40-41.

HD 20. Drucker, Peter F. "What We Can Learn from
Japanese Management." HARVARD BUSINESS REVIEW v.49
Mar./Apr. 1971 pp.110-122.

HD 21. English, C. W. "How Japanese Work Out as
Bosses in U.S." U.S. NEWS AND WORLD REPORT v.98 May 6,
1985 pp.75-76.

HD 22. England, G. W. "Managers and Their Value
Systems: A Five-Country Comparative Study." COLUMBIA
JOURNAL OF WORLD BUSINESS v.13 no.2 1978 pp.35-44.

HD 23. England, G. W., and Lee, R. "Organization
As an Influence on Perceived Organizational Goals: A
Comparative Study Among American, Japanese and Korean
Managers." ORGANIZATIONAL BEHAVIOR AND HUMAN
PERFORMANCE v.9 1973 pp.48-58.

HD 24. England, G. W., and Lee, R. "Organizational
Goals and Expected Behavior Among American, Japanese
and Korean Managers--A Comparative Study." ACADEMY OF
MANAGEMENT JOURNAL v.14 no.4 1971 pp.425-438.

HD 25. England, G. W., and Lee, R. "The
Relationship Between Managerial Values and Managerial
Success in the United States, Japan, India, and
Australia." JOURNAL OF APPLIED PSYCHOLOGY v.59 no.4
1974 pp.411-419.

HD 26.   Everett, J. E., and Stening, B. W.
"Intercultural Interpersonal Perceptions: A Study of
Japanese and Australian Managers." JAPANESE
PSYCHOLOGICAL RESEARCH v. 22 no. 1 1980 pp. 42-47.

HD 27.   Everett, J. E.; Stening, B. W.; and
Longton, P. A. "Stereotypes of the Japanese Manager in
Singapore." INTERNATIONAL JOURNAL OF INTERCULTURAL
RELATIONS v. 5 no. 3 1981 pp. 277-289.

HD 28.   Everett, J. E., and Stening, B. W.
"Japanese and British Managerial Colleagues--How They
View Each Other." JOURNAL OF MANAGEMENT STUDIES v. 20
Oct. 1983 pp. 467-475.

HD 29.   Everett, J. E., et al.   "Some Evidence for
an International Managerial Culture." JOURNAL OF
MANAGERIAL STUDIES v. 19 p. 153-62 Apr. 1982.

HD 30.   Franklin, W. H., Jr. "What Japanese
Managers Know That American Managers Don't."
ADMINISTRATIVE MANAGEMENT v. 42 Sep. 1981 pp. 36-39+.

HD 31.   Freedman, Audrey. "Learning from New
U.S.-Based Neighbors: Japanese Management of American
Work Forces." JOURNAL OF JAPANESE TRADE AND INDUSTRY
v. 1 Sep. 1982 pp. 31-33.

HD 32.   Friedman, T., and Solman, T. "Is American
Management Too Selfish?" FORBES v. 131 Jan. 17, 1983
pp. 75-77.

HD 33.   Fukuda, K. J. "Transfer of Management:
Japanese Practices for the Orientals?" MANAGEMENT
DECISIONS v. 21 no. 4 1983 pp. 17-26.

HD 34.   Gemmel, A. "Management in a Cross-cultural
Environment: the Best of Both Worlds." MANAGEMENT
SOLUTIONS v. 31 June 1986 pp. 28-33.

HD 35.   Georget, A. "They Stoop to Conquer." FAR
EAST ECONOMIC REVIEW v. 120 May 12, 1983 pp. 64-65.

HD 36. Hopkins, M. E. et al. "Japanese and American Managers." JOURNAL OF PSYCHOLOGY v. 96 1977 pp. 71-72.

HD 37. Horvath, Dezso; Azumi, K.; Hickson, D. J.; McMillan, Charles J. "Bureaucratic Structures in Cross-National Perspective: A Study of British, Japanese and Swedish Firms." in Dlugos, G., and Weiermair, K., eds. MANAGEMENT UNDER DIFFERING VALUE SYSTEMS: POLITICAL, SOCIAL AND ECONOMICAL PERSPECTIVES IN A CHANGING WORLD. Berlin: Walter de Gruyter, 1981. pp. 537-563.

HD 38. "How the Japanese Manage in the U. S." FORTUNE v. 103 June 15, 1981 pp. 97-98+.

HD 39. Howard, N. and Teramoto, Y. "Really Important Difference Between Japanese and Western Management." MANAGEMENT INTERNATIONAL REVIEW v. 21 no. 3 1981 pp. 19-30.

HD 40. Ibuka, M. "By Merging American Techniques with Japanese Cultural Philosophies Better Management can Develop." ADMINISTRATIVE MANAGEMENT v. 41 May 1980 pp. 86.

HD 41. Iida, Tsuneo. "Transferability of Japanese Management Systems and Practices into Australian Companies." HUMAN RESOURCE MANAGEMENT AUSTRALIA v. 21 no. 3 1983 pp. 23-27.

HD 42. Itami, H. "A Japanese-American Comparison of Management Productivity." JAPANESE ECONOMIC STUDIES v. 7 no. 1 1978 pp. 3-41.

HD 43. Jacobs, B. A. "Western Europe is Also Looking East." INDUSTRY WEEK v. 212 Mar. 22, 1982 pp. 44+.

HD 44. "Japan: the Japanization of an IBM Subsidiary." BUSINESS WEEK Apr. 6, 1981 p. 42.

HD 45.　"The Japanese Manager Meets the American Worker." BUSINESS WEEK Aug. 20, 1984 pp.128-129.

HD 46.　"Japanese Management in the United States." RESEARCH MANAGEMENT v.25 Jan. 1982 pp.3-4.

HD 47.　"Japanese Management Not for U.S." AUTOMOTIVE NEWS Apr. 25, 1983 p.13.

HD 48.　"Japanese Management Style Wins Converts." INDUSTRY WEEK v.201 Apr. 16, 1979 pp.19-20.

HD 49.　"Japanese-Style Management on Trial in America." ORIENTAL ECONOMIST v.51 Sep. 1983 pp.8-13.

HD 50.　Johnson, Richard T., and Ouchi, W. G. "Made in America (Under Japanese Management)." HARVARD BUSINESS REVIEW v.52 Sep./Oct. 1974 pp.61-69.

HD 51.　Kagono, T., et al.　"Mechanistic vs. Organic Management Systems: A Comparative Study of Adaptive Patterns of U.S. and Japanese Firms." KOBE ANNUAL REPORTS 1980 pp.115-139.

HD 52.　Kaufmann, F. "Decision Making Eastern and Western Style." BUSINESS HORIZONS v.13 no.6 1970 pp.81-86.

HD 53.　Kelley, L., and Worthley, R. "The Role of Culture in Comparative Management: A Cross-Cultural Perspective." ACADEMY OF MANAGMENT JOURNAL v.24 no.1 1981 pp.164-173.

HD 54.　Kono, Toyohiro. "Long Range Planning of U.K. and Japanese Corporations--A Comparative Study." LONG RANGE PLANNING v.17 Apr. 1984 pp.58-76.

HD 55.　Kuwahara, T. "An Understanding of the International Applicability of the Japanese Management System." KSU ECONOMIC AND BUSINESS REVIEW v.5 1978 pp.22-33.

HD 56. Licker, P. S. "On Beyond Z: Japanese Management Style Might Suit Us Just Fine." JOURNAL OF SYSTEMS MANAGMENT v.34 pp.10-13 Oct. 1983.

HD 57. McAbee, Michael. "Can Japanese Magic Work Here?" INDUSTRY WEEK v.218 Aug. 8, 1983 pp.46-48.

HD 58. McGovern, T. "Why Japan's Management Styles May Not Fit Here." NATION'S BUSINESS v.71 Aug. 1983 pp.30-31.

HD 59. McMillan, Charles J. "Is Japanese Management Really So Different?" BUSINESS QUARTERLY v.45 Autumn 1980 pp.26-31.

HD 60. Maguire, Mary Ann, and Pascale, Richard T. "Communication, Decision Making, and Implementation Among Managers in Japanese and American Managed Companies in the United States." SOCIOLOGY AND SOCIAL RESEARCH v.63 1978 pp.1-23.

HD 61. Muczyk, Jan P., and Hastings, Robert E. "The Management Club: A Quality Circle for Managers." BUSINESS HORIZONS v.27 Jan./Feb. 1984 pp.36-41.

HD 62. Nadler, L. "What Japan Learned from the U.S.--That We Forgot to Remember." CALIFORNIA MANAGEMENT REVIEW v.26 Summer 1984 pp.46-61.

HD 63. Nakayama, N. "United States and Japan: Some Management Contrasts." COMPUTERS AND PEOPLE v.29 Nov./Dec. 1980 pp.8-10+.

HD 64. Orpen, C. "Risk-Taking Attitudes Among Indian, United States and Japanese Managers." JOURNAL OF SOCIAL PSYCHOLOGY v.120 no.2 1983 pp.283-284.

HD 65. Ouchi, William G. "Theory Z: An Elaboration of Methodology and Findings." JOURNAL OF CONTEMPORARY BUSINESS v.11 no.2 1982 pp.27-42.

HD 66.   Ouchi, William G. "Theory Z Corporations: Straddling U.S. and Japanese Molds." INDUSTRY WEEK v.209 May 4, 1981 pp.48-50+.

HD 67.   Parkanskii, A. "Export of American Methods of Management to Japan." JAPANESE ECONOMIC STUDIES v.2 no.2 1973 pp.65-76.

HD 68.   Pascale, Richard Tanner. "Communication and Decision Making Across Cultures: Japanese and American Comparisons." ADMINISTRATIVE SCIENCE QUARTERLY v.23 1978 pp.91-110.

HD 69.   Pascale, Richard Tanner. "Personnel Practices and Employee Attitudes: A Study of Japanese-and American-Managed Firms in the United States." HUMAN RELATIONS v.31 no.7 1978 pp.597-615.

HD 70.   Peterson, Richard B., and Schwind, H. F. "A Comparative Study of Personnel Problems in International Companies and Joint Ventures in Japan." JOURNAL OF INTERNATIONAL BUSINESS STUDIES v.8 no.1 1977 pp.45-55.

HD 71.   Peterson, Richard B., and Shimada, J. Y. "Sources of Management Problems in Japanese-American Joint Ventures." ACADEMY OF MANAGEMENT REVIEW v.3 no.4 1978 pp.796-804.

HD 72.   Peterson, Richard B., and Sullivan, J. "Applying Japanese Management in the United States." JOURNAL OF CONTEMPORARY BUSINESS v.11 no.2 1982 pp.5-15.

HD 73.   Rehder, R. R. "Japanese Management: An American Challenge." HUMAN RESOURCE MANAGEMENT v.18 Winter 1979 pp.63-70.

HD 74.   Rehder, R. R. "What American and Japanese Managers are Learning from Each Other." BUSINESS HORIZONS v.24 Mar./Apr. 1981 pp.63-70.

HD. Comparative Management

HD 75. Reichel, A. "Values in Transition: an Empirical Study of Japanese Managers in the U.S." MANAGEMENT INTERNATIONAL REVIEW v.23 no.4 1983 pp.63-72.

HD 76. Reitsperger, W. "British Employees: Responding to Japanese Management Philosophies." JOURNAL OF MANAGEMENT STUDIES v.23 Sep. 1986 pp.563-586.

HD 77. Reitz, H. J., and Groff, G. K. "Economic Development and Belief in Locus of Control Among Factory Workers in Four Countries." JOURNAL OF CROSS-CULTURAL PSYCHOLOGY v.5 no.3 1974 pp.344-355.

HD 78. Saleh, S. D. "Management Systems in Japan and in North America." INDUSTRIAL MANAGEMENT v.24 Sep./Oct. 1982 pp.10-14.

HD 79. Schein, H. "SMR Forum: Does Japanese Management Style Have a Message for American Managers?" SLOAN MANAGEMENT REVIEW v.23 Fall 1981 pp.55-68.

HD 80. Schonberger, Richard J. "The Transfer of Japanese Manufacturing Management Approaches to U.S. Industry." ACADEMY OF MANAGEMENT REVIEW v.7 July 1982 pp.479-487.

HD 81. Sim, A. B. "Decentralized Management of Subsidiaries and Their Performance--Comparative Study of American, British and Japanese Subsidiaries in Malaysia." MANAGEMENT INTERNATIONAL REVIEW v.17 no.2 1977 pp.45-51.

HD 82. Smith, J. M. "The Japan Syndrome: Demystifying Japanese Management." MANAGEMENT DECISIONS v.21 no.3 1983 pp.25-33.

HD 83. Smith, L. "Japan's Autocratic Managers." FORTUNE v.111 Jan. 7, 1985 pp.56-65.

HD 84. Sorge, M. "Japanese System Can't Be Copied." AUTOMOTIVE NEWS p.12+ June 7, 1982.

HD 85. "Stamping Association Studies U.S./Japan Management Styles." AUTOMOTIVE INDUSTRIES v.162 May 1982 pp.25-26.

HD 86. Stening, B. W.; Everett, J. E.; and Longton, P. A. "Mutual Perceptions of Managerial Performance and Style in Multinational Subsidiaries." JOURNAL OF OCCUPATIONAL PSYCHOLOGY v.54 no.4 1981 pp.255-264.

HD 87. "Strategic Planning vs. Trial and Error in the U.S. and Japan." MANAGEMENT REVIEW v.71 Jun. 1982 pp.5-6.

HD 88. Sullivan, J.; Peterson, R. B.; Kameda, N.; and Shimada, J. "The Relationship Between Conflict Resolution Approaches and Trust: A Cross-Cultural Study." ACADEMY OF MANAGEMENT REVIEW v.24 no.4 1981 pp.803-815.

HD 89. Sullivan, J. J., and Nonaka, I. "The Application of Organizational Learning Theory to Japanese and American Management." JOURNAL OF INTERNATIONAL BUSINESS STUDIES v.17 Fall 1986 pp.127-147.

HD 90. Tavernier, Gerard. "Applying Japanese Techniques in the West." INTERNATIONAL MANAGEMENT June 1976 pp.35-40.

HD 91. Taylor, W. A., and Tanakadate, H. "Why Japan, Inc. Might Not Work in U.S." U.S. NEWS AND WORLD REPORT v.96 Jan. 30, 1984 pp.41+.

HD 92. "True Lessons from Japan." DIRECTOR Oct. 1981 p.9.

HD. Comparative Management

HD 93.   Tsurumi, Yoshi. "The Best of Times and the Worst of Times: Japanese Management in America." COLUMBIA JOURNAL OF WORLD BUSINESS v.13 Summer 1978 pp.56-61.

HD 94.   Tsurumi, Yoshi. "U.S. Managers Are Technologically Illiterate." CREATIVE COMPUTING v.10 Aug. 1984 pp.168-169.

HD 95.   Tung, Rosalie L. "Selection and Training Procedures of U.S., European, and Japanese Multinationals." CALIFORNIA MANAGEMENT REVIEW v.25 Fall 1982 pp.57-71.

HD 96.   "U.S. Concept Revives Oki." BUSINESS WEEK Mar. 1, 1982 p.112-13.

HD 97.   Yang, Charles Y. "Demystifying Japanese Management Practices." HARVARD BUSINESS REVIEW v.62 Nov./Dec. 1984 pp.172-174+.

HD 98.   Yang, Charles Y. "Management Styles: American Vis-a-Vis Japanese." COLUMBIA JOURNAL OF WORLD BUSINESS v.12 Fall 1977 pp.23-31.

XII.

CHAPTER 9

I. PRODUCTIVITY; QUALITY; QUALITY CONTROL

IA. Productivity (The Issue)

Monographic Works

IA 1.   Bernolak, Imre, ed.   PRODUCTIVITY
MEASUREMENT AND ANALYSIS: NEW ISSUES AND SOLUTIONS. APO
Study Meeting in Sri Lanka, 1982. Tokyo: Asian
Productivity Organization, 1983. 568 pp.

IA 2.   Burnham, John M., ed.   JAPANESE
PRODUCTIVITY: A STUDY MISSION REPORT. Falls Church,
Va.: American Production & Inventory Control Society,
1983. 76pp.

IA 3.   FACTORS WHICH HINDER OR HELP PRODUCTVITY
IMPROVEMENT IN THE ASIAN REGION--A REVIEW AND PROSPECT:
NATIONAL REPORT--JAPAN. Tokyo: Asian Productivity
Organization, 1981. 111pp.

IA. Productivity (The Issue)

IA 4.   The Japanese Standards Association.
RELIABILITY GUIDEBOOK. 8th ed.   Tokyo: Asian
Productivity Organization, 1972. 136pp.

IA 5.   MEASURING PRODUCTIVITY: TRENDS AND
COMPARISONS FROM THE FIRST INTERNATIONAL PRODUCTIVITY
SYMPOSIUM. New York: UNIPUB, 1984. 288pp.

IA 6.   METHODS FOR MEASURING PRODUCTIVITY:
INTERNATIONAL COMPARISONS. New York: UNIPUB, 1984.
250pp.

IA 7.   Mundel, Marvin E. MEASURING AND ENHANCING
THE PRODUCTIVITY OF SERVICE AND GOVERNMENT
ORGANIZATIONS. Tokyo: Asian Productivity Organization,
1980. 296pp.

IA 8.   Ross, Joel E. PRODUCTIVITY, PEOPLE, AND
PROFITS. Reston, Va.: Reston, 1981. 388pp.

IA 9.   Sadler, George E.; Steidtmann, Carl E.; and
Thor, Carl G. PRODUCTIVITY PERSPECTIVES. Houston:
American Productivity Center, 1981. 32pp.

IA 10.   STRATEGIES FOR PRODUCTIVITY: INTERNATIONAL
PERSPECTIVES. Sponsored by the Japan Productivity
Center. New York: UNIPUB, 1984. 158 pp.

IA 11.   United States. Congress. Joint Economic
Committee. JAPANESE AND AMERICAN ECONOMIC POLICIES AND
U.S. PRODUCTIVITY: HEARINGS, JUNE 23 AND JULY 28, 1981,
BEFORE THE SUBCOMMITTEE ON MONETARY AND FISCAL POLICY
AND THE SUBCOMMITTEE ON TRADE, PRODUCTIVITY, AND
ECONOMIC GROWTH. 97th Congress, 1st Session.
Washington, D.C.: Government Printing Office, 1981.
254pp.

IA 12.   Warburton-Brown, Derek. INVESTING IN VALUE.
Tokyo: Asian Productivity Organization, 1975. 164 pp.

IA. Productivity (The Issue)

Articles

IA 13.   "An Alternate Explanation for the
U.S.--Japan Productivity Gap." MANAGEMENT REVIEW v.72
Jan. 1983 pp.56-57.

IA 14.   Alvarez, D. and Cooper, B. "Productivity
Trends in Manufacturing in the U.S. and 11 Other
Countries." MONTHLY LABOR REVIEW v.107 Jan. 1984
pp.52-58.

IA 15.   "Business Studies Views of Managers and
Workers on Productivity and Quality." MONTHLY LABOR
REVIEW v.105 Apr. 1982 pp.58-59.

IA 16.   "Challenge of Increased Productivity." EDP
ANALYZER v.19 Apr. 1981 pp.1-12.

IA 17.   Christainsen, Gregory B. and Hogendorn, Jan
S. "Japanese Productivity: Adapting to Changing
Comparative Advantage in the Face of Lifetime
Employment Commitments." QUARTERLY REVIEW OF ECONOMICS
AND BUSINESS v.23 Summer 1983 pp.23-39.

IA 18.   Clutterbuck, David. "What Makes Japan(ese
Carmakers) So Productive?" INTERNATIONAL MANAGEMENT
v.33 April, 1978 pp.17-20.

IA 19.   Domar, Evsey David, et al. "Economic
Growth and Productivity in the United States, Canada,
United Kingdom, Germany and Japan in the Post-War
Period." REVIEW OF ECONOMICS AND STATISTICS v.46 no.1
Feb. 1964 pp.33-40.

IA 20.   Flynn, Michael S. "U.S. and Japanese
Automotive Productivity Comparisons: Strategic
Implications." NATIONAL PRODUCTIVITY REVIEW v.4 Winter
1984/1985 pp.60-71.

IA. Productivity (The Issue)

IA 21. Hatvany, Nina and Pucik, Vladimir.
"Japanese Management Practices and Productivity."
ORGANIZATIONAL DYNAMICS v.9 Spr. 1981 pp.4-21.

IA 22. Hecker, Gundolf. "A Comparison of
Productivity in the Federal Republic of Germany, Japan
and the U.S.A." INTERECONOMICS v.17 Nov./Dec. 1982
pp.286-90.

IA 23. Jacobs, B. A. "Quality Circles Alone Can't
Hike Productivity." INDUSTRY WEEK v.212 Feb. 8, 1982
pp.28-29.

IA 24. "Japanese Techniques Boost Productivity."
NEW ENGLAND BUSINESS Aug. 16, 1979 pp.10-11.

IA 25. Keegan, Warren J. "Productivity: Lessons
from Japan." LONG RANGE PLANNING v.8 April 1975
pp.61-71.

IA 26. Latham, G. P., and Saari, L. M. "The
Importance of Union Acceptance for Productivity
Improvement through Goal Setting." PERSONNEL PSYCHOLOGY
v.35 Winter 1982 pp.781-787.

IA 27. MacBeth, D. "Winning Production's Battle."
MANAGEMENT TODAY Apr. 1982 pp.76-78+.

IA 28. McNamara, Carlton P. "Productivity is
Management's Problem." BUSINESS HORIZONS v.26 Mar./Apr.
1983 pp.55-61.

IA 29. Mansfield, E. et al. "New Findings in
Technology Transfer, Productivity and Economic Policy."
RESEARCH MANAGEMENT v.26 Mar./Apr. 1983 pp.11-20.

IA 30. Mateyka, J. A. "Productivity Pressure is
Global: Will Technology become an Automotive
Commodity?" AUTOMOTIVE NEWS Feb. 28, 1983 pp.E17-E18.

IA 31. Miller, L. "Tearing Down the Barriers Between Management and Labor Leads to Increased Productivity and Greater Profits." MANAGEMENT REVIEW v.73 May 1984 pp.8-15.

IA 32. Muson, H. "The Patron Saint of Japanese Productivity." PSYCHOLOGY TODAY v.16 Dec. 1982 p.7. (re: Ninomiya Sontoku).

IA 33. Nellerman, David O. "Productivity--the Japanese Formula." Arthur Anderson and Company, Working Paper, New York, 1981.

IA 34. Okamo, Yukihide, and Okabe, Mitsuaki. "The Conditions for Labour Productivity--Japan." in Addison, John, et al. JOB CREATION--OR DESTRUCTION. London: Institute of Economic Affairs, 1979. pp.91-102.

IA 35. Patrick, Hugh Talbot. "The Future of the Japanese Economy: Output and Labor Productivity." JOURNAL OF JAPANESE STUDIES v.3 no.2 1977 pp.219-249.

IA 36. "Production Concentration in Japanese Industries." ORIENTAL ECONOMIST v.34 no.669 July 1966 p.412+.

IA 37. "Productivity." FORBES v.130 Nov. 8, 1982 pp.181-196 (advertisment section).

IA 38. "Productivity and Japan." BEVERAGE INDUSTRIES v.71 Nov. 20, 1981.

IA 39. Riggs, J. L., and Seo, K. K. "Wa: Personal Factor of Japanese Productivity." INDUSTRIAL ENGINEERING Apr. 1976 pp.32-35.

IA 40. Thurow, Lester C. "Productivity: Japan Has a Better Way." NEW YORK TIMES Feb. 8, 1981 Business Sect., p.2.

IA. Productivity (The Issue)

IA 41. Tsurumi, Yoshi. "Productivity: The Japanese Approach." PACIFIC BASIN QUARTERLY Summer 1981 pp. 7-9.

IA 42. Ueno, Ichiro; Blake, Robert R.; and Mouton, Jane S. "The Productivity Battle: A Behavioral Science Analysis of Japan and the United States." JOURNAL OF APPLIED BEHAVIORAL SCIENCE v. 20 no. 1 1984 pp. 49-56.

IA 43. Werther, William B., Jr. "Out of the Productivity Box." BUSINESS HORIZONS v. 25 Sep./Oct. 1982 pp. 51-59.

IA 44. White, James A. "Importing Productivity: Xerox Expects to Learn a Thing or Two from Successful Japanese Imitators." WALL STREET JOURNAL v. 200 July, 30, 1982 p. 40.

IA 45. Williamson, Nicholas C. "Japanese Productivity: Advances in Production and Marketing." BUSINESS (Atlanta) v. 34 Apr./June 1984 pp. 16-21.

IA 46. Williamson, Nicholas C. "Productivity--Another Japanese export." BUSINESS (Atlanta) v. 33 Oct./Dec. 1983 pp. 3-10.

IB. Production Management; Kanban;
Inventory Control

Monographic Works

IB 1. Fukuda, Ryuji. MANAGERIAL ENGINEERING: TECHNIQUES FOR IMPROVING QUALITY AND PRODUCTIVITY IN THE WORKPLACE. Cambridge, Mass.: Productivity Inc., 1983. 179pp.

IB 2.   Hall, Robert W. ZERO INVENTORIES. Homewood, Ill.: Dow Jones-Irwin, 1983. 329pp.

IB 3.   Hartley, John. FLEXIBLE AUTOMATION IN JAPAN. Bedford: IFS, 1984. 264pp.

IB 4.   Levy, Dana, and Sneider, Lea. KANBAN: SHOP SIGNS OF JAPAN. New York: Weatherhill, 1983. 167pp.

IB 5.   MANUAL ON PLANT LAYOUT AND MATERIALS HANDLING. Tokyo: Asian Productivity Organization, 1971. 80 pp.

IB 6.   Marsh, Robert M., and Mannari, Hiroshi. MODERNIZATION AND THE JAPANESE FACTORY. Princeton, N.J.: Princeton University Press, 1976. 437pp.

IB 7.   Monden, Yasuhiro. TOYOTA PRODUCTION SYSTEM: PRACTICAL APPROACH TO PRODUCTION MANAGEMENT. Norcross, Ga.: Institute Engineering and Management Press, Institute of Industrial Engineers, 1983. 247pp.

IB 8.   Ogawa, Eiji. MODERN PRODUCTION MANAGEMENT: A JAPANESE EXPERIENCE. Tokyo: Asian Productivity Organization, 1985. 132pp. (Including a special emphasis on the Toyota Production System.)

IB 9.   ORGANIZING FOR HIGHER PRODUCTIVITY: AN ANALYSIS OF JAPANESE SYSTEMS AND PRACTICES. New York: Unipub, 1982. 75pp.

IB 10.   PRODUCTION ENGINEERING. Part 1: PRODUCTION ENGINEERING COURSE, by Niebel, Benjamin. Part 2: MANUFACTURING ENGINEERING TRAINING MANUAL, by Ghesdahl, Maurice S. Tokyo: Asian Productivity Center, 1971. 148 pp.

IB 11.   Schonberger, Richard J. JAPANESE MANUFACTURING TECHNIQUES: NINE HIDDEN LESSONS IN SIMPLICITY. New York: The Free Press, 1982. 260pp.

IB. Production Management; Kanban

IB 12. Schonberger, Richard J. WORLD CLASS MANUFACTURING: THE LESSONS OF SIMPLICITY APPLIED. New York: Free Press, 1986. 252pp.

Articles

IB 13. "APICS Tours Japan." PRODUCTION AND INVENTORY MANAGEMENT REVIEW AND APICS NEWS v.2 no.5 May 1982 p.7.

IB 14. "Auto Makers Have Trouble with Kanban." WALL STREET JOURNAL April 7, 1982 pp.1, 32.

IB 15. Baker, E. F. "The Changing Scene on the Production Floor" MANAGEMENT REVIEW v.72 Jan. 1983 pp.8-11.

IB 16. Barks, J. V. "Some Words of Caution Arrive Just In Time." DISTRIBUTION v.83 Jan. 1984 p.30.

IB 17. Baxter, J. D. "Kanban Works Wonders, But Will It Work in U.S. Industry?" IRON AGE v.225 June 7, 1982 pp.44-45+.

IB 18. Bernstein, J. "How Japanese Hype Productivity." AUTOMOTIVE NEWS May 25, 1981 pp.24+.

IB 19. Bierman, M. G. "Flying for Just-In-Time." HANDLING AND SHIPPING MANAGEMENT v.25 Oct. 1984 pp.44-46+.

IB 20. Biermeier, F. "JIT: a Timely Lesson from the Japanese." CHAIN STORE AGE SUPERMARKET EDITION v.59 Apr. 1983 p.44.

IB 21. Brownstein, V. "The War on Inventories is Real this Time." FORTUNE v.109 Jun. 11, 1984 pp.20-24.

IB 22. "Can Kanban Ban Inventory Blues?" INDUSTRY WEEK v.214 July 26, 1982 pp.21-22.

IB 23. Donlan, T. G. "Yen for Productivity: an Inside View of Why Japan Inc. Works." BARRON'S v.62 Aug. 2, 1982 pp.28-29.

IB 24. Farrell, J. W. "Lessons from the East." TRAFFIC MANAGEMENT v.23 Jan. 1984 p.83.

IB 25. Feldman, Joan M. "Transportation Changes-- Just In Time." HANDLING AND SHIPPING MANAGEMENT v.25 Sep. 1984 pp.46-48+.

IB 26. Hahn, C. K., et al. "Just-In-Time Production and Purchasing." JOURNAL OF PURCHASING MATERIALS MANAGEMENT v.19 pp.2-10 Fall 1983.

IB 27. Hartley, John R. "Let's Get Kanban Right." AUTOMOTIVE INDUSTRIES v.161 Oct. 1981 pp.37-39.

IB 28. Harvey, R. E. "Is Japan Doing a Better Job Managing Inventory?" IRON AGE v.224 June 1, 1981 pp.38-41.

IB 29. Heydt, B. "Made in Japan." DISTRIBUTION v.83 Apr. 1984 pp.49-50+.

IB 30. Huang, P. Y. et al. "A Simulation Analysis of the Japanese Just-In-Time Technique (with Kanbans) for a Multiline, Multistage Production System. DECISION SCIENCES v.14 Jul. 1983 pp.326-344.

IB 31. Hunt, R., et al. "Direct Labor Cost Not Always Relevant at H-P." Hewlett-Packard MANAGEMENT ACCOUNTING v.66 Feb. 1985 pp.58-62.

IB 32. Monden, Yasuhiro. "Adaptable Kanban System Helps Toyota Maintain Just-In-Time Production." INDUSTRIAL ENGINEERING v. May 1981 pp.29-46.

IB. Production Management; Kanban

IB 33. Mondon, Yasuhiro. "Smoothed Production Lets Toyota Adapt to Changes and Reduce Inventory (Part I)." v. 13 Aug. 1981 pp. 42-51.

IB 34. Mondon, Yasuhiro. "Toyota's Production-Smoothing Methods: Part II." INDUSTRIAL ENGINEERING v. 13 Sep. 1981 pp. 22-30.

IB 35. Monden, Yasuhiro. "What Makes the Toyota Production System Really Tick?" INDUSTRIAL ENGINEERING v. 13 Jan. 1981 pp. 36-46.

IB 36. Morecraft, J. D. W. "A Systems Perspective on Material Requirements Planning." DECISION SCIENCES v. 14 Jan. 1983 pp. 1-18.

IB 37. Moskal, B. S. "Manufacturing: Just in Time; Putting the Squeeze on the Suppliers." INDUSTRY WEEK v. 222 July 9, 1984 pp. 59-60+.

IB 38. Moskal, B. S. "Kanban Changes Material Planning." INDUSTRY WEEK v. 218 July 25, 1983 pp. 73+.

IB 39. Pegels, C. Carl. "Critical Aspects of Japanese Component Suppliers and Employment Subcontractors." INTERNATIONAL JOURNAL OF OPERATIONS AND PRODUCTION MANAGEMENT v. 3 no. 1 1983 pp. 3-9.

IB 40. Pegels, C. Carl. "The Toyota Production System--Lessons for American Management." INTERNATIONAL JOURNAL OF OPERATIONS AND PRODUCTION MANAGEMENT v. 3 no. 2 1983.

IB 41. Schonberger, Richard J. "Applications of Single-Card and Dual-Card Kanban." INTERFACES v. 13 Aug. 1983 p. 56-67.

IB 42. Schonberger, Richard J., and Ansari, A. "Just-In-Time Purchasing Can Improve Quality." JOURNAL OF PURCHASING AND MATERIALS MANAGEMENT v. 20 Spring 1984 pp. 2-7.

IB 43.   Schonberger, Richard J., and Schniederjans, M. J. "Reinventing Inventory Control." INTERFACES v.14 May-June 1984 pp.76-83.

IB 44.   Seglund, R., and Ibarreche, S. "Just-In-Time: the Accounting Implications." MANAGEMENT ACCOUNTING v.66 Aug. 1984 pp.43-45.

IB 45.   Smith, C., and Frazelle, E. "Soko Circles: the Gateway to Improved Warehouse Productivity." HANDLING AND SHIPPING MANAGEMENT v.25 Sep. 1984 pp.69-70+.

IB 46.   Sorge, M. "Just In Time Cuts GM Inventory." AUTOMOTIVE NEWS Sep. 6, 1982 p.36.

IB 47.   Sorge, M. "Just-In-Time Requires Lots of Trust." AUTOMOTIVE NEWS Nov. 22, 1982 p.28.

IB 48.   Sorge, M. "Kanban Timing Stirs Disagreement." AUTOMOTIVE NEWS July 25, 1983 p.18.

IB 49.   Sugimori, Y.; Kusunoki, K.; Cho, F.; Uchikawa, S. "Toyota Production System and Kanban System: Materialization of Just-In-Time and Respect-For-Human System." INTERNATIONAL JOURNAL OF PRODUCTION RESEARCH v.15 no.6 1977 pp.553-64.

IB 50.   Teplitz, C. J. "Manufacturers Shift the Inventory Carrying Function." INDUSTRIAL MARKETING MANAGEMENT v.11 Jul. 1982 pp.225-230.

IC. Quality Control; Quality Circles

Monographic Works

IC 1.   Amsden, Davida M., and Amsden, Robert T. QC CIRCLES: APPLICATIONS, TOOLS, AND THEORY. Milwaukee, Wis.: American Society for Quality Control, 1967. 174pp.

IC 2.   Amsden, Davida M., et al, eds. QUALITY CIRCLES PAPERS: A COMPILATION. Milwaukee, Wis.: American Society for Quality Control, 1983. 252pp.

IC 3.   Crocker, Olga L., et al. QUALITY CIRCLES: A GUIDE TO PARTICIPATION AND PRODUCTIVITY. New York: Facts On File, 1984. 294pp.

IC 4.   Crosby, Phillip B. QUALITY WITHOUT TEARS: THE ART OF HASSLE-FREE MANAGEMENT. New York: McGraw-Hill, 1984, 205pp.

IC 5.   Dewar, Donald L. QUALITY CIRCLES: ANSWERS TO 100 FREQUENTLY ASKED QUESTIONS. Rev. ed.   Red Bluff, Calif.: Quality Circle Institute, 1984, c1979.   48pp.

IC 6.   Gryna, Frank M., Jr. QUALITY CIRCLES: A TEAM APPROACH TO PROBLEM SOLVING. New American Management Associations, 1981. 96pp.

IC 7.   Ingle, Sud. QUALITY CIRCLES MASTER GUIDE: INCREASING PRODUCTIVITY WITH PEOPLE POWER. Englewood Cliffs, NJ: Prentice-Hall, 1982. 246pp.

IC 8.   Ishikawa, Kaoru. GUIDE TO QUALITY CONTROL. 2nd rev. ed.   Tokyo: Asian Productivity Organization, 1982. 226pp.

IC 9. Ishikawa, Kaoru. QC CIRCLE ACTIVITIES. QC in Japan Series no.1. Tokyo: Union of Japanese Scientists & Engineers, 1968, c1958. 120pp.

IC 10. Japan External Trade Organization. (JETRO) PRODUCTIVITY AND QUALITY CONTROL: THE JAPANESE EXPERIENCE. Now in Japan, no.30/1981. Tokyo: Japan External Trade Organization, 1981. 40pp.

IC 11. JAPAN QUALITY CONTROL CIRCLES: QUALITY CONTROL CIRCLE CASE STUDIES. Tokyo: Asian Productivity Organization, 1982, c1972. 208pp.

IC 12. QUALITY CONTROL CIRCLES AT WORK. Introduction by Ishikawa, Kaoru. Tokyo: Asian Productivity Organization, 1984. 226 pp.

IC 13. Robson, Mike. QUALITY CIRCLES IN ACTION. Brookfield, Vt.: Gower Publishing Co., 1984. 176pp.

IC 14. Ross, Joel E., and Ross, William C. JAPANESE QUALITY CIRCLES AND PRODUCTIVITY. Reston, Va.: Reston, 1982. 205pp.

IC 15. Shingo, Shigeo. ZERO QUALITY CONTROL: SOURCE INSPECTION AND THE POKA-YOKE SYSTEM. Stamford, Conn.: Productivity Press, 1986. 303pp.

Articles

IC 16. Alexander, C. P. "A Hidden Benefit of Quality Circles." PERSONNEL JOURNAL v.63 Feb. 1984 pp.54+.

IC 17. Ambler, A. R., and Overholt, M. H. "Are Quality Circles Right for Your Company?" PERSONNEL JOURNAL v.61 Nov. 1982 pp.829-31.

IC. Quality Control; Quality Circles

IC 18.   Arbose, J. R. "Is Japan Cornering the
Market on Product Quality?" INTERNATIONAL MANAGEMENT
v. 36 Jan. 1981 pp. 22-25.

IC 19.   Archibald, R. B. "Quality, Price,
Advertising, and Published Quality Ratings." JOURNAL OF
CONSUMER RESEARCH v. 9 Mar. 1983.

IC 20.   Bank, John, and Wilpert, Bernhard. "What's
So Special About Quality Circles?" JOURNAL OF GENERAL
MANAGEMENT v. 9 Autumn 1983 pp. 21-27.

IC 21.   "Behind Japan's Economic Success." CANADIAN
BUSINESS REVIEW v. 8 Summer 1981 pp. 22-26.

IC 22.   Behrens, C. K., and Sollenberger, J. R.
"The National Labor Relations Act: a Potential Legal
Constraint Upon Quality Circles and Their
Employer-Sponsored Employee Committees." LABOR LAW
JOURNAL v. 34 Dec. 1983 pp. 776-80.

IC 23.   Blotnick, S. "If It's American, It Must Be
Bad." FORBES v. 129 Feb. 1, 1982 p. 146.

IC 24.   Bocker, H. J. and Overgaard, H. O.
"Japanese Quality Circles: a Managerial Response to the
Productivity Problem. MANAGEMENT INTERNATIONAL REVIEW
v. 22 no. 2 1982 pp. 13-19.

IC 25.   "Can Quality Circles Boost Your
Productivity?" PURCHASING v. 90 May 14, 1981 pp. 77+.

IC 26.   "Circle of Quality." FLEET OWNER v. 76 Feb.
1981 pp. 88-90.

IC 27.   Cole, Robert E. "Made in Japan--Quality
Control Circles." ACROSS THE BOARD v. 16 Nov. 1979
pp. 72+.

IC 28.   Crosby, Philip B. "The Management of Quality.
RESEARCH MANAGEMENT v. 25 July 1982 pp. 10-12.

IC. Quality Control; Quality Circles

IC 29. Cronin, W. "QCs: a Roundtable Process to Expose and Strengthen Weaknesses." TELEPHONY v. 204 Feb. 14, 1983 pp. 38+.

IC 30. Dailey, J. J. and Kagerer, R. L. "Primer on Quality Circles." SUPERVISORY MANAGEMENT v. 27 June 1982 pp. 40-43.

IC 31. Dubois, Pierre. "Quality Circles: a Valuable Tool for Effective Management." CANADIAN BANKER v. 90 Apr. 1983 pp. 38-43.

IC 32. Dumas, R. A. "The Shaky Foundations of Quality Circles." TRAINING v. 20 Apr. 1983 pp. 32-33.

IC 33. Geistfeld, L. V. "The Price-Quality Relationship--Revisited" JOURNAL OF CONSUMER AFFAIRS v. 16 Winter 1982 pp. 334-46.

IC 34. George, W. W. "How Honeywell Takes Advantage of National Cultural Differences." MANAGEMENT REVIEW v. 72 Sep. 1983 pp. 30-31.

IC 35. Gillett, D. "Better QCs: a Need for More Manager Action." MANAGEMENT REVIEW v. 72 Jan. 1983 pp. 19-25.

IC 36. Gray, Christopher S. "Total Quality Control in Japan--Less Inspection, Lower Cost." BUSINESS WEEK July 16, 1981 pp. 23-44.

IC 37. Hiraoka, Hirosuke. "Total Quality Control at Komatsu." JAPANESE MANAGEMENT no. 20 Spring/Summer 1982 pp. 14-18.

IC 38. "How MRP and JIT Do Work together." (Material Requirements Planning and Just-In-Time) PURCHASING v. 97 Nov. 29, 1984 pp. 43+.

IC 39. Hranac, Jo Anne. "Quality Control Circles for Small Business." JOURNAL OF SMALL BUSINESS MANAGEMENT v. 21 Jan. 1983 pp. 21-27.

IC. Quality Control; Quality Circles

IC 40. Imberman, W. "A Manager's Guide: Making
Quality Control Circles Work." DATA MANAGEMENT v. 20
p. 24-7 Nov. 1982.

IC 41. Imberman, W. "Why Quality Control Circles
Don't Work." CANADIAN BUSINESS v. 55 May 1982
pp. 103-4+.

IC 42. "In Sony--So UnJapanese that Even the
Quality Circles are Called Improvement Groups."
PERSONNEL MANAGEMENT v. 16 Jan. 1984 p. 41.

IC 43. Irving, R. R. "Quality Control by the
Numbers." IRON AGE v. 226 Aug. 1, 1983 pp. 37+.

IC 44. Irving, R. R. "Quality in Design." IRON AGE
v. 226 Aug. 1, 1983 pp. 35-37+.

IC 45. Ishikawa, Kaoru. "Quality Control in Japan:
Company-Wide Quality Control (CWQC)." DENTSU JAPAN
MARKETING/ADVERTISING Jan. 1982 pp. 4-8.

IC 46. Juran, J. M. "Japanese and Western
Quality--a Contrast." QUALITY PROGRESS v. 11 Dec. 1978
pp. 10-18.

IC 47. Juran, J. M. "Japanese and Western Quality:
a Contrast in Methods and Results." MANAGEMENT REVIEW
November 1978 pp. 26-45.

IC 48. Juran, J. M. "The QC Circle Phenomenon."
INDUSTRIAL QUALITY CONTROL v. 23 Jan. 1967 pp. 329-336.

IC 49. Karatsu, H. "What Makes Japanese Products
Better?" SAM ADVANCED MANAGEMENT JOURNAL v. 47 Spring
1982 pp. 4-7.

IC 50. Kobayshi, Y. "Quality Control in Japan: The
Case of Fuji Xerox." JAPANESE ECONOMIC STUDIES v. 11
no. 3 1983 pp. 75-104.

IC. Quality Control; Quality Circles

IC 51. Konz, Stephen. "Quality Circles: Japanese Success Story." INDUSTRIAL ENGINEERING Oct. 1979 pp. 24-27.

IC 52. Lawler, Edward E., III, and Mohrman, Susan. "Quality Circles After the Fad." HARVARD BUSINESS REVIEW v. 63 Jan./Feb. 1985 pp. 64-71.

IC 53. Lohr, Steve. "Consultant on Quality: W. Edwards Deming--He Taught the Japanese." NEW YORK TIMES May 10, 1981 p. 6.

IC 54. "The Long Road to Zero Defect Quality." INTERNATIONAL MANAGEMENT V. 38 July 1983 pp. 53-55+.

IC 55. Mahon, William A., and Dyck, Richard E. "Japanese Quality Systems from a Marketing Viewpoint." INDUSTRIAL MANAGEMENT AND SYSTEMS DATA Sep./Oct. 1982 pp. 8-14.

IC 56. Main, J. "The Curmudgeon Who Talks Tough on Quality." FORTUNE v. 109 June 25, 1984 pp. 118-122. (re: W. E. Deming.)

IC 57. Mroczkowski, Tomasz. "Quality Circles, Fine--What Next?" PERSONNEL ADMINISTRATOR v. 29 June 1984 pp. 173-174+.

IC 58. Rehder, R. R., and Ralston, F. "Total Quality Management: A Revolutionary Management Philosophy." ADVANCED MANAGEMENT JOURNAL v. 49 Summer 1984 pp. 24-33.

IC 59. Ringbe, William M. "The American Who Remade 'Made in Japan'." NATION'S BUSINESS Feb. 1981 pp. 67-70. (re: W. E. Deming.)

IC 60. Sato, Norikazu. "Behind Japan's Economic Success: Workers Form Quality Control Circles to Ensure Total Quality Control, Improve Product Quality and Increase Worker Morale." CANADIAN BUSINESS REVIEW v. 8 Summer 1981 pp. 22-23.

IC. Quality Control; Quality Circles

IC 61. Seidel, L. E. "Will Quality Circles Come
Full Cycle?" TEXTILE INDUSTRIES v.147 Mar. 1983
pp.48-50.

IC 62. Smeltzer, Larry R., III, and Kedia, Ben L.
"Knowing the Ropes: Organizational Requirements for
Quality Circles." BUSINESS HORIZONS v.28 July/Aug. 1985
pp.30-34.

IC 63. Temin, T. R. "How Quality Circles have
Fared in Japan." PURCHASING v.91 Nov. 25, 1981 pp.29+.

IC 64. "Test Your Company's Climate Before
Installing Quality Circles." TRAINING v.19 Nov. 1982
p.13.

IC 65. Thompson, Donald B. "Crucible Steel Molds
Problem-Solving Teams." INDUSTRY WEEK v.206 Sep. 29,
1980 pp.26-27+.

IC 66. Thompson, W. "Is the Organization Ready for
Quality Circles?" TRAINING AND DEVELOPMENT JOURNAL v.36
Dec. 1982 pp.115-18.

IC 67. Trevor, M. "Quality Control--Learning from
the Japanese." LONG RANGE PLANNING v.19 Oct. 1986
pp.46-53.

IC 68. Tribus, M. "Prize-Winning Japanese Firms'
Quality Management Programs Pass Inspection."
MANAGEMENT REVIEW v.73 Feb. 1984 pp.31-32+.

IC 69. Uemura, K. "Circle Activities and
Productivity at the Fuji Bank." BANKER'S MAGAZINE v.165
Nov./Dec. 1982 pp.32-34.

IC 70. Yamada, Y., and Ackerman, N.
"Price--Quality Correlations in the Japanese Market."
JOURNAL OF CONSUMER AFFAIRS v.18 Winter 1984
pp.251-265.

IC. Quality Control; Quality Circles

IC 71.   Zahra, S. A. "How To Be an Effective QC
Leader." SUPERVISORY MANAGEMENT v.28 Sep. 1983
pp.19-23.

ID. High Technology; Robotics

Monographic Works

ID 1.   Baranson, Jack. ROBOTS IN MANUFACTURING: KEY
TO INTERNATIONAL COMPETITIVENESS. Mt. Airy, Md.: Lomond
Pub., 1983. 152pp.

ID 2.   Cusumano, Michael A. THE JAPANESE AUTOMOBILE
INDUSTRY: TECHNOLOGY AND MANAGEMENT AT NISSAN AND
TOYOTA. Harvard East Asian Monographs, 122. Cambridge,
Mass.: Harvard University Press, 1986. 487pp.

ID 3.   Feigenbaum, Edward A., and McCorduck,
Pamela. THE FIFTH GENERATION: ARTIFICIAL INTELLIGENCE
AND JAPAN'S COMPUTER CHALLENGE TO THE WORLD. Reading,
Mass.: Addison-Wesley, 1983. 275pp.

ID 4.   Kansai Productivity Center. MECHATRONICS.
Tokyo: Asian Productivity Organization, 1985. 200pp.

ID 5.   Takagi, Noboru, et al.   CAD--CAM AND MIS IN
JAPAN: COMPUTER APPLICATIONS IN JAPANESE INDUSTRY.
London: Academic Press, 1986. 432pp.

ID 6.   Tatsuno, Sheridan. THE TECHNOPOLIS STRATEGY:
JAPAN, HIGH TECHNOLOGY AND THE CONTROL OF THE
TWENTY-FIRST CENTURY. New York: Prentice-Hall, 1986.
298pp.

ID 7.   United States. Congress. House. Committee on
Science and Technology. Subcommittee on Science,
Research and Technology. THE ROLE OF TECHNICAL

363

ID. High Technology; Robotics

INFORMATION IN U.S. COMPETITIVENESS WITH JAPAN;
HEARINGS BEFORE THE SUBCOMMITTEE ... JUNE 26, 27, 1985.
Washington, D.C.: U.S. Government Printing Office,
1985. 295pp.

ID 8.   Wright, J. C. TECHNOECONOMICS: CONCEPTS AND
CASES. Tokyo: Asian Productivity Organization, 1983.
178 pp.

Articles

ID 9.   Bell, John; Johnstone, Bob; and Nakaki,
Setsuko. "The New Face of Japanese Science." WORLD
PRESS REVIEW v.32 June 1985 pp.23-25.

ID 10.   Blumenthal, Tuvia. "Factor Proportions and
Choice of Technology: The Japanese Experience."
ECONOMIC DEVELOPMENT AND CULTURAL CHANGE v.28 Apr. 1980
pp.547-559.

ID 11.   Blumenthal, Tuvia, and Teubal, Morris. "The
Role of Future Oriental Technology in Japan's Economic
Development." HITOTSUBASHI JOURNAL OF ECONOMICS v.20
June 1979 pp.33-43.

ID 12.   "Factor Proportions and Choice of
Technology: The Japanese Experience." (discussion: T.
Blumenthal) ECONOMIC DEVELOPMENT AND CULTURAL CHANGE
v.29 July 1981 pp.842-888.

ID 13.   Goland, M. "Technological Cooperation with
the Japanese." SCIENCE v.223 Jan. 20, 1984 p.241.

ID 14.   Gralinski, Christian. "Information and
Documentation in Science and Technology in Japan."
JOURNAL OF INFORMATION SCIENCE v.5 Nov. 1982 pp.63-77.

ID 15.   Gregory, G. "Japan's Industrial
Revolution." FUTURIST v.16 Aug. 1982 pp.30-32.

ID 16. Gregory, G., et al. "Japan's Third Revolution." WORLD PRESS REVIEW v.29 Mar. 1982 pp.23-25.

ID 17. Gregory, Gene A., and Etori, Akio. "Japanese Technology Today." SCIENTIFIC AMERICAN v.245 Oct. 1981 pp.75-130.

ID 18. Hoos, Ida R., and Jones, Brownie Lee. "Office Automation in Japan." INTERNATIONAL LABOR REVIEW v.87 July 1963 pp.551-572.

ID 19. "Japan 2000." OMNI v.7 June 1985 pp.6+.

ID 20. "Japan's High-Tech Challenge." NEWSWEEK v.100 Aug. 9, 1982 pp.48-56+. (special section).

ID 21. Junnosuke, Kishida. "Japanese Technology, Its Strengths and Future Challenge." JAPAN QUARTERLY v.29 Dec. 1982 pp.426+.

ID 22. Lee, A. M. "A Tale of Two Countries: Some Systems Perspectives on Japan and the United Kingdom in the Age of Information Technology." JOURNAL OF THE OPERATIONAL RESEARCH SOCIETY v.34 Aug. 1983 pp.753-63.

ID 23. Lehner, Urban C. "Japanese Factories are Points of Interest to Foreign Tourists Studying Technology." WALL STREET JOURNAL v.198 Sep. 3, 1981 p.44.

ID 24. Lynn, Leonard. "Japanese Technology: Successes and Strategies." CURRENT HISTORY v.82 Nov. 1983 pp.366-370+.

ID 25. Machida, Y. "The General Trends in Japan's High Technology Industries." GESTION 2000 v.4 no.4 1985 pp.87-128.

ID. High Technology; Robotics

ID 26. Marsh, Robert M., and Mannari, Hiroshi.
"Technological Implications Theory: A Japanese Test."
ORGANIZATION STUDIES v. 1 1980 pp. 161-183.

ID 27. Meyers, K. A. et al. "Requirements
Planning for Control of Information Resources."
DECISION SCIENCES v. 14 Jan. 1983 pp. 19-33.

ID 28. Minami, Ryoshin. "Industrialization and
Technological Progress in Japan." ASIAN DEVELOPMENT
REVIEW v. 2 no. 2 1984 pp. 69-79.

ID 29. Ohmae, Kenichi. "The New Technologies:
Japan's Strategic Thrust." McKINSEY QUARTERLY Winter
1984 pp. 20-35.

ID 30. Onosko, Tim. "Japan and Technology: a
Nation Looks to the Future." CREATIVE COMPUTING v. 10
Aug. 1984 pp. 82-90.

ID 31. "Oriental Hospitality: Japanese Factories
Are Points of Interest to Foreign Tourists Studying
Technology." WALL STREET JOURNAL Sep. 3, 1981 pp. 40.

ID 32. Pura, Raphael. "Japanese Electronic 'Smart'
Tools Are Gaining in Europe and the U.S." WALL STREET
JOURNAL v. 201 Apr 15, 1981 pp. 33.

ID 33. Raloff, Janet. "Nipponese Know-How."
SCIENCE NEWS v. 122 Nov. 6, 1982 pp. 296-299.

ID 34. Reich, R. B. "Hi-Tech Warfare." NEW
REPUBLIC v. 187 Nov. 1, 1982 pp. 17-21.

ID 35. "Science and Technology in Japan." NEW
SCIENTIST v. 448 Mar. 21, 1985 pp. 30-61.

ID 36. "Science and Technology in Japan." SCIENCE
AND PUBLIC POLICY v. 13 Feb. 1986 pp. 3-51.

ID 37. Smith, A. "End of the Miracle Economy?"
ESQUIRE v. 97 May 1982 pp. 10-12.

ID 38. Stokes, H. S. "Japan's Love Affair with the Robot." NEW YORK TIMES MAGAZINE Jan. 10, 1982 pp. 24-27+.

ID 39. Teresko, John. "In Robots the Cry is Banzai." INDUSTRY WEEK v. 199 Nov. 27, 1978 pp. 85-88.

ID 40. Tharp, M. "Tokyo, After Buying Technology for Years Now Exports Its Own." WALL STREET JOURNAL v. 195 June 23, 1980 p. 1.

ID 41. Tsuda, Masumi. "Impact of Industrial Robots and Office Automation on Employment." DENTSU JAPAN MARKETING/ADVERTISING Jan. 1983 pp. 16-18+.

ID 42. Wilson, J. W. "America's High-Tech Crisis: Why Silicon Valley is Losing its Edge." BUSINESS WEEK Mar. 11, 1985 pp. 56-60.

IE. Invention; Innovation;
Research and Development

Monographic Works

IE 1. Lynn, Leonard H. HOW JAPAN INNOVATES; A COMPARISON WITH THE U.S. IN THE CASE OF OXYGEN STEELMAKING. Boulder, Colo.: Westview Press, 1982. 211pp.

IE 2. Rosow, Jerome M., and Zager, Robert. PRODUCTIVITY THROUGH WORK INNOVATIONS. New York: Pergamon, 1982. 161pp.

IE. Invention; Innovation; R&D

Articles

IE 3. Abegglan, James C., and Etori, Akio.
"Japanese Technology Today." SCIENTIFIC AMERICAN v.249
Nov. 1983 pp.J10-J11.

IE 4. Blumenthal, Tuvia. "A Note on the
Relationship Between Domestic Research and Development
and Imports of Technology." ECONOMIC DEVELOPMENT AND
CULTURAL CHANGE v.27 Jan. 1979 pp.303-306.

IE 5. Casement, R. "Japan's Creativity Drive."
WORLD PRESS REVIEW v.29 Aug. 1982 pp.28-30.

IE 6. Davidson, William H. "Factor Endowment,
Innovation and Industrial Trade Theory." KYKLOS v.32
1979 pp.764-774.

IE 7. Deguchi, Hiromu. "Energy Consumption and
Technological Innovation in Japan." ECONOMIA
INTERNAZIONALE v.16 Feb. 1963 pp.75-94.

IE 8. Deming, W. Edwards, and Gray, Christopher S.
"Japan: Quality Control and Innovation." BUSINESS WEEK
July 13, 1981 pp.17-44.

IE 9. Gerstenfeld, A. and Sumiyoshi, K. "The
Management of Innovation in Japan: Seven Forces that
Make the Difference." RESEARCH MANAGEMENT v.23 no.1
1980 pp.30-34.

IE 10. Holden, Constance. "Innovation: Japan Races
Ahead as U.S. Falters." SCIENCE v.210 Nov. 1980
pp.751-754.

IE 11. "Japan Calls for Creative Thinkers."
ECONOMIST v.288 Aug. 6-12, 1983 pp.65-66+.

IE 12. Joseph, J., and Hall, A. "Japan Focuses on
Basic Research to Close the Creativity Gap." BUSINESS
WEEK Feb. 25, 1985 pp.94+.

IE 13.   Karger, D. W., and Fujita, T. "R. and D. in
Japan Revisited: The 1970 Decade." MANAGEMENT
INTERNATIONAL REVIEW v. 14 no. 4-5 1974 pp. 31-38.

IE 14.   Marshall, E. "Japan and the Economics of
Invention." SCIENCE v. 228 Apr. 12, 1985 pp. 157-158.

IE 15.   Oshima, Keichi. "Technological Innovation
and Industrial Research in Japan." RESEARCH POLICY v. 13
Oct. 1984 pp. 285-301.

IE 16.   Prochaska, R. J. "The Management of
Invention in Japan--Why It Is Successful." RESEARCH
MANAGEMENT v. 23 no. 1 1980 pp. 35-38.

IE 17.   "Research Center: Japan Seeks Expertise
Abroad." BUSINESS JAPAN v. 29 Dec. 1984 pp. 25+.

IE 18.   Shoji, Takase. "What Star Wars Mean to
Japan." JAPAN QUARTERLY v. 32 Sep. 1985 pp. 240-247.

IE 19.   Treece, J. B. "Companies Cut the Budget But
Spare the R&D." BUSINESS WEEK Apr. 14, 1986 p. 50.

IE 20.   Valery, N. "Challenging the Yankees: Let's
Be Creative." ECONOMIST v. 288 Jul. 9-15, 1983 pp. survey
18+.

XIII.

CHAPTER 10

J. DIMENSIONS AND CONSIDERATIONS OF
THE JAPANESE ECONOMIC CHALLENGE

JA. American Perspectives

Monographic Works

JA 1. Baranson, Jack. THE JAPANESE CHALLENGE TO
U.S. INDUSTRY. Lexington, Mass.: Lexington Books, D.C.
Heath, 1981. 188p.

JA 2. Barnds, William J., ed. JAPAN AND THE
UNITED STATES, CHALLENGES AND OPPORTUNITIES. New York:
New York University Press, 1979. 286pp.

JA 3. Destler, I. M., and Sato, Hideo, eds.
COPING WITH U.S.-JAPANESE ECONOMIC CONFLICTS.
Lexington, Mass.: Lexington Books, D.C. Heath, 1982.
293pp.

JA. American Perspectives

JA 4.   Destler, I. M., et al.   MANAGING AN
ALLIANCE: THE POLITICS OF U.S-JAPANESE RELATIONS.
Washington, D.C.: Brookings Institution, 1976. 224 pp.

JA 5.   Destler, I. M.; Fukui, Harahiro; and Sato,
Hideo. THE TEXTILE WRANGLE: CONFLICT IN
JAPANESE-AMERICAN RELATIONS, 1969-1971. Ithaca, N.Y.:
Cornell University Press, 1979. 394pp.

JA 6.   Hollerman, Leon, ed.   JAPAN AND THE UNITED
STATES, ECONOMIC AND POLITICAL ADVERSARIES. Boulder,
Colo.: Westview Press, 1980. 245pp.

JA 7.   Morrison, David T., and Bendahmane, Diane
B., eds.   ROBOTICS AND FOREIGN AFFAIRS: A SYMPOSIUM.
Washington, D.C.: U.S. Government Printing Office,
1985. 93pp.

JA 8.   Morse, Ronald A., and Yoshida, Shigenobu,
eds.   BLIND PARTNERS: AMERICAN AND JAPANESE RESPONSES
TO AN UNKNOWN FUTURE. Lanham, MD.: University Press of
America, 1985. 141pp.

JA 9.   Simmons, John, and Mares, William. WORKING
TOGETHER. New York: Knopf, 1983. 319pp.

JA 10.   United States. Central Intelligence Agency.
National Foreign Assessment Center. U.S. EXPORT
COMPETITIVENESS: A REVIEW AND EVALUATION; A RESEARCH
PAPER. (ER 81-10044) Washington, DC.: National
Technical Information Service, Feb. 1981. 10p.

JA 11.   United States. Congress. Joint Economic
Committee. INTERNATIONAL COMPETITION IN ADVANCED
INDUSTRIAL SECTORS: TRADE AND DEVELOPMENT IN THE
SEMI-CONDUCTOR INDUSTRY; A STUDY. Borrus, Michael et
al.   97th Congress, 2d Session, Joint Committee Print.
Washington: Government Printing Office, 1982. 183pp.

JA 12. United States. Congress. Joint Economic
Committee. U.S. EXPORT COMPETITIVENESS: HEARING BEFORE
THE JOINT ECONOMIC COMMITTEE, CONGRESS OF THE UNITED
STATES, NINETY-SIXTH CONGRESS, SECOND SESSION, JULY 29,
1980. Washington: U.S. Government Printing Office,
1981. 66pp.

JA 13. United States. Congress. Joint Economic
Committee. Subcommittee on International Trade,
Finance, and Security Economics. JAPANESE PRODUCTIVITY:
LESSONS FOR AMERICA: HEARING, NOVEMBER 4, 1981. 97th
Congress, 1st Session. Washington, DC: U.S. Government
Printing Office, 1982. 94pp.

JA 14. United States. Congress. House. Committee
on Energy and Commerce. Subcommittee on Commerce,
Transportation, and Tourism. FUTURE OF THE AUTOMOBILE
INDUSTRY: HEARING, FEBRUARY 8, 1984. 98th Congress, 2nd
Session. Washington, D.C.: U.S. Government Printing
Office, 1984.

JA 15. United States. Congress. House. Committee
on Foreign Affairs. UNITED STATES--JAPAN RELATIONS:
HEARINGS, MAY 2-JUNE 12, 1984 BEFORE THE SUBCOMMITTEES
ON ASIAN AND PACIFIC AFFAIRS AND ON INTERNATIONAL
ECONOMIC POLICY AND TRADE. 98th Congress, 2nd Session.
Washington, D.C.: U.S. Government Printing Office,
1984. 490pp.

JA 16. United States. Congress. House. Committee
on Foreign Affairs. UNITED STATES--JAPAN ECONOMIC
RELATIONS: HEARING AND MARKUP, SEPTEMBER 16--OCTOBER
16, 1980, BEFORE THE SUBCOMMITTEES ON ASIAN AND PACIFIC
AFFAIRS AND ON INTERNATIONAL ECONOMIC POLICY AND TRADE,
ON H. CON. RES. 363. 96th Cong., 2nd Session.
Washington, D.C.: U.S. Government Printing Office,
1981.

JA. American Perspectives

JA 17. United States. Congress. House. Committee
on Ways and Means. Subcommittee on Trade. HIGH
TECHNOLOGY AND JAPANESE INDUSTRIAL POLICY: A STRATEGY
FOR U.S. POLICYMAKERS. 96th Congress, 2nd Session.
Committee Print 96-74. Washington, D.C. : U.S.
Government Printing Office, 1980. 73pp.

JA 18. United States. Congress. Joint Economic
Committee. JAPANESE AND AMERICAN ECONOMIC POLICIES AND
U.S. PRODUCTIVITY: HEARINGS, JUNE 23 AND JULY 28, 1981,
BEFORE THE SUBCOMMITTEE ON MONETARY AND FISCAL POLICY
AND THE SUBCOMMITTEE ON TRADE, PRODUCTIVITY, AND
ECONOMIC GROWTH. 97th Congress, 1st Session.
Washington, D.C. : U.S. Government Printing Office,
1981. 254p.

JA 19. United States. Congress. Office of
Technology Assessment. U.S. INDUSTRIAL COMPETITIVENESS:
A COMPARISON OF STEEL, ELECTRONICS, AND AUTOMOBILES.
Washington, D.C. : U.S. Office of Technology Assessment,
July 1981. 206pp.

JA 20. United States. Congress. Senate. Committee
on Banking, Housing, and Urban Affairs. Subcommittee on
International Finance and Monetary Policy. FOREIGN
INDUSTRIAL TARGETING: HEARING, JULY 7, 1983, ON FOREIGN
INDUSTRIAL TARGETING, ITS RESULTS AND ITS LESSONS FOR
THE UNITED STATES. (98th Congress, 1st Session, Senate
Hearing 98-246.) Washington, D.C. : U.S. Government
Printing Office, 1983. 113pp.

JA 21. Vogel, Ezra F. JAPAN AS NUMBER ONE: LESSONS
FOR AMERICA. Cambridge, Mass. : Harvard University
Press, 1979. 272pp.

JA 22. Watts, William. THE UNITED STATES AND
JAPAN: A TROUBLED PARTNERSHIP. Prepared by the Potomac
Association, Washington, D.C. Cambridge, Mass. :
Ballinger, 1984. 118pp.

JA 23.   Wolf, Marvin J.   THE JAPANESE CONSPIRACY:
THE PLOT TO DOMINATE INDUSTRY WORLDWIDE--AND HOW TO
DEAL WITH IT. New York: Empire Books, 1983. 336pp.

Articles

JA 24.   "America Starts Looking Over Japan's
Shoulder." BUSINESS WEEK Feb. 13, 1984 p. 136+.

JA 25.   Anderson, William S. "What We Are Learning
from Japan." NATION'S BUSINESS v. 69 Mar. 1981
pp. 39-41.

JA 26.   "Anyway You Measure It, Japan Outproduces
America." ELECTRONIC BUSINESS v. 12 Oct. 15, 1986
pp. 144+.

JA 27.   Baden, John, and Blood, Tom. "Abracadabra
Prosperity: Advocates of an Industrial Policy Are
Curiously Like Primitive Melanesians, Who Thought that
the Magic of Ritual Could Bring Them Wealth." REASON
v. 16 Sep. 1984 pp. 38-42.

JA 28.   Baranson, Jack. "The Japanese Challenge to
U. S. Industry." ANNALS OF THE AMERICAN ACADEMY OF
POLITICAL AND SOCIAL SCIENCE v. 465 Jan. 1983
pp. 176-177.

JA 29.   Bright, S. L., and McKinney, J. A. "The
Economics of the Steel Trigger Price Mechanism."
BUSINESS ECONOMICS v. 19 July 1984 pp. 40-46.

JA 30.   "Competing with Japan." (entire issue) LONG
RANGE PLANNING v. 17 Apr. 1984 pp. 12-156.

JA 31.   Davies, D. "Find a Good Market, Then Look
for Technology." FAR EASTERN ECONOMIC REVIEW v. 112 June
12-18, 1981 p. 56.

JA. American Perspectives

JA 32. "Detroit's Jobs that Will Never Come Back."
BUSINESS WEEK May 23, 1983 pp.168+.

JA 33. Doe, P. "A Japanese Economist Grades the
U.S.: We Get an A." ELECTRONIC BUSINESS v.9 July 1983
pp.50+. (re: Hiroyuki Itami)

JA 34. Fierman, J. "The Selling Off of America."
FORTUNE v.114 Dec. 22, 1986 pp.44-50+.

JA 35. Garvin, David A. "Quality on the Line."
HARVARD BUSINESS REVIEW v.61 Sep./Oct. 1983 pp.64-75.

JA 36. Givens, William L., and Rapp, William V.
"What It Takes to Meet the Japanese Challenge." FORTUNE
v.99 June 18, 1979 pp. 104-120.

JA 37. Gomez-Ibz, J. A., and Harrison, D., Jr.
"Imports and the Future of the U.S. Automobile
Industry." AMERICAN ECONOMIC REVIEW PAPERS AND
PROCEEDINGS v.72 May 1982 pp.19-23.

JA 38. Grover, R. "Congress is Losing Its Temper
with Japan." BUSINESS WEEK Apr. 15, 1985 p.43.

JA 39. Hadley, Eleanor M. "Is the U.S.--Japan
Trade Imbalance a Problem? Economists Answer 'No,'
Politicians 'Yes.'" JOURNAL OF NORTHEAST ASIAN STUDIES
v.1 Mar. 1982 pp.35-56.

JA 40. Hampton, W. J. "Can Detroit Cope this Time?
Output and Jobs Will Suffer--But the Industry May
Emerge Stronger." BUSINESS WEEK Apr. 22, 1985
pp.78-81+.

JA 41. "Hate Japan Mood Develops in Recent U.S.
Publications." BUSINESS JAPAN v.29 April 1984
pp.14-16.

JA 42. Hollerman, Leon. "Japan's Economic Impact on the United States." ANNALS OF THE AMERICAN ACADEMY OF POLITICAL AND SOCIAL SCIENCE v.460 Mar. 1982 pp.127-135.

JA 43. Ingersoll, Robert S. "Japan--United States Relations: Economic Challenge and Mutual Benefits." TRIALOGUE Summer/Fall 1981 pp.21-26.

JA 44. "Japan and America: An Offer You Won't Refuse." ECONOMIST v.285 Nov. 13, 1982 p.45.

JA 45. "Japan: Can You Plan a Global Strategy Without It?" SITE SELECTION HANDBOOK v.31 Oct. 1986 pp.1093-1106.

JA 46. Leffler, K. B. "Ambiguous Changes in Product Quality." AMERICAN ECONOMIC REVIEW v.72 Dec. 1982 pp.956-67.

JA 47. Main, J. "The Battle for Quality Begins." FORTUNE v.102 Dec. 29, 1980 pp.28-33.

JA 48. Markley, H. E. "Quality: a Way to Cut Costs." INDUSTRY WEEK v.216 Feb. 7, 1983 p.88.

JA 49. Mattill, J. "Winning the Quality Revolution." TECHNOLOGY REVIEW v.85 May/June 1982 pp.80-81.

JA 50. Mino, Hojaki. "Japan, U.S. Both Require More Balanced Economies." BUSINESS JAPAN v.31 Oct. 1986 pp.28-29.

JA 51. Neely, B., and Nevens, M. "Politics Won't Cure the U.S. Chip Industry's Woes." ELECTRONIC BUSINESS v.12 Nov. 15, 1986 pp.114-116.

JA 52. Prentice, John. "Competing with the Japanese Approach to Technology." LONG RANGE PLANNING v.17 Apr. 1984 pp.25-32.

JA. American Perspectives

JA 53. "Putting a Japanese Face on American Business." DATA MANAGEMENT v.19 Oct. 1981 pp.27-54.

JA 54. "Quality: the U.S. Drives to Catch Up." BUSINESS WEEK Nov. 1, 1982 pp.66-69+.

JA 55. Riemer, B., and Glasgall, W. "The Risks of a Free-Fall: the Allies Face Big Trouble If They Don't Come Up with a Dollar Strategy." BUSINESS WEEK Feb. 2, 1987 pp.28-29.

JA 56. Rohan, T. M. "U.S. May Have Found Potent Import-Fighter." INDUSTRY WEEK v.215 Nov. 15, 1982 pp.19-21.

JA 57. Sato, Hideo. "The Political Dynamics of U.S.-Japan Economic Conflicts." JOURNAL OF NORTHEAST ASIAN STUDIES v.3 Spring 1984 pp.3-15.

JA 58. "Say Japan to Remain Major International Trade Force." ELECTRONICS NEWS v.32 Aug. 25, 1986 p.6. (re: Pacific Rim Study for the Joint Congressional Economic Committee.)

JA 59. Thackray, J. "America's Japanese Jitters." MANAGEMENT TODAY Jun. 1982 pp.70-73.

JA 60. Tsongas, Paul E., and Tyson, Mitchell G. "Washington Versus Tokyo: the Technorivalry." CREATIVE COMPUTING v.10 Aug. 1984 pp.31-38.

JA 61. "U.S. Reprisals Loom as Trade Reforms Stall." BUSINESS WEEK Aug. 23, 1982 p.44.

JA 62. "Ways U.S. Can Cope with the Japanese Challenge." U.S. NEWS AND WORLD REPORT v.95 Nov. 28, 1983 pp.43-44. (Interview with Mike Mansfield).

JA 63. Weil, Ulric. "Evaluating the Japanese Challenge." DATAMATION v.29 Jan. 1983 pp.122-133.

JA 64. "What the U.S. Can Learn from Its Rivals." BUSINESS WEEK June 30, 1980 pp. 138-142.

JA 65. White, G. et al. "A Drive to Put Quality Back into U.S. Goods." U.S. NEWS AND WORLD REPORT v. 93 Sep. 20, 1982 pp. 49-50.

JA 66. Wilson, J. W., and Dryden, S. J. "The Truce in the Chip War May Be Temporary." BUSINESS WEEK Feb. 23, 1987 pp. 46-47.

JA 67. Wingis, C. "New Connections in the Silicon Valley." INDUSTRIAL MARKETING v. 66 Mar. 1981 pp. 82+.

JA 68. Wishard, W. V. D. "Productivity and American World Competitiveness." (Address given December 1, 1981) VITAL SPEECHES OF THE DAY v. 48 Mar. 1, 1982 pp. 316-320.

JA 69. Wolfowitz, Paul D. "Taking Stock of U.S.-Japan Relations." DEPARTMENT OF STATE BULLETIN v. 84 Sep. 1984 pp. 28-34.

JA 70. Wozniak, C. "Meeting the Japanese Challenge." INTERNAL AUDITOR v. 40 Feb. 1983 pp. 14-18.

JA 71. Zippo, M. "Working for the Japanese: Views of American Employees." PERSONNEL v. 59 Mar./Apr. 1982 pp. 56-58.

JA 72. Zussman, Y. M. "Learning from the Japanese: Management in a Resource-Scarce World" ORGANIZATIONAL DYNAMICS v. 11 p. 68-80 Winter 1982.

JB. Global Perspectives

Monographic Works

JB 1.   Bogdanov, A. THE U.S.A., WESTERN EUROPE,
JAPAN: A TRIANGLE OF RIVALRY. Moscow: Progress
Publishers, 1985. 252pp.

JB 2.   European Communitites Committee--Directorate
General for Information. THE EUROPE--UNITED STATES--
JAPAN TRADE CONTROVERSY. Luxembourg: European
Communities Official Publications Office, May 1983.
7pp.

JB 3.   Frame, J. Davidson. INTERNATIONAL BUSINESS
AND GLOBAL TECHNOLOGY. Lexington, Mass.: Lexington
Books, D. C. Heath, 1983. 206pp.

JB 4.   Franko, Lawrence G. THE THREAT OF JAPANESE
MULTINATIONALS: HOW THE WEST CAN RESPOND. New York:
Wiley, 1983. 148pp.

JB 5.   Guillain, Robert. THE JAPANESE CHALLENGE.
Philadelphia: Lippincott, 1970. 352pp.

JB 6.   Hanabusa, Masamichi. TRADE PROBLEMS BETWEEN
JAPAN AND WESTERN EUROPE. Farnborough, Eng.: Saxon
House, 1979. 125pp.

JB 7.   Smith, Michael, et al.   ASIA'S NEW
INDUSTRIAL WORLD. London; New York: Methuen, 1985.
136pp.

JB 8.   Striner, Herbert E. REGAINING THE LEAD:
POLICIES FOR ECONOMIC GROWTH. 2nd ed.   Millwood, N.Y.:
Associated Faculty Press, 1987. 205pp.

Articles

JB 9. Berney, K. "Competing in Japan." NATION'S
BUSINESS v. 74 Oct 1986 pp. 28-30.

JB 10. Davies, D. "Are the Europeans Ready to
Listen to the Japanese?" FAR EASTERN ECONOMIC REVIEW
v. 112 June 12-18, 1981 pp. 54+.

JB 11. Nussbaum, B. "Badgering Its Allies Won't
Cure America's Ills." BUSINESS WEEK Oct. 6, 1986 p. 29.

JB 12. Peterson, T., et al. "The Europeans Start
To Play a Little Rough." BUSINESS WEEK Feb. 9, 1987
p. 47.

JC. Adaptation of Japanese Production and
Management Techniques in America

Monographic Works

JC 1. Crosby, Philip B. QUALITY IS FREE: THE ART
OF MAKING QUALITY CERTAIN. New York: McGraw-Hill, 1979.
309pp.

JC 2. Harris, Philip R. NEW WORLD, NEW WAYS, NEW
MANAGEMENT. New York: American Management Associations,
1983. 324pp.

JC 3. Skrovan, Daniel J., ed. QUALITY OF WORK
LIFE: PERSPECTIVES FOR BUSINESS AND THE PUBLIC SECTOR.
Reading, Mass. : Addison-Wesley, 1983. 192pp.

JC. Adaptations of Japanese Methods

JC 4.   Thompson, Philip C. QUALITY CIRCLES: HOW TO
MAKE THEM WORK IN AMERICA. New York: AMACOM, 1982.
198pp.

Articles

JC 5.   Alexander, C. P. "Learning From the
Japanese." PERSONNEL JOURNAL v.60 Aug. 1981
pp.616-619.

JC 6.   Anderson, William S. "Meeting the Japanese
Economic Challenge." BUSINESS HORIZONS v.24 Mar./Apr.
1981 pp.56-62.

JC 7.   "Armand Feigenbaum: Making Quality a Way of
Life." (an interview) INTERNATIONAL MANAGEMENT v.39
Jan. 1984 pp.30-31+.

JC 8.   Bernstein, J. "GM Exec Discusses Commitment
to Kanban." AUTOMOTIVE NEWS Nov. 19, 1984 p.48.

JC 9.   Blair, J. D., and Whitehead, C. J. "Can
Quality Circles Survive in the United States?" BUSINESS
HORIZONS v.27 Sep./Oct. 1984 pp.17-23.

JC 10.   Bobbe, Richard A., and Schaffer, Robert H.
"Productivity Improvement: Manage It or Buy It?"
BUSINESS HORIZONS v.26 Mar./Apr. 1983.

JC 11.   Boulton, W. R., and Saladin, B. A. "Let's
Make Production/Operations Management Top Priority For
Strategic Planning in the 1980s." MANAGEMENT PLANNING
v.32 July/Aug. 1983 pp.14-21.

JC 12.   Bowen, William. "Lessons from Behind the
Kimono." FORTUNE v.102 June 15, 1981 pp.247-248+.

JC 13.   Brannen, Kathleen C., and Hranac, Jo Anne.
"Quality Control Circles for Small Business." JOURNAL
OF SMALL BUSINESS v.21 Jan. 1983 pp.21-27.

JC 14.   Brown, M. "An American Version of Theory
Z." HEALTH CARE MANAGEMENT REVIEW v.7 Fall 1982
pp.23-25.

JC 15.   Bruce-Briggs, B. "The Dangerous Folly
Called Theory Z." FORTUNE v.105 May 17, 1982 pp.41+.
Same, abridged, "Why We Can't Imitate the Japanese."
READER'S DIGEST v.121 Nov. 1982 pp.255-56.

JC 16.   Callahan, J. M. "Just-In-Time a Winner."
AUTOMOTIVE INDUSTRIES v.165 Mar. 1985 p.78.

JC 17.   "Can America Copy Japanese Methods--or
Should We Simply Borrow Some Useful Ideas?" MANAGEMENT
REVIEW v.71 Mar. 1982 pp.4-5.

JC 18.   Chironis, N. P. "Quality Circles Raise
Efficiency." COAL AGE v.88 Jan. 1983 v.80-82+.

JC 19.   Cole, Robert E. "How to Gain the
Competitive Edge: Improving Product Quality through
Continuous Feedback." MANAGEMENT REVIEW v.72 Oct. 1983
pp.8-12.

JC 20.   Cole, Robert E. "Learning From the
Japanese: Prospects and Pitfalls." MANAGEMENT REVIEW
Sep. 1980 pp.22-28.

JC 21.   Cook, J. "Kanban, American-Style." FORBES
v.134 Oct. 8, 1984 pp.66+.

JC 22.   Cosier, R. A., and Dalton, D. R. "Search
for Excellence, Learn from Japan--Are These Panaceas or
Problems?" BUSINESS HORIZONS v.29 Nov./Dec. 1986
pp.63-68.

JC. Adaptations of Japanese Methods

JC 23. Courtenay, V. "Glitches Aside, Just-In-Time Coming Along Just Fine." WARD'S AUTO WORLD v.20 Apr. 1984 pp.49-50.

JC 24. Dickinson, D. "Foreign Competition: From Shop Floor to Japan." INDUSTRY WEEK v.221 May 14, 1984 pp.77+.

JC 25. Diebold, J. "Management Can Learn From the Japanese." BUSINESS WEEK no.2299 Sep. 29, 1973 pp.14-19.

JC 26. Dillon, L. S. "Adopting Japanese Management: Some Cultural Stumbling Blocks." PERSONNEL v.60 July/Aug. 1983 pp.73-77.

JC 27. Flax, S. "An Auto Man Tunes Up Warner-Lambert." FORTUNE v.111 Mar. 4, 1985 pp.70-72+.

JC 28. Gadon, Herman. "Making Sense of Quality of Work Life Programs: Quality Circles, Flextime, and Wellness in the Workplace Are But a Few of the Plethora of New, and Often Confusing, Ideas About Improving America's Business." BUSINESS HORIZONS v.27 Jan./Feb. 1984 pp.42-46.

JC 29. "GM Turns to Just-In-Time." AUTOMOTIVE INDUSTRIES v.162 June 1982 p.21.

JC 30. Gorovitz, E. S. "Adapting Japanese Management to American Organizations." TRAINING AND DEVELOPMENT JOURNAL v.36 Sep. 1982 pp.9-10.

JC 31. Gottschalk, Earl C., Jr. "U.S. Firms, Worried by Productivity Lag, Copy Japan in Seeking Employees' Advice." WALL STREET JOURNAL v.195 Feb. 2, 1980 p.4.

JC 32. Harbron, J. D. "Why the U.S. Executive Must Change His Ways." BUSINESS QUARTERLY v.46 Spring 1981 pp.10-12.

JC 33. Hoeffer, E. "GM Tries Just-In-Time American Style." PURCHASING v.93 Aug. 19, 1982 pp.67+.

JC 34. Hoffman, F. O. "A Quality Atmosphere: Quality Circles Demand a Supportive Business Philosophy." MANAGEMENT WORLD v.12 Jan. 1983 pp.44+.

JC 35. "In Quest of Quality ." TIME v.123 Mar. 26, 1984 pp.52. (Views of Philip B. Crosby)

JC 36. Irving, R. R.; Banter, J.; and McManus, G. L. "What Can American Manufacturers Learn From the Japanese?" IRON AGE v.223 Oct. 6, 1980 pp.45-51.

JC 37. Jones, W. G. "Quality's Vicious Circles." MANAGEMENT TODAY Mar. 1983 pp.97-98+.

JC 38. Kelderman, J. "New Role for Workers in K Quality." AUTOMOTIVE NEWS July 7, 1980 pp.3+.

JC 39. Leventhal, R. B. "Working Hard to Make QWL Look Easy." TRAINING AND DEVELOPMENT JOURNAL v.38 June 1984 pp.59-60.

JC 40. Levine, H. Z. "Participation Programs." PERSONNEL v.61 May-June 1984 pp.4-13.

JC 41. Lippert, F. G. "Quality with Economy." SUPERVISION v.45 July 1983 pp.16-17.

JC 42. List, Charles E. "How to Make Quality Circles Work for Your Organization." PERSONNEL JOURNAL v.61 Sep. 1982 pp.652+.

JC 43. McClenahen, J. S. "Bringing Home Japan's Lessons." INDUSTRY WEEK v.208 Feb. 23, 1981 pp.69-73.

JC 44. McClenahen, J. S. "Japan's Lessons." INDUSTRY WEEK v.208 Feb. 23, 1981 pp.69-73.

JC. Adaptations of Japanese Methods

JC 45. McClenahen, J. S. "More Quality Circles Sporting White Collars." INDUSTRY WEEK v.213 May 31, 1982 pp.28-29+.

JC 46. MacMillan, Charles J. "From Quality Control to Quality Management: Lessons from Japan." BUSINESS QUARTERLY v.47 May 1982 pp.31-40.

JC 47. Myers, Edith. "Learning From the Japanese." DATAMATION v.27 Jan. 1981 pp.63-65.

JC 48. Nelson, Joani. "Quality Circles Become Contagious." INDUSTRY WEEK v.205 Apr. 14, 1980 pp.99-103.

JC 49. "New Way of Managing People." BUSINESS WEEK May 11, 1981 pp.89-90+.

JC 50. "Not a Cure-All But Worth a Try Says New Guide to Quality Circles." PERSONNEL MANAGEMENT v.13 July 1981 p.10.

JC 51. O'Donnell, M., and O'Donnell, R. J. "Quality Circles--The Latest Fad or a Real Winner." BUSINESS HORIZONS v.27 May-June 1984 pp.48-52.

JC 52. O'Neal, C. R. "U.S. Firms Adopting Kanban System: Devise New Marketing Strategies to Serve JIT Producers." MARKETING NEWS v.18 Sep. 14, 1984 pp.20-21.

JC 53. Pascarella, P. "Quality Circles: Just Another Management Headache?" INDUSTRY WEEK v.213 June 28, 1982 pp.50-55.

JC 54. "Productivity and Morale Sagging? Try the Quality Circle Approach." PERSONNEL v.57 May/June 1980 pp43-44.

JC 55. "QC Facilitator: Not Just a Turgid Title." TRAINING v.21 Jan. 1984 pp.84+.

JC. Adaptations of Japanese Methods

JC 56. "A QC Success Story." TRAINING v.21 Jan. 1984 p.84.

JC 57. "QCs--Much More than Rap Sessions." TRAINING v.20 Sep. 1983 pp.84-85.

JC 58. "Quality and Productivity: America's Revitalization." (advertisement) BUSINESS WEEK Nov. 8, 1982 pp.19-20+.

JC 59. "Quality Circle Boom Part of Growing American Trend." SUPERVISION v.43 Sep. 1981 pp.8-11.

JC 60. "Quality Circles." BUSINESS v.32 Jul./Aug./Sep. pp.56-57.

JC 61. "Quality Circles: How Chemical Companies Use a Japanese Tool." CHEMICAL WEEK v.131 Dec.8, 1982 pp.36-39.

JC 62. Randall, E. "Quality Circles--a Third Wave Intervention." TRAINING AND DEVELOPMENT JOURNAL v.35 Mar. 1981 pp.28-31.

JC 63. Ransey, D., and Kirk, D. "Lessons from Japan, Inc." NEWSWEEK v.46 Sep. 8, 1980 pp.61-62.

JC 64. Rice, B. "Square Holes for Quality Circles." PSYCHOLOGY TODAY v.18 Feb. 1984 p.17.

JC 65. Rowand, R. "Chrysler Grooms a Revolution--One Step Beyond Kan-Ban." AUTOMOTIVE NEWS Aug. 29. 1983 p.2.

JC 66. Rowand, R. "New Just-In-Time Systems Called Boon for Midwest." AUTOMOTIVE NEWS Oct. 11, 1982 pp.1+.

JC 67. Shaw, Robert J. "Keeping the Commitment to Quality Circles: Does Management Commitment Mean Never Having To Say You're Sorry?" MANAGEMENT FOCUS v.29 Nov./Dec. 1982 pp.25-32.

387

JC. Adaptations of Japanese Methods

JC 68. Sorge, M. "Chrysler to Try for Japanese
Style." AUTOMOTIVE NEWS Aug. 16, 1982 p.14.

JC 69. Steingraber, F. G. "Improving Productivity
in the U.S." (Address, Oct. 27, 1981) VITAL SPEECHES OF
THE DAY v.48 Jan. 15, 1982 pp.219-21.

JC 70. Strier, Franklin. "Quality Circles in the
United States: Fad or Fixture?" BUSINESS FORUM v.9
Summer 1984 pp.19-23.

JC 71. Stone, F. "To QC or Not To QC." ADVANCED
MANAGMENT JOURNAL v.48 Spring 1983 pp.50-51.

JC 72. Takeuchi, Hirotaka. "Productivity: Learning
from the Japanese." CALIFORNIA MANAGEMENT REVIEW v.23
Summer 1981 pp.5-19.

JC 73. Takeuchi, Hirotaka, and Quelch, John A.
"Quality Is More than Making a Good Product: It's Also
a Matter of Keeping Close Tabs on Changing Customer
Values and After-Sale Servicing." HARVARD BUSINESS
REVIEW v.61 July/Aug. 1983 pp.139-45.

JC 74. Tersine, R. J., and Price, R. L.
"Productivity Improvement Strategies: Technological
Transfer and Upgrading." JOURNAL OF SYSTEMS MANAGEMENT
v.33 Nov. 1982 pp.15-23.

JC 75. Uretsky, Myron. "Japanese Lessons for U.S.
Productivity." FREEDOM ENTERPRISE Spring 1981 pp.5-6.

JC 76. Versagi, Frank J. "What American
Labor/Management Can Learn from Japanese Unions."
MANAGEMENT REVIEW v.71 June 1982 pp.24-28.

JC 77. Visser, Carla. "What We Can Learn from the
Japanese About QCs." ADVANCED MANAGEMENT JOURNAL v.47
Summer 1982 pp.55-63.

JC 78.   Werter, William B., Jr.   "Quality Circles:
Key Executive Issues." JOURNAL OF CONTEMPORARY BUSINESS
v.11 no.2 1982 pp.17-26.

JC 79.   "Why Quality Circles Failed at 21 Firms."
MANAGEMENT REVIEW v.71 Sep. 1982 p.56.

JC 80.   "Why QCs Don't Always Work--And What To Do
About It." MANAGEMENT REVIEW v.71 May 1982 pp.6-7.

JC 81.   Wood, R. C.   "Squaring Off on Quality
Circles." INC. v.4 Aug. 1982 pp.98+.

JC 82.   Yager, E.   "Quality Circle: a Tool for the
'80s." TRAINING AND DEVELOPMENT JOURNAL v.34 Aug. 1980
pp.60-62.

JC 83.   Yager, E.   "Quality Control Circle
Explosion." TRAINING AND DEVELOPMENT JOURNAL v.35 Apr.
1981 pp.98-99+.

JC 84.   Yamada, Mitsuhiko.   "Japanese-Style
Management in America: Merits and Difficulties."
JAPANESE ECONOMIC STUDIES v.10 no.1 1981 pp.1-30.

JD. Japanese Methods in the World

JD 1.   Arbose, J. R.   "Quality Control Circles: the
West Adopts a Japanese Concept." INTERNATIONAL
MANAGEMENT v.35 Dec. 1980 pp.31-32+.

JD 2.   Brown, G. F., and Read, A. R.   "Personnel and
Training Policies--Some Lessons for Western Companies."
LONG RANGE PLANNING v.17 Apr. 1984 pp.48-57.

JD 3.   Juran, J. M.   "International Significance of
the QC Circle Movement." QUALITY PROGRESS v.13 Nov.
1980 pp.18-22.

JD. Japanese Methods in the World

JD 4. Juran, J. M. "Product Quality--A Prescription for the West: Part I: Training and Development Programs." MANAGEMENT REVIEW v.70 no.6 June 1981 pp.8-14.

JD 5. Trevor, M. "Does Japanese Management Work in Britain?" JOURNAL OF GENERAL MANAGEMENT v.8 no.4 1983 pp.28-43.

JD 6. "Western Culture Makes Life Difficult for Quality Circles." PERSONNEL ADMINISTRATOR v.28 Oct. 1983 p.13.

JD 7. White, M. "Japanese Management and British Workers." POLICY STUDIES v.1 1981 pp.49-58.

XIV.

CHAPTER 11

K. RESPONSE TO THE JAPANESE CHALLENGE

Monographic Works

K 1. Baumol, William J., and McLennan, Kenneth, eds. PRODUCTIVITY GROWTH AND U.S. COMPETITIVENESS. Committee on Economic Development, Supplementary Paper no. 245. New York: Oxford University Press, 1985. 228pp.

K 2. Halberstam, David. THE RECKONING. New York: William Morrow & Co., 1987. 752pp.

K 3. Hayes, R. H., and Wheelwright, S. C. RESTORING OUR COMPETITIVE EDGE: COMPETING THROUGH MANUFACTURING. New York: Wiley, 1984. 427pp.

K 4. Hitchcock, Terrance S. AMERICAN BUSINESS: THE LAST HURRAH? CAN WE REGAIN OUR COMPETITIVE EDGE? Homewood, Ill.: Dow Jones-Irwin, 1982. 199pp.

K 5. Kanter, Rosabeth Moss. THE CHANGE MASTERS: INNOVATIONS FOR PRODUCTIVITY IN THE AMERICAN CORPORATION. New York: Simon and Shuster, 1983. 432pp.

K. Response to Challenge

K 6. Lawrence, Paul R. and Dyer, Davis. RENEWING
AMERICAN INDUSTRY. New York: Free Press, 1983. 384pp.

K 7. McGrath, John. CAN THE UNITED STATES BECOME
A MORE COMPETITIVE INTERNATIONAL TRADER? A SUMMARY
REPORT. Public Affairs Series 16. New York: Japan
Society, Inc., 1981. 82p.

K 8. O'Toole, James. MAKING AMERICA WORK:
PRODUCTIVITY AND RESPONSIBILITY. New York: Continuum
Pub. Co., 1981. 216pp.

K 9. Ouchi, William G. THEORY Z: HOW AMERICAN
BUSINESS CAN MEET THE JAPANESE CHALLENGE. Reading,
Mass.: Addison-Wesley. 1981. 283pp.

K 10. Richmond, Frederick W., and Kahan, Michael.
HOW TO BEAT THE JAPANESE AT THEIR OWN GAME. Englewood
Cliffs, N.J.: Prentice-Hall, 1983. 175pp.

K 11. Riccomini, Donald R. UNEXPECTED JAPAN; WHY
AMERICAN BUSINESS SHOULD RETURN TO ITS OWN TRADITIONAL
VALUES--AND NOT IMITATE THE JAPANESE. New York: Walker
& Co., 1985. 144pp.

K 12. Vogel, Ezra F. COMEBACK: CASE BY CASE:
BUILDING THE RESURGENCE OF AMERICAN BUSINESS. New York:
Simon and Shuster, 1985. 320pp.

Articles

K 13. Burton, Daniel F., Jr., and Hewlett, Sylvia
Ann. "Labor-Management Relations and Productivity: A
Framework for Success." NATIONAL PRODUCTIVITY REVIEW
v.2 Spring 1983 pp.185-94.

K 14. Bylinsky, G. "America's Best-Managed
Factories." FORTUNE v.109 May 28, 1984 pp.16-24.

K 15.   "Can Workplace Democracy Boost
Productivity?" BUSINESS AND SOCIETY REVIEW no.43 Fall
1982 pp.10-15.

K 16.   Coleman, B. "A Misguided View of American
Industry." INC v.5 Oct. 1983 pp.23-26.

K 17.   Collard, R. "How to Go One Better Than
Japan." MANAGEMENT TODAY Jan. 1982 pp.27+.

K 18.   "Fighting Back: It Can Work; Some Companies
Are Finding Ways to Keep Japan from Always Winning."
BUSINESS WEEK Aug. 26, 1985 pp.62-68.

K 19.   Freund, W. C. "Reindustrialization--A New
Name for an Old Prescription." JOURNAL OF ACCOUNTING,
AUDITING AND FINANCE v.6 Spring 1983 pp.275-80.

K 20.   Friesecke, R. F. "The Quality Revolution: a
Challenge to Management." MANAGERIAL PLANNING v.32
July/Aug. 1983 pp.7-9+.

K 21.   "The Furor Over America's Ability to
Compete." BUSINESS WEEK Sep. 10, 1984 pp.89-90.

K 22.   Gall, N. "Innovate or Die." FORBES v.128
Nov. 9, 1981 pp.155+.

K 23.   Greene, J. A. "The New Trading Stratagems."
McKINSEY QUARTERLY Summer 1984 pp.45-54.

K 24.   Iacocca, Lee A. "Making U.S. Business
Competitive." JOURNAL OF BUSINESS STRATEGY v.5 Summer
1984 pp.26-28.

K 25.   Irving, R. R. "Is America Turning Around in
Quality?" IRON AGE v.226 July 22, 1983 pp.40-41+.

K 26.   "A Japan-like Surge in Labor Productivity."
FORTUNE v.107 May 30, 1983 p.42.

K. Response to Challenge

K 27. Judson, Arnold S. "The Awkward Truth About Productivity: At Last Managers Are Admitting, 'We Have Met the Enemy and They Is Us.'" HARVARD BUSINESS REVIEW v.60 Sep./Oct. 1982 pp.93-97.

K 28. Krugman, P. R. "The U.S. Response to Foreign Industrial Targeting." BROOKINGS PAPERS ON ECONOMIC ACTIVITY no.1 1984 pp.77-131.

K 29. "Leaders for the 21st Century?" TIME v.115 Jan. 28, 1980 p.81.

K 30. "Look Out, Japan, the Americans Are Coming." ECONOMIST v.294 Mar. 30, 1985 pp.37-38.

K 31. McNamara, Carleton P. "A Strategic Response To the Productivity Challenge." BUSINESS AND ECONOMIC REVIEW v.30 Jan. 1984 pp.29-36.

K 32. Park, J. C. "Need for Managerial Changes in U.S. Corporations." MANAGERIAL PLANNING v.30 May/June 1982 pp.26-30.

K 33. Rapp, William V. "Industrial Structure and Japanese Trade Friction: U.S. Policy Responses." JOURNAL OF INTERNATIONAL AFFAIRS v.37 Summer 1983 pp.67-79.

K 34. "The Revival of Productivity." BUSINESS WEEK Feb. 13, 1984 pp.92-95+.

K 35. Sherrid, P. "Good News on the Productivity Front." FORBES v.132 Oct. 10, 1983 p.124+.

K 36. Soros, George. "A Global New Deal." NEW YORK REVIEW OF BOOKS v.34 no.13 Aug. 13, 1987 pp.52-53.

K 37. Statile, Lorraine. "United States--Japan Trade Relations: Meeting the Japanese Challenge." BROOKLYN JOURNAL OF INTERNATIONAL LAW v.10 Winter 1984 pp.157-191.

K 38. Thurow, Lester C. "Revitalizing American
Industry: Managing in a Competitive World Economy."
CALIFORNIA MANAGEMENT REVIEW v.27 Fall 1984 pp.9-41.

K 39. Tregoe, T. T. "Productivity in America:
Where It Went and How to Get It Back." MANAGEMENT
REVIEW v.72 Feb. 1983 pp.23+.

K 40. "A Work Revolution in U.S. Industry."
BUSINESS WEEK May 16, 1983 pp.100-103+.

K 41. Yamawaki, H. "Exports, Foreign Market
Structure, and Profitability in Japanese and U.S.
Manufacturing." REVIEW OF ECONOMIC STATISTICS v.68 Nov.
1986 pp.18-27.

AUTHOR INDEX

397

Author Index

Author Index

Author Index

Author Index

Author Index

Author Index

Author Index

Author Index

EF-25, JA-6, JA-42
Holstein, W. J.   EC-78, EF-26
Honjo, Eijiro   CA-21
Hoos, Ida R.   ID-18
Hopkins, M. E.   HD-36
Hori, Takeaki   CH-8
Horie, Yasuzo   CB-40, CB-41, CB-42
Horiuchi, Toshihiro   DA-70
Horne, James   DH-6
Horvath, Dezso   DA-29, HD-37
Hoshii, Iwao   CA-22
Hoshino, Yasuo   DA-30, GA-4
Hotani, Rokuro   FD-10
Houser, M.   BD-48
Hout, Thomas   EC-17, DA-7
Howard, N.   HD-39
Hranac, Jo Anne   IC-39, JC-13
Hsieh, D. A.   EA-36
Huang, P. Y.   IB-30
Hubbard, Gilbert E.   BF-5
Huh, Kung-Mo   CH-9
Hulbert, J.   GC-3
Hunsburger, Warren S.   CD-6, EC-8, GA-1
Hunt, E. H.   HB-37
Hunt, R.   IB-31
Iacocca, Lee A.   EC-79, K-24
Ibarreche, S.   IB-44
Ibe, Kyonosuke   FA-11
Ibuka, M.   HD-40
Ichimuro, Muto   BB-43
Ichimura, Shinichi   CF-53, DG-11, EA-71, EH-5
Iida, Tsuneo   CF-54, HD-41
Iizuka, A.   HA-22
Ike, Brian   BD-34
Ike, Nobutaka   BB-16
Ikeda, Katsuhiko   DA-31
Ikeda, Kotaro   DG-12
Ikegami, Jun   DG-13
Ikemoto, K.   DG-14
Ikoma, Albert R.   BD-21
Ilgen, Thomas L.   EA-5
Imai, Kenichi   CA-60

412

413

Author Index

Author Index

Author Index

418

Author Index

Author Index

Author Index

Author Index

430

Author Index

Author Index